ATTITUDE CHANGE

Consulting Editor

JEROME L. SINGER
City College, CUNY
PSYCHOLOGY

The Editor

PETER SUEDFELD is Professor and Chairman, Department of Psychology, University College, Rutgers University. He has also taught at Princeton University, where he received his Ph.D., Trenton State College, and the University of Illinois. A specialist in the environmental, cognitive, and personality aspects of attitude change, Professor Suedfeld has contributed widely to professional journals and is co-editor of *Personality Theory and Information Processing*.

ATTITUDE

EDITED BY

CHANGE

THE COMPETING VIEWS

Peter Suedfeld

Aldine · Atherton
Chicago/New York

First published 1971 by
Aldine • Atherton, Inc.
529 South Wabash Avenue
Chicago, Illinois 60605

Library of Congress Catalog Number 74-159604

ISBN 202-25081-4, cloth; 202-25082-2, paper

Printed in the United States of America
DESIGNED BY LORETTA LI

Contents

1

Models of Attitude Change: Theories That Pass in the Night

PETER SUEDFELD

The inclusion of a book on attitude theory in a series devoted to controversies is highly justified by the state of the field. In any controversy there are at least two opposing views on the subject in question—and a recent survey counted thirty-four distinguishable models of attitude change (Ostrom, 1968)! When the controversy occurs in a field of science, the ultimate outcome depends on which side proves to be closer to empirical fact; the tremendous amount of effort that has gone into attitude research in the past two decades is therefore not surprising.

Theoretical controversies are beneficial to scientific progress to the extent that they lead to critical experiments—experiments that clearly show that one theory predicts events more accurately

I am grateful to Yakov M. Epstein, Richard Pargament, and Christa Wyzykowski for critical reading and helpful comments.

1

than another. Platt (1964) describes the best course of development as a series of alternative hypotheses (this is the controversy
stage) followed by empirical tests designed so that each possible
outcome will support only one hypothesis—and so on to finer
and finer predictions.

There are few psychological theories that can be posed against
each other so neatly as to produce this logical tree. The complex
array of statistical techniques needed by psychologists to distinguish between relevant and irrelevant influences on their data
testifies to theoretical imprecision (Platt, 1964) and inadequate
experimental control (Skinner, 1956). Attitude theories and experiments share these characteristics, which in a relatively young
science, dealing with highly variable phenomena, may be una-
voidable and may in fact help to generate novel and increasingly
fruitful hypotheses (Hafner and Presswood, 1965).

The problem with attitude theories is that they seldom stand in
clear opposition to each other. Some models are so vague that
while almost any outcome can be related to the theory in some
way, prediction is highly speculative. In such a situation, a critical test is impossible to achieve. Others are so similar to each
other that experiments could test only trivial differences, or so
dissimilar in scope, language, and approach that one is hard put
to identify areas in which their predictions or methods are comparable. Even when such areas are found, and empirical data do
exist, one can usually find alternative interpretations that save
each of the theories from having to admit inadequacy. That is
the reason for the title of this essay: models that can so seldom
be pitted against each other conclusively are indeed like ships
that pass in the night.[1] This may be (as Charlie Brown once put
it) not a fault, but a character trait. Quite probably there is no
metatheory that can ever explain every aspect of attitude change.
In that case, many theories may have parts of the truth, and each
can be utilized in the specific situation for which it is most useful
(like the wave and quantum theories, which are used to explain
different aspects of the physical nature of light). Such a multi-

plicity of theories has been proposed for social psychology in general (Deutsch and Krauss, 1965). Even if this is the appropriate solution, however, we must identify the domain in which each theory is most powerful; and for that effort we need more specificity and greater overlap than are available to us now.

One may ask whether, in view of these difficulties, it is worth while to study the theories of attitude change. While there is some disagreement on the value of theorizing *per se,* the weight of scientific opinion is favorable. Science strives to explain, predict, and control events. Theories are necessary as an explanatory framework, since if there are no explicitly stated conceptual linkages among events, their actual relationship to each other may easily be overlooked. Good empirical research tells us the facts; a good theory tells us what the facts mean. In the same way, theoretical constructs are used to predict the future: once we have an idea of the ways in which antecedent conditions influence the outcome, their pattern can be fitted into a theoretical framework that points to the most likely consequence. If the theory is explicit enough, its strong and weak points can be identified by the accuracy of its predictions. Finally, a good theory defines its components so precisely and is so closely related to experimental operations that the relevant antecedents can be deliberately manipulated to obtain a predicted result. Not until it has reached this stage has the theory attained its full power and utility. The fact that no attitude theory has arrived at this point so far indicates that our understanding of the phenomena of attitude change is at present inadequate; the actual shortcomings should serve to indicate areas in which more research and thinking are needed.

SOME AREAS OF DISAGREEMENT

The very definition of "attitude" has been embroiled in controversy. To many workers the concept has three components: cog-

4 : Models of Attitude Change

nition, affect, and behavior. Some writers restrict the term to the first two dimensions, and view behavior as an independent dimension that may be but does not have to be a function of attitude. Still others use "attitude" to mean only emotional reactions, and refer to cognitive responses as "beliefs." These distinctions are by no means trivial. For example, many cigarette smokers admit that smoking is harmful to their health. While they accept this idea intellectually and emotionally, they continue to smoke. If we define behavior as part of attitude, then we see this situation as an attitude with components that are either inconsistent (in which case we are moved to investigate how this internal conflict developed) or differentially relevant to a variety of circumstances (in which case we turn our attention to the determinants of relevance). From the second viewpoint, the attitude is internally consistent; the reason it did not lead to action resides in other attitudinal, personality, and environmental factors.[2]

Another area of lively disagreement is that of attitude measurement. Problems of scoring and interpreting evaluations and beliefs have vexed numerous investigators. Just what, for example, is the meaning of a response of "zero" or "neutral" on a "plus-minus" or "like-dislike" attitude scale? A number of answers are possible:

1. The subject has no attitude on the issue.
2. The subject is a middle-of-the-roader.
3. The subject is ambivalent.
4. The subject is being reticent or uncooperative.
5. The subject is afraid to answer because of the possible interpretation that might be put on his real feelings if he revealed them.

Quite obviously, these reasons for a neutral response have very different antecedents and consequences; yet no attitude instrument can differentiate adequately among them.

Scaling is the most common method of measuring attitudes, and many of the techniques developed for psychophysics find social application here. Other measures, such as the semantic dif-

ferential (Osgood, Suci, and Tannenbaum, 1957), were specifically developed for evaluating concepts and symbols. As usual,
there are several unresolved issues. An obvious one is whether a
given measurement technique is accurate; or rather, how accurate it is in comparison with others. There is the question of how
widespread certain response tendencies are (giving "extreme"
answers on rating scales, for example), and how personality may
be related to such tendencies. Still another problem is the effect
on attitude scaling of the difference between the rater's own position and other positions sampled by the test. How well can a
person who takes a strong stand on a subject discriminate among
items representing divergent viewpoints?[3]

Some attitude researchers concentrate on persuasive technol-
ogy. Whether one-sided or two-sided messages are better,
whether the strongest arguments should be presented first or last,
whether conclusions should be stated or only implied—these
questions will not concern us here. They have been intensively
investigated by a group of researchers at Yale University (Hovland et al., 1957), and their findings as well as those of other investigators were summarized in a how-to book by H. I. Abelson
(1959; revised, Karlins and Abelson, 1970). Neither shall we
cover the factors of source prestige and credibility, of environ-
ments which facilitate the task of the persuader, or of the ways in
which susceptibility to the message can be decreased.[4] When
we turn to the major theoretical systems on which this book focuses, it becomes clear that "major" is difficult to define and is to
a large extent a matter of personal choice. There is one obvious
dichotomy in the literature, between theories that propose that
attitude change occurs because of a need for cognitive and emotional consistency, on the one hand, and theories based on other
psychological concepts (mostly learning and perception) on the
other. The first sort of explanation is the more widely used, and
has led to the greater amount of research; four of the eight selec-
tions in this book concentrate on consistency theories (two of
them on cognitive dissonance, the dominant construct in this

group). Other chapters use the learning, perception, and utility models. The research relevant to the theories is covered only briefly.[5]

CONSISTENCY THEORIES

Explications of attitude change often invoke motivational constructs. Theorists assume that attitudes serve some function—to provide cognitive structure, to facilitate the processing of information, to fit the individual into his group, to maintain self-esteem, or whatever. Once an attitude succeeds in gaining the goal for which the individual intended it, it will not change without some reason. The reason must go beyond a mere encounter with new information; the new attitude must be more pleasing or useful in some way than the old. As in other motivational models, there are two alternative emphases: an internal need that is reduced by a response and an external reward that the response may make attainable. The parallel to drive and incentive theories in general is obvious. We would be well advised, however, to suppress the associations that terms such as "drive" are likely to call forth; the accumulated connotations of forty years of traditional experimental psychology should not be transferred blindly into the attitude area.

Motivational theories of attitude change have undoubtedly been the most important propositions offered over the past decade or so, and the experimental literature reflects their popularity. Among these approaches, consistency theories represent a dominant trend. The key assumption of these models is that human beings require their attitudinal systems to be internally consistent, and that a state of inconsistency is (by analogy) non-homeostatic. Attitude change then follows as a way to restore the stable state.

Theorists do not agree unanimously on the motivational basis of consistency. Some workers ignore the issue for various reasons (see Singer, 1966), while others propose a variety of answers to such questions as whether the "consistency motive" is one motive or several, absolute or relative, innate or learned, aimed at eliminating inconsistency or at maintaining some optimal level (McGuire, 1966). These questions need not delay us here, but the lack of agreement—or rather the lack of empirical resolution —is a serious flaw in the consistency literature.

In the paper reprinted as Chapter 2 of this book, Zajonc (1960) describes three important versions of consistency theory. He also discusses research based on these formulations, and therefore I shall not treat it in detail here.

Balance Theory

Balance theory, as it was originated by Heider (1946, 1958), analyzes systems consisting of two or three persons (or two persons and an object), with any two of these entities related to each other by either positive or negative sentiments, or not related at all. The model is most relevant when belongingness (the unit relation) does exist; then, the sentiment relations are balanced if they provide a good Gestalt—if a liked person agrees and a disliked person disagrees with one's own sentiments toward the third entity. Newcomb (1953) enlarged the model to include communicative acts as linkages; Cartwright and Harary (1956) mathematicized it, clearing up some ambiguities and extending it to systems of more than three entities. Feather (1967) built further upon Cartwright and Harary's improvements in a communication context.

While the basic idea was persuasive, the theory was vague and incomplete. For example, the three-entity relationship did not take into account the fact that liking and disliking usually flow in two directions (with only two people involved, mutual liking or disliking represents balance). Though in many situations there are both positive and negative feelings toward a person or object, and though affects vary greatly in intensity (both "like" and "adore" are positive, but they are hardly equivalent), there was no way to assess the relative or absolute strength of sentiments. Furthermore, as Insko (1967) points out, experimenters have inferred imbalance when a subject rates himself as feeling uneasy, tense, or unpleasant on a scale from pleasant to unpleasant; but a stable-unstable rating of the relationship would seem more relevant to the theory, and certainly to attitude change. Unfortunately, such ratings of stability may not be very reliable, and (a major flaw) there are no unequivocal behavioral measures of imbalance. But other consistency theories have not even tried to develop an independent measure of the hypothetical state; honor is due at least for the recognition of the problem.

Another problem is that the unit relationship introduces a high degree of vagueness. For one thing, "belonging together" can be inferred from many relationships: ownership, causation, proximity, responsibility, membership, and so on. If an experimental finding can be explained by a bond that unites two entities, the experimenter can surely find a definition of unity that is plausible in the particular situation. And there is another problem: while things may either belong together or not, there seems to be no equivalent of like–not like–dislike. The best candidate seems to be "belong apart," and the effects of such a relationship on attitudes need to be investigated.

Insko (1967, pp. 162–63) cites some proverbs that contradict balance theory ("Opposites attract"; "Familiarity breeds contempt") and gives Heider's resolution of these dilemmas (for example, dissimilarity can result in liking if the characteristics of the two people involved complement each other). Other theories could offer less tortuous explanations; as an exercise, the reader might work out a balance interpretation of the Arab saying "The enemy of my enemy is my friend" as applied to the average American's strong dislike of both Nazis and Communists, who are mutual enemies. This is a losing game: if it could not be done, the exercise would show a striking exception to a basic aspect of the theory (which supports the proverb). But it can (by emphasizing the Nazis' and Communists' joint hostility to the United States). The room for semantic maneuvering is obvious, and the consequent loss of precision greatly weakens the theory.

While Cartwright and Harary have resolved a few of these problems, most of them remain. In short, balance theory is relevant to a great number of areas—among them friendship development (Newcomb, 1961), conformity (Brown, 1965, pp. 673–77), and reactions to criticism (Pilisuk, 1962)—but it explains the past much better than it predicts the future.

COGNITIVE AND AFFECTIVE CONSISTENCY

A much more sophisticated version of balance theory was developed by M. J. Rosenberg and R. P. Abelson. An early version of the model emphasizes consistency between attitudes (affect) and beliefs (cognition) toward a given object (Rosenberg, 1956, 1960a). Objects are liked to the extent that they are believed to be helpful or harmful to the individual's other significant attitude objects. If an object is positively valued and is seen as advancing other preferred objects (if an integrationist Democrat, for example, believes that his party is working for racial equality), the structure is consistent; but if the same liked object is believed to be hindering the attainment of other such objects (if our Democrat looks at some southern Democratic congressmen), there is inconsistency. And, according to the homeostatic model, when inconsistency exceeds the individual's tolerance limits, change occurs to restore consistency. In a similar vein, McGuire (1960) has analyzed Socratic questioning to show how it makes the individual aware of logical inconsistency among his beliefs, with a consequent striving for consistency.

In another version (Abelson and Rosenberg, 1958; Rosenberg and Abelson, 1960), cognitive elements (mental representations) are affectively related to each other in one of four ways: positively, negatively, ambivalently, or not at all. Positive and negative relationships are analogous to Heider's two sentiment relationships combined with unity, while ambivalence is a combination of positive and negative relationships (a step forward in allowing for complexity). In the null relationship, there is no connecting affect. A pair of cognitive elements linked in one of these ways is a cognitive unit, which thus has both cognitive and affective components.

In Chapter 3,[6] Abelson and Rosenberg list eight rules of "psycho-logic" (the test of which is psychological, not formal, acceptability), which predict new cognitive units from existing units. (If a student likes a certain professor, and the professor recommends a particular book, the student will expect to like the book. It's not logical, since one can like a man without sharing his taste in literature—but it's psycho-logically consistent.) When units are in accord with these predictions, balance exists; when there is ambivalence or inconsistency, there is imbalance. If the imbalance is recognized, and if the individual is motivated to think about the situation (note that these are further improvements in specifying relevant factors), cognitive steps are taken to resolve it. Motivation to reduce inconsistency is comparatively low when the existing relationship is to the individual's advantage (people are less bothered by the statement "Someone you dislike likes you" than by "Someone you like dislikes you," although both statements involve imbalance). The model provides for several balancing techniques (Abelson, 1959), adding complexity (which is good) and reducing precision (which is bad). The techniques include ceasing to think about the inconsistency, "denial" (the alteration of cognitive relations, similar to the resolution process described by Heider), bolstering (strengthening a cognitive unit to overwhelm the perceived inconsistency), differentiation (redefining a cognitive element), and transcendence (relating the inconsistent components to a larger concept that subsumes them both). Resolution techniques are used hierarchically, with the simplest ones (those requiring the fewest cognitive steps) attempted first. Incidentally, it may be a commentary on the state of the field that the recognition of "ceasing to think" as a way to resolve the problem represented a significant contribution.

Among the research efforts relevant to the theory, Rosenberg's (1960*b)* experiment deserves special honors for ingenuity. In this study, subjects were given posthypnotic suggestions to induce changes in the affective component of attitudes ("When you awake . . . [the] idea of Negroes moving into white neighborhoods will give you a happy, exhilarated feeling"); when they were awakened and asked to describe their attitudes, the perceived utility of the attitude object had changed to restore consistency with the altered affect. While hypnosis experiments should be evaluated with care, this is a striking and novel approach to consistency.

Another study (Rosenberg and Abelson, 1960) gave support to the hypothesis that the resolution of inconsistency follows the path of least resistance—that is, the technique that requires the least change is the one that is used. The subjects were told that the manager of the rug department in a department store, a man named Fenwick, had in the past raised the volume of rug sales. Now, however, Fenwick was planning a modern art display in his department, and such displays were known to reduce sales. The subjects were asked to play the roles of the owners of the store, with positive attitudes toward sales and either positive or negative attitudes toward Fenwick and modern art. In these roles they were to rate three messages. One of the messages argued that modern art increases sales, one denied that Fenwick was planning the display, and one said that Fenwick had not maintained sales. As predicted, in each case the message that led to restored balanced by changing only one sign was rated highest. If a subject was pretending to like Fenwick, modern art, and high sales, the original situation was "imbalanced" because Fenwick was in effect planning to hurt sales; the message that art displays increase sales would change the display-sales relationship to positive, restoring balance. This message was in fact rated most pleasant, persuasive, and accurate by the subjects whose roles called for positive attitudes toward Fenwick and modern art. Again, a somewhat unclean technique was used to good effect.

This approach is in several ways a great improvement over the original balance theory. It states explicitly that imbalance leads to change only if the individual is aware of it and is motivated to reduce it; the approach also recognizes (although it does not investigate thoroughly) individual differences in the ability to tolerate imbalance. The interrelationships possible among cognitive units become increasingly complex. Perhaps most important, ways of reducing inconsistency are defined and a principle is stated for predicting their order of preference. There is still no way to measure gradations in affect, and the definition of cognitive relations is somewhat vague, although some recent work (summarized in Abelson, 1968) is making inroads on the relationships implied by various connective verbs. In general, however, the theory is a powerful one worthy of further empirical consideration. Sad to say, it has not caught the imaginations of many researchers, and is to a great extent lying dormant—not an uncommon fate among psychological theories, many of which remain only partially explored. Which formulation will suffer this fate and which will arouse widespread furor and experimentation seems to be a matter of style and perhaps of the spirit of the times rather than of intrinsic value.

Congruity Theory

The second major consistency approach described by Zajonc (1960 and Chapter 2 of this volume) is Osgood and Tannenbaum's congruity theory (Osgood and Tannenbaum, 1955; Tannenbaum, 1967). This theory is integrally involved with a measurement technique proposed by Osgood et al. (1957) and known as the semantic differential, the first such close relationship between a theory and a scaling technique. One important component of the semantic differential is the evaluative dimension. Objects are evaluated on a seven-point scale, one pole representing "good" and the other "bad." The theory proposes that attitudes tend toward simplicity—that is, they tend to lie at the extremes of the good-bad dimension. A second proposition states that when two objects that are rated differently become related, they are subsequently given ratings more nearly alike. Thus if Mr. Smith, who dislikes President Nixon (rating of -3 on the evaluative dimension) and likes the idea of withdrawing American troops from Vietnam ($+3$), reads that President Nixon advocates troop withdrawal, congruity theory would predict that Smith's rating of Nixon would move from -3 toward the positive end of the scale and his ratings of troop withdrawal would move down from $+3$ toward the negative end. The relation between Nixon and troop withdrawal is associative, or positive. Relations may also be negative or dissociative, as in balance theory.

Tendency toward simplicity is a highly dubious proposition. Even if extreme judgments are "simpler"—and, while this proposition may seem likely, it is difficult to test—the general scaling literature shows that most judgments made by most people are not extreme. One may also question the adequacy of a seven-point scale to investigate this problem, since so small a dimension may lump a wide range of potential ratings from -3 to $-\infty$ and from $+3$ to $+\infty$ into the "extremes." At any rate, it seems clear that no "tendency" can be shown to exist without specification of the personality and situational variables that affect its activation.

The second hypothesis, known as the principle of congruity, is more testable as well as more interesting. Following this principle, we would predict that if a positively rated and a negatively rated object are linked, the ratings of both would move toward neutrality; if both of two linked objects are either positive or negative, but differently so, their subsequent ratings would be between their original ratings. Pressure toward congruity is a function of the polarity of the original scale values. In all cases of incongruity, the more polarized object (that is, the one closer to ± 3) will change less than the other. There is an "assertion constant," calculated ad hoc from data (Osgood and Tannenbaum, 1955), which is applied to rating results to allow for the fact that attitude toward the source of an assertion changes less than that toward the object of the assertion. In other words, if President Nixon (-3) endorses a troop withdrawal ($+3$), the rating of the President will improve less than the rating of withdrawal will deteriorate. There is also an ad hoc "correction for incredulity" to explain the reduction in obtained change when the subject does not wholly accept the link that is claimed to exist ("I don't believe he really meant it!").

The theory is particularly relevant to that old area of attitude research, prestige suggestion. The congruity model predicts that the more prestigious the source of an assertion or message—that is, the higher the source's evaluative rating—the greater the change of attitude toward the object of the assertion. The research results are not clear-cut, however; other variables affect the relationship between the source's prestige and the efficacy of a persuasive attempt. In fact, cognitive dissonance theory predicts that in some situations a negatively rated source is the most potent changer of attitude (Smith, 1961): when we agree to do what a disliked person asks, our attitude toward the task becomes more favorable than when a liked person makes the request. (An interesting experiment reported by Smith is described below, under "Dissonance Theory.")

Incidentally, there is a source of ambiguity here. While reviewers sometimes write as if a high evaluative rating were synonymous with prestige, this is not necessarily the case. Any reader —and any writer, too—can think of people whom he likes very much but whom he would not consider a prestigious source of arguments. Furthermore, prestige is seldom universal: a respected speaker on politics may be widely known as ignorant, biased, or both on the subject of art (see Feldman, 1966a). Thus the rating scale must be specified somewhat more exactly than it is in the prestige suggestion literature before this material can be interpreted in terms of congruity.

Osgood and Tannenbaum's use of the seven-point semantic differential eliminates one objection to balance theory, the oversimplified positive vs. negative categories of affective relations. Unfortunately, the third relationship, "assertion," remains not only dichotomous (either associative or dissociative), but vaguely defined as well. The concept that the evaluation of the source changes along with the attitude toward the object of the assertion is novel, interesting, and empirically challenging. Another improvement is the fact that any number of assertions can be included in the prediction formula; their overall effect is the average rating of the characteristics that each imputes to the object.

An alternative hypothesis, that overall change is a function of the summed ratings (Anderson and Fishbein, 1965), has some empirical support but has been criticized on methodological grounds (S. Rosenberg, 1968). The congruity model predicts both the direction and the amount of attitude change, but—except for the incredulity provision—ignores alternative methods for reducing imbalance or incongruity, such as those posited by R. P. Abelson (1959).

The use of mathematical formulae is generally considered a significant step forward in explicitness, and the congruity model has provided this to some extent. The facts remain, however, that the relationships underlying the numbers are still somewhat vague and that some of the formulae represent ad hoc patchwork. It may be that even such relatively primitive mathematics is more precise than our concepts and measures now warrant.

BELIEF CONGRUENCE

Rokeach (1968) has proposed a principle of belief congruence as a substitute for the Osgood and Tannenbaum congruity principle. This model measures the importance of a given belief by the number of other beliefs with which it is connected ("centrality") rather than by its usefulness for goal attainment (as in Rosenberg and Abelson's balance model). Beliefs are important to the extent that they concern one's own identity, are shared with other people, are learned by encounter with the belief object rather than at secondhand, and are not merely matters of taste. Using hypnosis to induce a change in belief, Rokeach found that beliefs categorized *a priori* as differing in centrality were to some extent distinguishable by factor analysis, that central beliefs resist change, and that when central beliefs do change, they produce changes in the rest of the belief system.

The Gestalt foundation of Rokeach's theory implies an interactive pattern that differs from a simple additive or averaging effect. In this approach, assertions are "unique configurations cognitively representing a *characterized subject* (S), capable of being characterized in many ways, and a *characterization* (C), capable of being applied to many subjects" (Rokeach, 1968, p. 84). If C and S are relevant to each other, there is cognitive interaction between them (CS). The resolution of incongruence between C and CS and between S and CS depends upon their relative centrality. For example, if a fervent enemy of "the world-wide Communist conspiracy" encounters a Yugoslav Communist, the C (Communist) is more important to his attitude than either the S (Yugoslav) or the CS (Yugoslav Communist). For a person who is interested in national differences within the Eastern bloc, the S may be of paramount importance. This consideration of incongruence and relative importance in context results in a number of possible resolutions and in the abandonment of the assertion constant and the correction for incredulity. The emphasis on configuration or pattern rather than on mere averaging or summing increases the complexity—and probably the realism—of the view. It has also led to interesting research on the interplay of racial and attitudinal similarity as factors in interpersonal relations. For example, under some circumstances racially prejudiced religious whites prefer religious Negroes to atheistic whites (Rokeach, 1968).

Insko (1967) points out the vagueness of the interaction construct as well as other conceptual and methodological inadequacies in the Rokeach model; and for a Gestalt approach, the definition of context is rather restricted. Helson (1964) has done a more thorough analysis of contextual factors in his adaptation-level formulation, which is discussed in a later section on cognitive and perceptual theories. While there is some evidence in support of Rokeach's predictions, no persuasive data have appeared in an attitude change paradigm. At the moment, belief congruence is at best a potentially useful modification of the consistency construct, its particular contribution being its emphasis on configuration rather than additivity. Its real worth awaits the clarification of ideas (the idea of interaction, for example) and of measures (such as those of centrality), followed by rigorous research and interpretation.

Cognitive Dissonance Theory

Of the formulations based on the concept of consistency, cognitive dissonance theory (Festinger, 1957) is the most lively one in today's literature. In fact, it is probably the most lively of all attitude theories: it has originated the largest number of experiments, it has attracted the most adherents, and it has aroused the greatest controversy. The supporters of dissonance theory have a penchant for surprising predictions, for cute experimental designs, and for just enough loopholes in procedure and interpretation to provide attractive targets for their opponents. We shall have a look at some examples of the nonobvious hypothesis, the ingenious experiment, and the inviting weakness.

The theory was first presented by Festinger (1957) and extended by, among others, Brehm and Cohen (1962) and Lawrence and Festinger (1962). Briefly, it focuses on the consequences of incompatibility between two related cognitions, which may be thoughts, memories, beliefs, or attitudes. Such incompatibility, or dissonance, is aroused when the opposite of one cognition is implied by the other. For example, studying for a test implies (is consonant with) getting a good grade; if one studies hard and then gets a bad grade, dissonance is aroused. This is a simple starting point not greatly different from those of other consistency theories and considerably less elegant than some; but from this acorn has grown an oak with very widespreading branches indeed.

More than any other homeostatic approach to attitude change, cognitive dissonance theory relates its hypotheses to overt action. In fact, its most intriguing aspect is its reversal of the usual question, "How do attitudes influence behavior?" Much of the research of cognitive dissonance adherents—or "dissonancers," as Rosenberg (1968) conveniently calls them—has to do with the effects of behavior on the behaver's attitudes. Aspects of this concern are the effects of acting in opposition to one's real beliefs (counterattitudinal performance, frequently mislabeled "forced compliance")[7] and of psychologically costly experiences such as severe embarrassment or intense effort. Research has also been done on the attitude change and the seeking of information that follow the making of a decision.

Counterattitudinal behavior is the context for what are probably the most famous nonobvious predictions of cognitive dissonance theory. Festinger and Carlsmith (1959) originally demonstrated that a person who received a small reward for lying to someone else eventually came to believe his own lies more firmly than did someone who had received a large reward. Festinger and Carlsmith's design asked the subject to convince someone else that an actually boring task was really interesting. One group of deceivers was offered $20 each and the other group $1 to perform this task. After their performance, the subjects were asked to evaluate the experiment. The $1 group rated it as interesting and worthwhile. The $20 group rated it quite negatively.

The theory predicted this outcome, since a large reward is sufficient justification for a small deception, while to mislead an innocent victim without significant compensation arouses dissonance (an interesting judgment on moral codes). The dissonance is reduced if the liar comes to believe himself, since then he retroactively (or perhaps concurrently) erases the untruth. Incidentally, the phenomenon had been found by Kelman in 1953, before the theory was published by Festinger.

An interesting variation has been the study of dissonance effects of hunger, thirst, and pain. High-dissonance subjects have reported less intense reactions after such unpleasant experimental manipulations than low-dissonance subjects; when subjects were paid only a small amount, they reduced their dissonance by minimizing the unpleasantness of the experience. Physiological and behavioral differences were compatible with self-ratings; for instance, high-dissonance subjects deprived of food not only reported being less hungry than low-dissonance subjects, but actually ate less (Brehm, 1962; Zimbardo, 1969). Bankart and Lanzetta (1968) extended this design to the reactions of heavy smokers who were deprived of tobacco, and their findings also supported the dissonance hypothesis: that is, high-dissonance subjects missed cigarettes less than low-dissonance subjects.

Dissonance theory predicts that people who obey to avoid being severely punished will evidence less attitude change than those who comply with a mildly threatening demand. Again, one can justify counterattitudinal behavior by citing a strong threat; but when the external consequences would not be very severe, the threat seems insufficient to explain the hypocrisy, so the attitude is changed (since one's actions are acceptable if they are not *really* counterattitudinal). This hypothesis was supported by the results of an experiment in which children were told they would be punished (either mildly or severely) for playing with a desirable toy (Aronson and Carlsmith, 1963). The findings imply that if we want to change people's attitudes toward the behavior we demand of them, we should induce them to comply by offering a small reward or threatening them with mild punishment if they refuse. On the other hand, if mere obedience or cooperation is all we want, we will get more people to comply by increasing our bribes and our threats.

Related to these experiments are studies that associate some unpleasant factor with an activity, a goal, or a demand for obedience. One famous article (Aronson and Mills, 1959) concerned girls who suffered through an embarrassing initiation in order to hear a supposedly exciting discussion that turned out to be quite dull. These girls evaluated the discussion more positively than subjects who did not experience a severe initiation (a finding of some relevance to fraternities). Dissonance was reduced by the rationalization that the discussion really was worth the price. Another aspect of the same process is the effect of obeying a disliked person. In an ingenious experiment (Smith, 1961), Army reservists were offered fifty cents each to eat a grasshopper. Supposedly the Army wanted to investigate the acceptability of unusual foods. When the request was made by an aloof and formal person, only half complied; when it was made by someone the reservists wanted to please, over 90% agreed to cooperate. But among all compliant subjects, those who obeyed the less likable persuader liked the grasshopper more! The dissonance mechanism, presumably, was: "Why would I do this for such an unlikable character? Obviously because what he asked me to do wasn't all that bad," versus "I'll eat the grasshopper because I like you; I don't have to like *it*."

An article by Myers (1963) tells of an experiment in which psychologists were presented with a hypothetical situation in which some subjects experienced victory and others defeat, and were asked to speculate on which subjects would be willing to go through the experiment again. Each psychologist was asked to make two predictions, one based on dissonance theory and one representing his own personal conjecture. On the basis of dissonance theory, most respondents predicted that the losers would come back; but their independent guess was that the winners would do so. This is not only an enjoyable study to read, but it demonstrates vividly the widespread feeling that dissonance theory always predicts an outcome that seems unlikely. As Myers points out, the information given was too incomplete to permit anyone to derive a dissonance hypothesis from it. Did all the hypothetical losers expect to win? If some of them did not, then they experienced no dissonance when they lost. And if dissonance has been aroused, there are alternate ways to reduce it. Volunteering for another session is one possible resolution, but not the only one. It is interesting, though, that most of the responding psychologists agreed on what the theory would predict, and also uniformly disagreed with that prediction.

The effects of effort represent a closely related dissonance analysis. We would expect that the more one has to work to reach a goal, the more valuable the goal will seem. While attempts to demonstrate the truth of this hypothesis are not very conclusive, there is some evidence to support it (Zimbardo, 1965). Lawrence and Festinger (1962) pointed out that dissonance theory predicts rat behavior: it takes longer to extinguish a response in a rat trained on a partial reinforcement schedule than in one trained on a 100 percent reinforcement schedule, and so on. Cognitive dissonance in rats—a thought to chill the rat-runner's soul!

Another noteworthy feature of dissonance theory is its treatment of what happens after a decision is made. Inner conflict before decision has long been studied by psychologists (Lewin, 1935; Miller, 1944). The general conclusion has been that both the desirable and the undesirable characteristics of an object or event seem stronger as one gets closer to it in space or time.

Thus ambivalence about a decision should reach its height just before a decision is made. But what happens immediately afterward?

Festinger (1957) indicates that the act of choosing is the demarcation between conflict (which leads to conflict resolution) and dissonance (which leads to dissonance reduction). Like the intensity of conflict, the intensity of dissonance increases with the similarity in the attractiveness of the possible choices. There is no problem if you choose a good job over a bad one; but when you have chosen one of several jobs that are almost equally good (or bad), the decision arouses dissonance. The choice may be revoked, or both alternatives may be incorporated into a larger category, or—most often—the chosen alternative is reevaluated as being really *much* better. This is contrary to Lewin's (1938) position, that once a choice has been made between two goals, the unchosen one begins to look better. To bolster dissonance reduction, information favorable to the preferred choice may be sought out while information favoring the rejected alternative is rejected. Evidence on the reevaluation issue supports dissonance theory fairly well (Festinger, 1964; Insko, 1967); but selective exposure to information, and particularly selective avoidance of information, have not been demonstrated at all adequately (Sears, 1968).

CRITICISMS AND ALTERNATIVES

There is probably no other critique so all-encompassing and so devastating as the paper by Chapanis and Chapanis (1964) which appears as Chapter 4 of this volume. One of the basic criticisms, which really applies to most consistency research, is that methodologically dissonance is used as an independent variable when theoretically it is an intervening or a dependent variable. That is, subjects in a "dissonance condition" are compared with those in a "no-dissonance condition," the experimenter's manipulations defining the conditions. But people no doubt differ in their reactions to those manipulations, and the subjects in both "conditions" are likely to represent a wide range of dissonance arousal. It would seem an urgent matter to develop specific measures of dissonance, either physiological or in paper-and-pencil format (as balance theorists have attempted to do; see the earlier section on balance theory, under "Consistency Theories"). Without these, the argument becomes circular: How does the experimenter *know* that subjects in the dissonance group really experienced dissonance? Because their attitudes changed. Why did the attitudes of these subjects change? Because the subjects had experienced dissonance. And when subjects in the dissonance group *don't* change their attitudes, the experimenter may conclude that they must be reducing dissonance in some other way, and therefore throw out their data—the basis of another serious criticism.

The Chapanis article makes three major points that must be considered in any examination of the cognitive dissonance literature: first, that experimental designs have been so confounded that alternative interpretations of the data are frequently plausible; second, that the data analysis is to some extent (sometimes a very great extent) invalidated by such improper practices as the selective dropping of subjects; and third, that these shortcomings are frequently ignored in later references to the experiments, with resultant exaggerated claims of support for the dissonance hypothesis. (See Insko, 1967, for some recent evidence on the third point.) Readers of secondary sources—students, for example—are easily misled by this last practice. Studies result in nonsignificant trends, or in mixed significant and nonsignificant outcomes, or in significant outcomes after highly questionable analyses, thus providing much less than clear-cut support for the theory. These weaknesses are seldom pointed out in sympathetic reviews or introducton sections. It should also be noted, but often is not, that when the theory makes absolute predictions, relative differences are not necessarily adequate evidence. For example, in the Festinger and Carlsmith (1959) study, the hypothesis was that high-dissonance subjects would enjoy the task while low-dissonance subjects would find it unpleasantly boring. Yet, while there were significant intergroup differences in the right direction, the absolute ratings of all groups were close to neutral. Similarly, an experiment that finds subjects preferring information that supports a decision to information that opposes the decision does not critically test the dissonance hypothesis that unfavorable information will be *avoided*.

Silverman's (1964) defense against the Chapanis' criticisms, which is reprinted as Chapter 5, takes up the first two kinds of objections separately. His major argument in response to the alternative explanations advanced by the Chapanises is that there is no empirical reason to prefer these explanations to one based on dissonance theory. For instance, while a certain result may be due to suspicion, no evidence is presented in support of the contention. This argument is an excellent impetus for further research, but not an impregnable defense of dissonance theory: the Chapanis article was not intended to be a research report, and the raising of other, equally plausible hypotheses seems a permissible attack on a theoretical system. Obviously the validity of the attack and of the theory then depend on further experiments that, through strong inference, pose the dissonance and the alternative hypotheses against each other. Adherence to dissonance theory is certainly more parsimonious than the multiplicity of alternative explanations; but parsimony is only a pragmatic guideline, not an empirical test. If several variables are necessary before a complex set of phenomena can be understood, devotion to only one leads to inadequate understanding.

Some of Silverman's criticisms of specific alternatives are also worthy of consideration. As an example, let us take the experiment in which subjects who worked hard for a reward did not show the secondary reinforcement effect (liking the color associated with a reward) found in a low-effort group (Aronson, 1961). Aronson's article maintained that secondary reinforcement and dissonance canceled each other with high effort: dissonance reduction led to preference for the unrewarded color. The Chapanis paper explained that effort and reward rate were confounded. Since with high effort there was less reinforcement, there was also less secondary reinforcement, and references to dissonance are unnecessary. Silverman's defense quotes Skinner to refute the Chapanis' implication that high reward rate leads to greater secondary reinforcement effects. However, the paper by Ferster and Skinner (1957) compares continuous with intermittent reinforcement, not different rates of intermittent reinforcement with each other—which was the nature of the Aronson procedure. When Silverman deals with the effects of reward on attitude change after lying (Festinger and Carlsmith's 1959 study), his citation of Lependorf's dissertation raises some interesting questions. Can it be that there is a real difference in the degree of self-justification after lying for fifty cents and for five cents? And how could it be that $1 is not sufficient justification for lying when another group gets $20 (Festinger and Carlsmith, 1959) but is enough when the other group gets fifty cents (Cohen, 1962)? Such questions cannot be answered adequately until degrees of dissonance arousal can be measured.

As for the methodological and statistical faults cited in the Chapanis review, the defense rests upon necessary compensation for lack of precision and upon the failure (with one exception) of the Chapanises to demonstrate how the flaws could have affected the conclusions. These, like the previous arguments, strongly indicate that while dissonance theory is by no means indefensible, it is in need of more convincing empirical support. The *post hoc* elimination of subjects, for example, is a tactic for getting the desired result artificially; and calling it "induction" does not exonerate the practice. Data based on such methods are highly suspect, and need to be confirmed before they can be accepted as convincing evidence.

In an important research contribution, Rosenberg (1965) not only suggested an alternative to some dissonance explanations, but also performed an experiment to test his hypothesis. The suggestion was that differential reward leads to different degrees of anxiety concerning the experimenter's opinion of a subject who agrees to lie for pay. Rosenberg called this particular kind of anxiety "evaluation apprehension." In the high-reward condition, suspicion and disbelief of the experiment's stated purpose are aroused and lead to apprehension. "Why would this psychologist offer me twenty dollars for such an easy task? Obviously, to see how I react to a bribe—so I will not indicate that my real attitude has changed." Rosenberg also pointed out (1966) that the agreement to be on call for future participation, far from being a justification for the high retainer, may arouse even more suspicion: "It may be true, as the experimenter claims, that his assistant has failed to show up and he really needs help, but why hire an inexperienced undergraduate like me as a permanent substitute if he expects future emergencies?" When evaluation apprehension was reduced by making the subject think that the counterattitudinal behavior and the attitude measurement were two separate experiments, and that neither experimenter would know the subject's performance on the other's study, dissonance effects were not found. It seems, then, that evaluation apprehension is an adequate alternative to cognitive dissonance in this particular design.

Other substitutes have been proposed to explain other dissonance findings: feelings of achievement, relief from embarrassment, sexual arousal, and expectation of future discomfort (Chapanis and Chapanis, 1964); self-judgment in which one infers his attitudes from his own behavior, but with no postulate of an intervening aversive state that causes attitude change (Bem, 1965 [Chapter 7 of this volume], 1967, 1968b); self-persuasion (Janis and King, 1954); defense against a feeling of having behaved improperly, and the anticipation of negative social consequences (Pepitone, 1966).

Conversely, dissonance adherents have been finding variables that tend to determine whether dissonance will in fact occur. It is quite clear that the theory is not always supported (see Insko, 1967). For example, Collins, with a number of associates, has done close to twenty experiments on forced compliance, mostly with nondissonance results (Collins, 1969). It now appears that support for the theory is more likely when there is little or no justification offered for complying (Freedman, 1963); when the subject perceives that he is free not to comply but does so of his own volition (Brock, 1968a); when he commits himself as publicly and firmly as possible (Brehm and Cohen, 1962; Carlsmith, Collins, and Helmreich, 1966); and when he feels that he is being asked to persuade an open-minded audience (Nel, Helmreich, and Aronson, 1969).

What can we say about dissonance theory in general? It obviously is not *the* solution to all problems of prediction and explanation in the attitude area. While it makes possible more direct empirical confrontations with other theories than most other approaches do, the crucial question for experimenter and student seems to be "not which but when" (Aronson, 1969, p. 20); in other words, which theory is better *in a particular situation*.

Internally, the model is vague in many of the same areas as other consistency theories. What are the "cognitions" among which dissonance can exist? Apparently, responses of almost every kind. How do we determine the relevance of a given cognition? When incompatible cognitions arouse dissonance, what factors in the cognitions are responsible for the magnitude of the dissonance? We don't know. Why do subjects comply if the justification is "insufficient"? Logically, the fact that they do comply would seem to indicate that there must be *some* adequate reason; and if there is, why should they experience dissonance? Dissonance is typically definable as a situation that the experimenter thinks is dissonant; is there a way to assess dissonance independently? How can we identify or control various methods of dissonance reduction? These questions have as yet no good answers.[8]

There has been much recent work on experimental artifacts —the tendency of experimenters to get the results they expect, and of subjects to act as they think the experimenter expects them to act (Rosenthal and Rosnow, 1969). Dissonance researchers have ignored this problem; to an unknown extent, therefore, dissonance results may be artifactual. The extent is quite likely to be large. Since the tasks given subjects are often unpleasant or fatiguing, and since noncompliers are thrown out, the group that is left consists of people who by definition are submissive to the experimenter's rather extreme demands. It is probable that such people will generally try to please the experimenter, and giving him the responses they think he wants is the most obvious way of pleasing him. Furthermore, the elaborateness of the staging and the great number of pilot studies required to get the production just right may result in experimental procedures that maximize the demands implied to the subject. It would be interesting to calculate the proportion of procedures with which an experimenter has succeeded in arousing dissonance (in his opinion) out of all the procedures with which he has attempted to do so. The difficulty of getting the effect may indicate the fragility of the phenomenon; the difficulty of explaining why some procedures are "successful" and other, similar ones are not shows the vagueness of the dissonance concept.

As for the effect of the experimenter's expectations, Cooper, Eisenberg, Robert, and Dohrenwend (1967) have found that they could wash out the dissonance effect by using experimenters whose expectations were systematically manipulated. This extremely serious warning seems so far to have gone unheeded. Rosnow and Robinson (1967, p. 307) have noted that "findings by supporters of dissonance theory seem consistently to confirm it, while findings by its opponents seem consistently to refute it." This does not seem to bother some of the disputants; Brehm (1965) has gone so far as to suggest that only a researcher who has previously confirmed the theory is fully qualified to disconfirm it, since only such a person has demonstrated a grasp of the conceptual and methodological problems involved. This argument has a kernel of merit: a grasp of the problems should be demonstrated by critic and supporter alike. However, it is a fallacious prescription in the light of what we know about experimental artifacts. From this point of view, the criterion is the opposite: confirmation should come from researchers who have previously obtained negative results.

The research is certainly copious, and this fact has been offered as a sort of a justification for the theory: "Happily, after more than 10 years, it is still not proven; all the theory ever does is generate research" (Aronson, 1969, p. 31). But that is not enough; what is needed is a formulation that accounts for attitude change of differing kinds, magnitudes, and persistence, at various stages of development, in a variety of situations, and which can be confirmed or disconfirmed by both experimental and field data (Koslin, 1967).

Deutsch and Krauss (1965), referring to the idea that originating research is what really counts, speculate that "undoubtedly Festinger would rather be stimulating than right" (p. 76). Considering the amount of commitment and work that the development of a good theory entails, I doubt that. (Festinger, too, disagrees, quite vehemently.)[9] From an empirical point of view, Festinger has been both stimulating *and* right; and also wrong. Of the theories discussed so far, dissonance is certainly the most wide-ranging. Its truth value cannot be judged on the basis of the existing data. An independent measure of dissonance appears to be a prerequisite for valid testing and for an authoritative assessment.

NONCONSISTENCY THEORIES

That there are consistency theories aplenty we have seen; they are dominant in number, in adherents, and in research. In comparison with this mainstream, other approaches seem mere rivulets unless we arbitrarily combine them in a category of theories that have little in common beyond the fact that they are not based on consistency. It is these theories, mostly centered around learning and cognition, that now concern us. (There is also a small, barely begun trickle of my own favorites, *anti*consistency theories: that is, theories asserting that man seeks variety, novelty, and excitement, even at the expense of balance, congruence, or consonance. Unfortunately, these approaches are as yet hardly evident in the attitude area, although they are gaining ground among theories of personality, motivation, and development.)

In general, the nonconsistency theories emphasize that attitudes have adaptive significance to the people who hold them.

They may be based on past reinforcements, or on the prospect of future reinforcements; they may be guidelines to make the world seem more understandable or more friendly; they may aid the individual to defend, express, or actualize himself. No intervening aversive state is needed to bring about attitude change; in fact, these theories are frequently concerned with attitude *formation* rather than change.

Learning Theories

One general view of attitude development is that attitudes are learned either through reinforcement or through contiguity. As learning theories have become increasingly important in experimental psychology, several psychologists have proposed learning theories of attitude change. The first systematic proposal of this sort was Doob's (1947), which considers attitude to be an implicit response intervening between stimuli and overt responses. In line with the theories of Hull and Spence, this implicit response has the properties of energizing and guiding behavior.

The specific nature of the cue provided by an attitude depends upon previous rewards and punishments: if an action has been rewarded in the past, the attitude that led to it is strengthened. Also, a stimulus similar to one that was present in a former favorable stimulus-attitude-action chain will tend to evoke the same response through the process of generalization. As we shall see, other derivations from learning theory have also been applied to the attitude area.

INCENTIVE THEORY

One extensive line of work based on the learning viewpoint is the incentive theory of the so-called Yale group, which was led by Carl I. Hovland. The conceptual framework is outlined in Hovland, Janis, and Kelley (1953), and many publications have described the group's research. The theory argues that a new opinion is accepted (assuming that the message is received and understood) if there is a potential reward or incentive for such acceptance. Working under this general rule, the researcher seeks to establish the likelihood of such a positive consequence in a given situation, to determine how to maximize its probability, and so on. For example, the Yale theorists proposed that being "right" on an issue is a rewarding experience; that in most people's experience, believing the statements of experts in their fields of expertise has usually led them to be right; and that therefore people will tend to believe a persuader whom they consider an expert on the issue in question. Specific details are explained by principles (such as generalization and extinction) based on general learning theory.

If this seems like a rather complex analysis of a simple situation, let us look at another problem. As we saw earlier, dissonance theory holds that arguing against one's real beliefs produces a change in those beliefs only if there is no strong external reason for engaging in the task to begin with. Reinforcement theory predicts just the opposite: that an argument will be accepted if it is associated with reward; that money or social approval or some sort of victory gained by counterattitudinal behavior should lead to attitude change in the direction of the behavior. There are empirical data supporting both hypotheses (Insko, 1967). Aronson, a staunch dissonancer, concludes that although high incentive in itself may lead to attitude change, under some conditions it produces dissonance instead (1966). The specific variables that determine the strength of these two conflicting tendencies are still to be identified. One relevant finding is that dissonance effects are found when subjects feel free not to comply, and incentive effects when they do not feel that they can refuse (Linder, Cooper, and Jones, 1967; Holmes and Strickland, 1970); this is the kind of research needed to define the issues clearly.

Another direct confrontation between incentive theory and dissonance theory occurs on the issue of effort. On the one hand, effort supposedly arouses dissonance and may lead to attitude change; on the other hand, the harder one has to work for a given outcome, the less pleasurable that outcome should seem—a matter of profit rather than of straight reward. If the profit is

PETER SUEDFELD : 31

little, there should be little attitude change. It appears that the two theories complement each other, and that both explain some of the data: Fromkin (1968) reported a reinforcement effect for rewarded stimuli (they were preferred to nonrewarded stimuli, particularly when effort was low, and their attractiveness declined as effort went up) and a weak dissonance effect for nonrewarded stimuli (they tended to become more attractive as effort increased).

PERSUASIVE COMMUNICATION MODELS

Chapter 6 (Weiss, 1967) presents a brief overview of the application of a strict learning approach to attitude change. The parallels between data derived from attitudinal and nonattitudinal learning studies are particularly interesting. Another point that should be noted is the ability of this model to explain such well-established phenomena as the tendency to remember arguments with which one agrees (selective learning). This particular paper (expanded in Weiss, 1968) gives specific empirical instances of the general analogues discussed by Hovland, Janis, and Kelley (1953) and others.

Weiss (1963) also offers a unique application of learning principles to a specific change in social attitude, defection from social movements. According to this analysis, four social situations, each associated with a learning process, explain defection and subsequent adherence to another movement. One of these situations is the unavailability of the movement when a member leaves the area where it is functioning or when the movement itself collapses. In this case, stimulus generalization leads the member to seek out another movement similar to the first. Failure of the member to gain rewards from membership is another such situation. It is followed by the extinction of belief, participation, or both, depending on which has not been reinforced, with little likelihood of recruitment into a new group. If the individual receives no rewards and in addition is mildly punished for belief and/or participation in the movement, he will leave it and transfer his allegiance to another group. If rewards are nonexistent and punishment is severe, he will leave the group and not join another. The selection of a new group is a function of severity and target of punishment, intergroup similarity, and the individual member's initial level of belief and participation. The final choice depends upon reinforcement and repetition. This ingenious presentation, with historical examples of the four categories, offers some interesting alternatives to other models of group membership as well as to the standard laboratory-centered attitude-learning approaches.

Weiss applies conditioning principles to an old dichotomy investigated by the Yale group—the difference between the effects of explicit and implicit conclusions in a persuasive message—and shows that the effects of explicit conclusions follow the rules of instrumental conditioning, while those of implicit conclusions follow the rules of classical conditioning (see Chapter 6, Figures 11 and 12). There is considerable evidence that the reinforcement of certain attitude-related responses by verbal approval will strengthen those responses by instrumental conditioning (see Bem, 1968b; Insko, 1967). It has also been demonstrated that the repeated coupling of an innocuous stimulus with either pleasant or unpleasant adjectives will make the originally neutral stimulus take on positive or negative meaning by classical conditioning. For example, nonsense syllables paired with favorable adjectives eventually are rated as more pleasant than nonsense syllables paired with unfavorable adjectives (Staats and Staats, 1958). The association between stimuli and such nonverbal reinforcers as food also changes attitudes toward the stimuli (Insko, 1967).

The attitude models based on learning theory reflect the variety of learning theory versions and emphases. Greenwald (1968), for example, argues that remembering—that is, having learned—a message and being persuaded by it do not necessarily to together. Rather, what is learned is a set of cognitive responses to the message. Attitude change is then a function of the acceptability of these responses on the basis of other beliefs, reinforcement history, and the like. An individual who encounters a message to which he has previously learned favorable responses and associations is more likely to find the message persuasive than one who has not. Similarly, a subject who generates and rehearses his own arguments is likely to be persuaded by the rehearsal (see also Insko, 1967). Here we have an alternative to the dissonance explanation of role-playing. It is the learning of such positive responses, not dissonance aroused by commitment or effort, that leads the persuader to believe his own argument. The superiority of this model to other learning theories (which emphasize attention to the argument, the impact of newly discovered points, or satisfaction engendered by the performance) remains to be tested. This approach emphasizes the existence of a relatively complex cognitive superstructure built upon a learning base. In this aspect, it is highly compatible with Bem's (1967) view that "dissonance" effects occur when subjects examine their past behavior.

SELF-PERSUASION THEORY

Bem's self-persuasion theory (1965, [Chapter 7 of this volume], 1967, 1968a, 1968b, 1968c) focuses on the information derived from observing one's own behavior. The individual who is receiving positive outcomes from performing a particular act will be likely to repeat the act, in accordance with the laws of learning; the fact that he is doing something over and over again indicates to him that he must like doing it. To use Bem's favorite example, the answer to the question "Do you like brown bread?" is "I guess I do, I'm always eating it." Note that the emphasis is on the behavior, as befits a theorist who calls himself a radical behaviorist. But the attitude does not undergo any change in order to match behavior, as in the dissonance postulate; rather, the attitude is inferred from the behavior, and the inference is made by the behaver himself. The implication is that attitudes as such are unimportant. In fact, they are perhaps nonexistent until we are asked (or ask ourselves) to explain our actions. When that happens, an appropriate attitude statement is formulated. Bem points out, however, that the individual cannot always identify the specific behavior on which his inference is based. This last point, made almost in passing, seems to dilute the rigor and testability of the model.

Research has supported Bem's arguments in two ways. First, it has demonstrated that learned behavior is used to infer attitudes about the stimuli associated with the behavior. It is important to note that the attitudes are not merely verbal responses associated with the stimuli, as in the Staats' classical conditioning approach. Thus in Chapter 7's Experiment III, when subjects were required to make extreme evaluations of originally neutral stimuli in the presence of a cue that they were to tell the truth, they later indicated that their "true" attitude was indeed relatively extreme ("I rated the cartoon as very funny and the truth light was on; I guess I think it *is* very funny"). Bem (1966) has also trained subjects to believe that the false statements they made when the truth light was on were really true.

The other line of evidence comes from a series of studies that Bem calls "interpersonal replications." These involve a written description of one or another of the popular dissonance scenarios. Each group of subjects reads the description of the situation as it was perceived by one group in the original experiment, and is informed that those particular subjects agreed to do as they were asked (to lie, to go hungry, and so on). The replication subjects are then asked to describe the attitude of the original participants. It turns out that these ratings are usually quite close to those obtained in the dissonance studies. If an external observer can infer the subject's attitude from a description of his behavior, there is no reason to think that the subject himself cannot make the same inference from observing his own behavior. Thus, Bem argues, there is no need to postulate intervening motivational processes such as dissonance.

So far, no attack has succeeded in refuting this explanation, although some contradictory data have been reported (see Jones, Linder, Kiesler, Zanna, and Brehm, 1968; Bem, 1968c). Whether the model will stand up under more detailed and possibly hostile testing remains to be seen. In spite of its originality and obvious strength, it has not attracted many adherents yet. One reason for this besides its newness, may be its simplicity: in this field, insistence on a behavioral focus and deemphasis of intervening processes are truly quite radical.[10] Such an insistence seems to many workers in the field not merely simple, but simplistic. Moreover, Bem has had very little to say about the determinants of the behavior on which attitudes are based. In one study (Bem, 1968a), operant conditioning techniques were used to train institutionalized children to say that they liked a lot of brown bread (Bem's interest in brown bread is intriguing, especially to a fellow enthusiast). Another group was repeatedly told that it liked a lot of brown bread. Both groups increased their consumption of brown bread about equally. Bem interprets these data as showing that self-instruction and external instruction are similar in their power to direct behavior. More work on these and other relevant factors is obviously needed.

TASK-EXPERIENCE THEORY

Breer and Locke (1965) have developed an interesting learning model that accepts the importance of reinforcement and generalization, but concentrates on the ways in which these factors affect the development of attitudes based upon the performance of various types of activity, or "task experience." Their thesis is that when one operates on certain stimuli to achieve an outcome, the nature of the stimuli (difficult or easy, for example), the nature of the operations (socially cooperative or individualistic), and the nature of the outcome (successful or failing) give rise to new attitudes. Task performances have four components: cognitive, affective, evaluative, and behavioral. The cognitive component involves the building of hypotheses and the selection of tactics. The affective component (which Breer and Locke call "cathectic") is the emergence of preference and attachment to certain responses. The evaluative component is the judgment of the legitimacy of given responses by social and individual norms. Behavior, of course, is the set of overt actions with which the other three components are concerned.

Let us see how the components are related. If a task necessitates social cooperation for success, then as a group progresses in its performance, the members will "(1) become *cognitively* aware that cooperation is instrumental to task success, (2) *behave* in a cooperative fashion, (3) develop a *cathectic* interest in co-operating with each other, and (4) establish *norms* defining cooperation as a legitimate and expected form of behavior" (Breer and Locke, 1965, p. 13; italics mine). Thus positive reinforcement or the prospect of positive reinforcement shapes all four components into an integrated orientation. Such orientations are then generalized to other, similar task situations ("lateral generalization") and to general cultural beliefs and norms ("vertical generalization"). So, for example, the members of the group described above will tend to have a cooperative attitude when they work at other tasks with other groups, at least until they are negatively reinforced as a result. They will also come to believe that cooperation is, in general, a desirable and useful characteristic.

This rather complex version of conditioning theory does not deal with the effects of verbal persuasion as such, and thus differs from most other theories of attitude change. Its broad definition of "tasks" enables it to deal with religious beliefs, societal factors and general social change, occupational choice and success, and many other areas of attitude and behavior. To date, task-experience theory has attracted very little attention among attitude workers, partly because of its sociological emphasis and partly because of its lack of interest in the more popular or traditional variables—persuasive messages, role-playing, and so on. It is worth pursuing, however, both for its own intrinsic value and as a means of delineating crucial boundaries between theories. For example, it predicts that only task performance, not mere commitment to the task, will result in the learning of new attitudes, and that reward and attitude change are positively correlated. Both predictions are contrary to those of dissonance theory. The concern with long-term everyday activity, in contrast to the laboratory orientation of most dissonancers, may underlie this disagreement. If so, we may start to identify the appropriate theory for a given situation.

STRENGTHS AND WEAKNESSES OF LEARNING MODELS

Learning theory has been widely used to explore the effects of motivational (especially fear) arousal on persuasibility, the differential power of one-and two-sided arguments or of earlier and more recent arguments, and so on. In order not to arouse dissonance, I shall retain my earlier restriction on such largely technological questions.

What good are these models? For one thing, the confrontations between learning theories and the dissonance school provide the largest proportion of critical experiments in the literature. Some of these tests have identified weaknesses or omissions in one theory or the other; others have given us ideas about the appropriate conditions and areas in which a given theory is most powerful. Learning models have also accomplished the translation of vague ideas into relatively concrete, operational, and sometimes even quantitative terms. Their emphasis on the parallels between attitudes and other behavioral and cognitive phenomena has also been of value.

As for their weaknesses, one is the refusal of most of the theorists to commit themselves to a system. From Hovland et al. (1953) through Weiss (1967), we have comments that the presentation is only preliminary, the parallels drawn are only analogies. While this may be justifiable at one point in time, it would be nice to see some progress toward stronger statements. A related shortcoming is the fragmentary nature of the general approach, which makes it difficult to evaluate the usefulness of learning theory as such. As Kiesler et al. (1969, p. 154) say of these theorists, "One thing is certain—they do not cite each other." Also, the research and theorizing alike tend to concentrate on relatively simple situations, such as original attitude acquisition. Here reinforcers are fairly easily manipulable, the cognitive and affective complexity of the issues is not formidable, there is no preexisting involvement, and the whole enterprise remains comparatively undemanding. Other problems arise from the nature of learning theory itself, and from the vagueness of its relevant variables when they are transferred to the attitude area: the difficulty of defining the nature of reinforcement independently and of measuring the reinforcing value of outcomes (particularly in complex, multi-outcome situations); the uncertain relationship between reinforcement and drive, and the question of identifying and measuring the drive that is operating; the dispute about the relative importance of association and reinforcement; and the evaluation of the role of other intervening variables, such as awareness and cognitive manipulation. All of these are questions to which learning theory has no clear-cut answers. Some faults, like the unevaluated role of experimental artifacts and the measurement problem, are shared with other attitude models.

There is no doubt that the learning approaches as a class currently offer the only good explanations of some attitude phenomena, such as the classical conditioning of attitudes. In other areas, they present plausible alternatives or complements, usually to consistency models. While I doubt that we shall soon see one integrated learning theory of attitude change (which Festinger [1968] discerns on the horizon), the book by Greenwald et al. (1968) has already stimulated research and thinking that may lead in that direction. At the very least, the consistency approaches are likely to become less dominant than they have been in the past decade, and the theories mentioned here may prove to be strong competitors.

Functional Theories

Somewhat related to learning theory is the functional approach. While functional theorists do not usually bother with the processes of learning, they are interested in the instrumental nature of attitudes. That is, an attitude serves some useful purpose; when the individual concludes that this usefulness has ended or that a change may be more useful, the attitude will be likely to change. Reinforcement and incentive, then, provide the common ground between the two schools. The major conceptual difference is that functional theorists emphasize the types of real-life adaptive values served by attitudes (Insko [1967] calls these approaches "type theories"). Learning adherents, while using many kinds of reinforcers in experimentation, have not tried to evaluate the general importance or relevance of these rewards. The task-experience analysis of Breer and Locke (1965), described earlier, is close to being a combination of these two emphases.

The functional approaches also have some relevance to the idea of consistency. For example, they deal with the conditions that lead the individual to experience inconsistency as a noxious state, with the reasons for choosing one of several alternative modes of inconsistency resolution, and with levels of relevant motivation. Most importantly, they ask the question: "Consistency for what?" (Katz, 1968).

MOTIVATIONAL CONSTRUCTS

Functional theories, obviously, involve motivational constructs. Thus Katz, beginning with three relevant motives (Sarnoff and Katz, 1954), eventually described four such factors (Katz, 1960). Of these, the adjustive function (also called the instrumental or utilitarian function) is closest to that emphasized by learning theorists: the motive is to obtain extrinsic reward (that is, to obtain useful objects and avoid painful ones), and attitudes are maintained or changed to the extent that they fulfill this function. The ego-defensive function is the protection of one's self-respect and feelings of worth and competence, the need to deny one's own shortcomings, and so on. The classical Freudian defense mechanisms are intricately involved with attitudes in this regard; for example, the role of projection in the development of racial prejudice, and of reaction formation in the pattern of authoritarianism.[11] Katz's "value-expressive" function —the desire to be true to one's beliefs and norms, to communicate these beliefs to others, and to defend them when appropriate

—is related to ego psychology in personality theory. Finally, the knowledge function fulfills man's need for a structured, certain, and predictable world. Here the theory may be closest to consistency hypotheses, and is certainly related to information-processing theories of personality (Mancuso, 1970; Schroder and Suedfeld, 1971). Incidentally, the relevance of this approach to various personality formulations is one of its attractive and useful characteristics. Katz also describes the dimensions of attitudes —their connections with other attitudes and with behavior, their intensity, and so on.

In a similar analysis, Smith, Bruner, and White (1956) use social adjustment, object appraisal, and externalization as their constructs. Social adjustment is the utility of an attitude in gaining social approval; object appraisal is the cognitive utility of the attitude in directing the individual to attend and respond to important aspects of the environment; and externalization is the equivalent of ego defense, which transfers the perceived source of anxiety from the self and its conflicts to the environment.

Smith et al. further discuss object-relevant characteristics of attitude. Their analysis is quite compatible with the one offered by Katz (1960). For instance, attitudes differ in the extent to which their objects are differentiated. An opinion that research in psychology is good or bad because science *per se* is good or bad is relatively undifferentiated. A more complex view might weigh research in psychology against the use of the same resources in other sciences, or in social projects, or in reducing taxes; or it might weigh the advantages of research against threats to privacy and nonconformity; or it might evaluate various kinds of research in various areas of psychology (research on psychopharmacology for clinical use, for example, as compared with learning studies using rats), and so on. While the resulting decisions—to support or not to support a research program, for instance—may be the same, there are obvious differences in the specific attitudes. Salience, time perspective, informational support, and object value are probably strongly related to this dimension of differentiation. Salience is the importance of the attitude object to the person; time perspective is the duration of his interest in it; informational support is the amount of knowledge he has that is relevant to it. Perceived complexity probably increases as these other three variables increase. The last characteristic, object value, is the positive or negative valence of the attitude object.

An attitude changes when its functional utility decreases. The decrease may be caused by a change in reinforcement contingencies or by the development of new needs (for the adjustive functions); by an increase in insight and self-acceptance (for ego defense and externalization); by the emergence of self-doubt or the discovery of more appropriate ways of expressing selfhood (for value expression); or by the impact of new information (for knowledge and object appraisal).

The formulation of Smith et al. has led to no empirical research, and that of Katz and Sarnoff to little more. Both have elements of several general theories—learning, psychoanalytic, and cognitive—and the Smith approach also emphasizes social consequences. This and their close connection to personality theory are intriguing advantages. Their major problem is to define clearly and operationally the unique combination of functions served by a specific attitude and the environmental characteristics that can be manipulated to frustrate these functions. If this last could be done experimentally and the resultant changes predicted, the theories would be on a firm footing. The theories give more attention to individual differences in motivation and perception than other approaches do, and recognize the multiple determinants of attitudes (the fact that a given attitude can serve a number of functions). Both are significant improvements compared to such overgeneralized approaches as consistency and reinforcement theories. On the other hand, these same qualities make experimental verification difficult unless the personal world of each subject is thoroughly understood. Both conceptual and operational specificity need to be increased.

PROCESSES OF ATTITUDE CHANGE—A FUNCTIONAL ANALYSIS

Chapter 8 presents the functional theory of Kelman (1961). Restricting itself to three instrumental roles of attitudes and attitude change, this approach is relatively specific. Kelman spells out the sources of the three processes of change: the power, the attractiveness, and the credibility of the communicator and the communication. This categorization links up well with analyses of social power in general (for example, Raven, 1965; see Suedfeld, 1966), thus embedding itself usefully in another important area of social psychology.

The description of the environmental factors that must be present for each process to work is also valuable. Note that the antecedents and consequents of each type of change are quite distinct, making the derivation of clear-cut testable hypotheses possible, with less opportunity for *post hoc* juggling than is provided by most theories. There are, of course, situations in which more than one process is operating—in brainwashing, for example (see Suedfeld, 1966); but it should not be too difficult to design experiments in which such overlap is eliminated.

Kelman's theory, like the other functional systems, is conceptually relevant to nonlaboratory situations; unlike some, it is also amenable to field *testing*. Identification with a liked communicator, compliance with the demands of a powerful one, and internalization of the message of a believable one can be measured in educational, political, military, religious, and other settings. The relative potency of each process and its interactions with other processes present interesting research problems. All in all, this appears to be the most promising of the functional theories; with the increasing interest in nonconsistency approaches, we may soon see the performance of more of the necessary empirical groundwork.

REACTANCE THEORY

More restricted discussions based on a functional approach have appeared recently. One interesting variant is the idea that adherence to existing attitudes in the face of persuasive pressure (or "reactance" against the pressure) serves to enhance one's feeling of personal freedom and self-reliance, even when the communicator is prestigious and trustworthy, the message is credible and informationally valuable, and the probable outcome of acceptance is positive (Brehm, 1966). This hypothesis may explain the resistance to change found in so many attitude studies, particularly in field research dealing with significant "real-life" attitudes, and the occasional boomerang effect, in which an attitude changes in the direction opposite to that advocated by the message (for instance, a rise in smoking rates after publication of figures linking smoking with disease). Although this model is as yet quite vague, it is nice to see social psychologists paying attention to people's striving toward freedom.

DISCREPANT ACTION THEORY

Baron (1968) reinterprets the consequences of counterattitudinal behavior (or "discrepant action") as the result of three factors. First, there may be a moral dilemma; many behaviors demanded of subjects in dissonance and related experiments are considered immoral in our society (talking someone into participating in an unpleasant experience, administering painful shocks, and so on). Now, if one has done this for a reward, the greater the "bribe," the greater the guilt; but the more embarrassment or effort associated with the act—that is, the more we suffer while doing these things—the less the guilt. Since guilt, like cognitive dissonance, implies discomfort, in such a simple situation Baron's hypothesis concerning subjective feelings is directly contradictory to explanations derived from dissonance theory. So is his conjecture that a liked communicator, being more likely to reduce guilt feelings, is a more powerful source of change than a disliked one. Hedonic dilemmas occur when one has made a bad bargain, expended too much effort for too little reward, chosen the wrong alternative. This should lead to discomfort, which is reduced by deciding that the choice, the reward, the bargain are really better than one supposed at first. Here dissonance theory agrees. Finally, consensual validation dilemmas occur when a person's counterattitudinal behavior makes him doubt his own previous beliefs, leading to awareness of inconsistency and to uncertainty.

Some interesting hypotheses can be derived from this approach. For example, characteristics that make a communicator effective in solving one kind of dilemma will be irrelevant in solving another: for advice in moral dilemmas, integrity and disinterest are important; in consensual validation dilemmas, expertise is best. Moral dilemmas may lead to problems with self-respect and to serious attitudinal changes; hedonic dilemmas are relatively easy to solve by selective memory or selective information seeking. Again, experiments delimiting the proper role of dissonance theory can be derived from this approach. In fact, the theory points out that inconsistency can function as a positive motivation. This is so because inconsistencies may lead to increased accuracy in the evaluation of oneself and others or to social relations with new and valued others—a step toward an anticonsistency viewpoint.

CONFLICT THEORY

A last functional approach, which also incorporates the importance of incentive, is the conflict theory of Janis and Mann (1968). It is based on the hypothesis that information (including attempts at persuasion) presents a challenge to existing attitudes and actions. This challenge and the resultant conflict motivate the individual to seek out and evaluate alternative courses of action. A five-stage process is proposed: appraisal of the challenge, appraisal of alternatives, selection of the best alternative, commitment to a new policy despite negative information (this fourth stage reflects the importance of commitment and of reactance), and, if the feedback becomes negative enough, a return to the first stage, whereupon the cycle will presumably be repeated.

Utilitarian reinforcement for oneself and for significant others, social reinforcement, and self-evaluation play important roles in the development of new attitudes in response to challenges to old ones. These factors represent the functions that attitudes are to serve, and conflicts revolve around the extent to which present and alternative attitudes do in fact serve them. Janis and Mann view conflict before and after a decision as a continuous process, with both objective and distorted evaluations occurring in both stages. Here the theory differs from that of Festinger, who takes the position that objective judgment predominates before a choice is made and distortions are dominant afterward.

The postulates of conflict theory are fairly specific and appear to be clearly testable. So far, the theory has not been very influential; it has not dealt with many of the standard questions of attitude change, has not been presented in detailed form, and has very little relevant evidence to offer.

STRENGTHS AND WEAKNESSES OF FUNCTIONAL MODELS

One important contribution of the functional theories is their emphasis upon purposiveness in attitude formation and change. Their lists of relevant factors vary, but they also overlap, and it is quite clear that these approaches are much more amenable to integration than other types of theories. Unfortunately, they have led to relatively little research so far, so that their validity and power are largely untested. The generality of many constructs makes empirical testing difficult, and there is always the problem of measuring the relative and joint strengths of the various motives; but some of the theories at least indicate appropriate paths toward this goal.

Cognitive and Perceptual Theories

The important variables in theories that concentrate on cognitive and perceptual factors are the discrepancy between the attitude advocated by a communication and the attitude held by the listener, the discrepancy between a message and previously encountered messages, and (as before) the perceived usefulness or value of the message itself.

ADAPTATION-LEVEL THEORY

An attempt to apply a comprehensive model of perception and attention to the attitude area has been made by Helson (1964), the originator of adaptation-level theory. In this model, stimuli are arranged on a unidimensional scale, and the response to any stimulus then varies in accordance with its position on the scale in relation to other stimuli with which the respondent has experience. In the perceptual realm, for example, a subject who has lifted a series of five- to ten-pound weights may judge a one-pound weight to be very light, while a subject who has been lifting one- to five-ounce weights (and therefore has a different adaptation level) may call that same one-pound stimulus quite heavy. The adaptation level is affected by the surrounding environment and previously encountered stimuli as well as by the characteristics of the objects being judged. This level is the scale point or range within which stimuli are evaluated as neutral, in between, midway between the two extremes of the dimension.

In generalizing this model to attitude change, Helson and his co-workers (see Helson, 1959; Insko, 1967) carried out a large number of studies. Helson assumes that the behaviors and attitudes that a person usually experiences or observes represent his adaptation level, and that this level will change if the subject encounters new stimuli. Most of the research has attempted to accomplish such change by providing models to whose behavior the individual could conform. These experiments verify common-sense assumptions, such as that when people are asked to contribute money toward some common enterprise, their contributions are larger when other donors give an average of seventy-five cents than when the average donation is a quarter. The theory is not the unique predictor of such results, nor has it led to any very striking predictions of other results. Because of the difficulty of quantifying attitudes, this extension of the theory has not been very successful. That part of the research which manipulates several variables simultaneously leaves unanswered the difficult question of how the various adaptation levels interact and combine; when an experiment involves models whose behavior affects adaptation level along several independent dimensions, the theory cannot predict the subject's performance. On the whole, this approach has been unexciting to attitude researchers. While change in adaptation level may in fact be the mediating mechanism in certain conformity situations, the theory offers no predictions or explanations that are superior to those offered by other systems. So far, no one has extended the theory to the many situations in which attitude change occurs independently of any aspect of conformity.

Nevertheless, some general characteristics of the approach are admirable. Helson insists on the importance of observable stimulus characteristics and of the effects of these characteristics on evaluative, cognitive, and emotional responses. To the extent that intervening variables are used, they are based on the same concepts: observed and recalled stimuli are dimensionalized alike. There is no need for constructs (such as inconsistency) that are neither observable nor measurable. If this behaviorist position could be made more powerful and stimulating, it might remove some of the fuzziness of attitude theories. Another good point is Helson's concept of the motivating nature of intellectual activity. He rejects the dominance of primary drives and reinforcers, and of aversive states brought on by inconsistency, and emphasizes the positive nature of problem-solving, insight, and the processing of information. In this he is allied with the "new look" in motivational theory, and has helped to lay the foundation for an anticonsistency explanation of attitude change (see Helson, 1966).

SOCIAL JUDGMENT THEORY

The social judgment or assimilation-contrast theory advanced by Sherif (Sherif and Hovland, 1961; Sherif, Sherif, and Nebergall, 1965) puts more emphasis on the cognitive scale than adaptation-level theory does, but it too uses dimensionality as the basic concept in judgment and emphasizes the importance of the stimuli that anchor the ends of a given scale. Sherif approaches the problems of sensory discrimination from the general direction of psychophysics, assigning stimuli to various places on a scale. Consistent differences between objective characteristics and subjective judgment, and between the judgments of various individuals, are important in psychophysics and perhaps even more important in this psychophysical model of attitude change. The relevant dimension is agreement or acceptance, and Helson's problem in identifying and combining a number of scales is avoided. The theory proposes that internal scales are developed through evaluation of stimuli (arguments) and through social influence. In this development both internal and external anchors have important parts to play. Internal anchors are reference points that have been established through experience, such as one's attitudes; external anchors are provided by the actual stimuli or by group consensus.

Sherif is concerned with the consequences of discrepancy between anchors. An attitude—an internal anchor—represents the portion of the reference scale with which the individual most agrees, which he likes and accepts. A persuasive message is a stimulus that covers a different portion of the same scale. If these two parts of the scale are close together or actually overlap, the new information is perceived as compatible with the existing attitude system, and is "assimilated" into it. The greater the discrepancy between the two anchors, the more change will occur—as long as the discrepancy remains within the latitude of acceptance. Once the difference is so great that the message is close to the opposite end of the scale (the least accepted, most disliked point of view), it enters the latitude of rejection. Then the new stimulus is evaluated as being so far from the recipient's own view that it cannot possibly be incorporated ("contrast"); there will be no attitude change, or the large discrepancy may even lead to a boomerang effect. It should be pointed out that explicitly partisan, extreme statements and statements of objective fact (rather than opinion) are not subject to assimilation-contrast effects (Sherif et al., 1965). Ego involvement in the issue—the centrality of the attitude—narrows the range of acceptance, reduces the neutral noncommitment range, and widens the latitude of rejection. This is why open-mindedness on a topic is usually associated with a relative lack of interest in it. Unfortunately, the lack of a good independent measure of involvement has led to problems.

While the research based on these concepts has had mixed results, the lack of consistent confirmation must be attributed
largely to gaps in the theory rather than to specific errors in it.
For example, the idea that there is a curvilinear relationship between discrepancy and attitude change (greater discrepancy increasing change in the region of acceptance and decreasing it in
the region of rejection) has been tested in many studies, and has
not always been supported. One problem is that discrepancy has
often been confounded with the subject's own position; to include subjects with varying attitudes while keeping discrepancy
constant calls for many subjects and many messages. When the
confounding occurs, it leads to ceiling effects on both discrepancy and attitude change. It also appears that independent variables not considered by the theory play a part—the credibility of
the communicator and of the message (an incredulity measure,
like Osgood and Tannenbaum's [1955], might help), confounding variables such as group pressure, and so on. This approach is
more closely tied to phenomena and measurement, and is more
testable, than most. Since the scale is very explicit, the fudge factors so useful to other theorists are not available. On the other
hand, the limitation of the model to a description of one set of
phenomena makes the label "theory" somewhat premature: the
implication of generality is misleading. The questions answered
by the assimilation-contrast concept have been of restricted
scope. It is clear that wider applicability, added complexity, and
more research are needed to establish social judgment theory as
an important explanation of attitude change.

Although the relationship of the empirical work to the theory
is sometimes vague, there has been much field research generated by supporters of this approach. The importance of studying
the individual in a realistic context and, above all, in the context
of his social environment never escaped Sherif, as it did so many
others. The reference group is always present, either physically
or symbolically. As a source of information and consensual validation, it continuously affects responses to persuasive attempts.
The work of social judgment theorists on voting behavior, on the

attitudes of socially committed individuals, and on intergroup relations has not had the artificiality and triviality of many experimentally "pure" programs.

PERSPECTIVE THEORY

Ostrom and Upshaw (1968), in their description of the perspective model, make explicit one of the implications of perceptual-cognitive theories in general: the idea that attitudes can change without any alteration of one's beliefs about the object. It is not necessary to persuade oneself that a previously disliked politician is really a paragon of virtue; it is sufficient to compare him with a new set of anchors. He is what we have always thought him to be, but compared to X, that's really not so bad!

While a change in beliefs is not necessary for a new attitude label, it may be required if that label is to be maintained. The decision that our politician is not so bad may then motivate us to reexamine his specific characteristics. "Perspective" is the range of attitudes that one considers before rating his own attitude as positive or negative. With changes in the ends of this range (end anchors), the place of the individual's own attitude is modified. The anchors may be changed by new information or by the reevaluation of existing stimuli. The increasing acceptance of social changes once considered radical as new, even more radical ones come along has been frequently observed.

The model is, on the whole, in accord with common sense, but its scope is restricted to only a portion of the situations relevant to attitude change. There is some work on mathematical expression and definition of possible outcomes, and its implications for attitude scaling (which is outside the province of this book) have challenged some older beliefs. For research on self-concepts, reference groups, and the like, it is an interesting thought that two people can have completely different specific beliefs and opinions on many topics and yet use the same label: a rural southern white and an urban black may both label themselves Democrats. The opposite can also occur: two people with basically similar beliefs may use contrasting labels; and to confound the issue further, these contrasting labels may confuse the nature of any agreement or disagreement that may exist between them. Of two adherents of the NAACP, for instance, one may have a perspective which includes organizations ranging from the Ku Klux Klan to the NAACP, and may label himself a radical, while the other, with a scale extending from the Klan to the Black Panthers, may call himself a moderate or even a conservative.

COMMODITY THEORY

Brock's commodity theory (1968b), new and only partially developed, deals with the availability of a class of objects as an important variable in many kinds of situations. Applied to the study of attitudes, the "objects" are messages or other informational communications. Their basic value depends on their utility: "The value of a commodity is . . . the extent to which it accounts for response variance when compared to other stimuli" (Brock, 1968b, p. 246).

If the information is hard to obtain, or if one must wait a long time for it, its value is enhanced—a change that Brock has unfortunately decided to call "commodification." The higher the perceived value of the information to the recipient, the more likely he is to modify his attitudes to bring them into harmony with it. The contrast with reinforcement and with some utility theories is apparent; the idea that cost increases value is more akin to dissonance theory.

While at this stage there is no real theory, and nothing much new, there are a few interesting thoughts. One is that, if information is to increase in value because it is difficult to obtain, the would-be recipient must be interested in the topic. This idea should be a truism to anyone not hopelessly trapped in the "I've got a secret" syndrome of our childhood, but not many theorists have been fully aware of it. Second, information increases in value with the perception that it is available to only a few people, or can be communicated by only a few people—the "inside dope" syndrome. Finally, information increases in value if the person who has it is reluctant to part with it or has difficulty in communicating it. These factors may reduce the effects of massive, obtrusive advertising campaigns.

Brock cites some research that tends to support his hypotheses, and there are relevant anecdotes and examples from history, economics, and other disciplines. At the moment the eventual contribution of the model is difficult to predict. A connection between attitude and general exchange theory would be desirable if it provided a meaningful contribution rather than merely another set of labels. Whether the commodity approach meets this criterion remains to be established. As usual, there is the problem of a general measure of value, to say nothing of effort and of what "scarcity" means—although it certainly seems possible to develop appropriate indices. I do recommend the evaluation of the theory that Brock provides at the end of his presentation: it's nice to see a theorist who recognizes criticisms as something other than straw men that he can knock down to enhance the image of his formulation. Students who read these passages will discover some good comments on the model; colleagues may find a model to follow.

THE UNCERTAINTY MODEL

Chapter 9, which was specially written for this volume, presents the uncertainty model originated by Koslin. This approach uses some of the constructs of social judgment theory. Specifically, it asserts that messages are judged on a dimension from one's own attitude to the attitude most dissimilar to it, and it recognizes latitudes of acceptance and rejection. But the function of attitudes as informational input is believed to mediate the differential effects of small and large discrepancy.

The attempt to construct a stable and sensible view of the world leads to the development of attitudes, a functional interpretation that may explain consistency models too. New information, including persuasive messages, may shake up that cognitive organization. The reference scale becomes confused. Once this confusion occurs, the relative locations of stimuli and the discrepancies between them shift; in this situation a new scale can make previously rejected statements acceptable. There is an interesting parallel between this view and the unfreezing-changing-refreezing sequence of the brainwashing process, as analyzed by Schein (1961).

In the induction of uncertainty, moderately discrepant messages are most effective. Small discrepancies provide information that agrees to some extent with the existing attitude, and thus stabilize the scale; highly discrepant statements are rejected as irrelevant or obviously wrong (see also Festinger, 1954). In general, there is a curvilinear relationship between discrepancy and confusion, and a positive linear relationship between confusion and attitude change. A prestigious communicator makes the message seem more useful as information, enhancing the reinforcing effect of a congruent statement and making moderately and greatly discrepant communications more potent as disorganizers of the scale. The portions of the scale where uncertainty will exist can be specified; as we have seen, such specificity is rare indeed.

This model is in its early stages of development. The relevant research is scarce, but what there is supports the hypotheses (see Koslin and Pargament, 1969). Like Sherif, Koslin has developed a scaling technique that is appropriate to test the induction of instability and is in its own right a contribution to attitude measurement. One of the great contributions of the theory is that its intervening variable, uncertainty, can be independently measured —unlike such intervening variables as cognitive dissonance. Furthermore, results obtained by this technique are much less liable to distortion by evaluation apprehension, suspicion, and other such factors than are those obtained by a simple rating. So far, the measure is a rather cumbersome one to take and to score; but that's still much better than no measure at all.

Like some of the reinforcement propositions and like the commodity approach, this model has yet to undergo serious development and testing. In its combination of judgment and utility and its linkage of these to current motivational theory (which emphasizes the importance of cognitive structuring, predicting, and coping with information), the model appears to be powerful. It seems to be testable, and should stimulate further research; it also appears applicable to a variety of attitude change problems.

CONCLUSION

To rehash the outlines and the criticisms of each theory at this point would be unkind to the reader. In general, it is clear that consistency theories have dominated the field in the past fifteen years or so. In spite of all their shortcomings of specificity and measurement, such models appear to be good explanations of certain aspects of attitude change. Now many leaders in the field agree that nonconsistency approaches are about to come into their own. These are usually much more crude than the consistency models; this is both a cause and an effect of the latter's influence.

For the near future, the internal development of alternative theories should be a prime task: the tightening of logic, the identification of relevant variables, the deduction of testable hypotheses, the extension into broader areas. Many of these propositions are minitheories. Their future may be to complement other, more general formulations, or they may grow into greater applicability. While this conceptual development occurs, empirical work will also emerge. We will see much more field research, the testing and application of attitude theory in socially important contexts as well as in the laboratory. The next fifteen years may see the meeting and merging of some theories and the delineation of the appropriate domain of each. If nothing else, the "glorious entertainment" (Barzun, 1964) will go on; but I think there will be much else.

NOTES

1. Cynics may suggest that several theories must have the sheltering darkness of night in order to pass, and that the light of day would cause them to fail; this is the beauty of metaphor.
2. The interested reader may turn to Katz and Stotland (1959), Fishbein and Raven (1962), and Triandis (1964). A comprehensive review is given in Fishbein (1966), and some implications of this controversy for research methodology are pointed out by Sechrest (1969).
3. The basic scaling methods used are described by Krech, Crutchfield, and Ballachey (1962); Fishbein (1967) offers a selection of more advanced analyses. Good presentations of specific viewpoints are offered by Stevens (1966) and by Koslin and Pargament (1969).
4. Information on these issues can be found in Hovland, Janis, and Kelley, 1953; Biderman and Zimmer, 1961; Schein, 1961; Suedfeld, 1966; and McGuire, 1964.
5. Readers who desire more detailed treatments may refer to the primary sources, or to the following collections: for general theoretical discussion, Insko (1967) and Kiesler, Collins, and Miller (1969); for theory and research based on the consistency model, Abelson, Aronson, McGuire, Newcomb, Rosenberg, and Tannenbaum (1968) (the size and quality of the volume justify the awesome array of editors) and Feldman (1966b); for work springing from other approaches, Greenwald, Brock, and Ostrom (1968); and for reprinted research articles on attitude change, Rosnow and Robinson (1967) and Fishbein (1967). Most texts and books of readings in general social psychology also contain relevant portions. To facilitate further reading on general principles and research topics, references in this book are made, whenever appropriate, to summaries, reviews, and compilations rather than to original reports.
6. The general structure and some specific derivations of the theory are discussed in detail in the first part of the chapter; the section on the mathematical system gives a more rigorous analysis, which some students will find useful.
7. The inaccuracy of this term lies in its implication that the subject is *forced* to do something. But he is usually bribed, or at worst fairly mildly threatened. Note, for example, the number of subjects who refuse to comply. Scientific ethics seldom permit serious coercion in the laboratory; for a discussion of the possible relevance of dissonance theory in a severely threatening situation, see Schein's (1961) book on brainwashing.
8. Zastrow (1969) discusses some of these and other aspects of the theory at greater length.
9. Personal communication, March 12, 1969.

56 :   *Models of Attitude Change*

10. A purist may ask how a "behavioristic" theory can feature subjects who infer their attitudes from self-observation. To *behaviorists* this may not be behavioristic; but to *attitude theorists*, it is. It's all a matter of perspective (see the section on Ostrom & Upshaw's perspective theory later in this chapter).
11. Sarnoff has built this particular aspect into a psychoanalytic theory of attitude change, using the constructs of Freudian theory (see Sarnoff, 1960; Insko, 1967).

R E F E R E N C E S

ABELSON, H. I. 1959. *Persuasion,* 1st ed. New York: Springer.

ABELSON, R. P. 1959. "Modes of Resolution of Belief Dilemmas," *Journal of Conflict Resolution,* 3, 343–52.

———. 1968. "Psychological Implication," in *Theories of Cognitive Consistency: A Sourcebook,* ed. R. P. Abelson et al., pp. 112–39. Chicago: Rand McNally.

———. E. ARONSON, W. J. McGUIRE, T. M. NEWCOMB, M. J. ROSENBERG, and P. H. TANNENBAUM, eds. 1968. *Theories of Cognitive Consistency: A Sourcebook.* Chicago: Rand McNally.

——— and M. J. ROSENBERG. 1958. "Symbolic Psycho-logic: A Model of Attitudinal Cognition," *Behavioral Science,* 3, 1–13.

ANDERSON, L. R., and M. FISHBEIN. 1965. "Prediction of Attitude from the Number, Strength, and Evaluative Aspects of Beliefs About the Attitude Object: A Comparison of Summation and Congruity Theories," *Journal of Personality and Social Psychology,* 3, 437–43.

ARONSON, E. 1961. "The Effect of Effort on the Attractiveness of Rewarded and Unrewarded Stimuli," *Journal of Abnormal and Social Psychology,* 63, 375–80.

———. 1966. "The Psychology of Insufficient Justification: An Analysis of Some Conflicting Data," in *Cognitive Consistency: Motivational Antecedents and Behavioral Consequents,* ed. S. Feldman, pp. 109–33. New York: Academic Press.

———. 1969. "The Theory of Cognitive Dissonance: A Current Perspective," in *Advances in Experimental Social Psychology,* ed. L. Berkowitz, vol. 4, pp. 1–34. New York: Academic Press.

——— and J. M. CARLSMITH. 1963. "Effect of the Severity of Threat on the Evaluation of Forbidden Behavior," *Journal of Abnormal and Social Psychology,* 66, 584–88.

——— and J. MILLS. 1959. "The Effect of Severity of Initiation on Liking for a Group," *Journal of Abnormal and Social Psychology,* 59, 177–81.

BANKART, C. P., and J. T. LANZETTA. 1968. "Dissonance and Desire for a Cigarette," *Psychological Reports,* 23, 1155–61.

BARON, R. M. 1968. "Attitude Change Through Discrepant Action: A Functional Analysis," in *Psychological Foundations of Attitudes,* ed. A. G. Greenwald et al., pp. 297–326. New York: Academic Press.

BARZUN, J. 1964. *Science: The Glorious Entertainment*. Toronto: University of Toronto Press.

BEM, D. J. 1965. "An Experimental Analysis of Self-persuasion," *Journal of Experimental Social Psychology*, 1, 199–218.

————. 1966. "Inducing Beliefs in False Confessions," *Journal of Personality and Social Psychology*, 3, 707–10.

————. 1967. "Self-perception: An Alternative Explanation of Cognitive Dissonance Phenomena," *Psychological Review*, 74, 183–200.

————. 1968a. "Dissonance Reduction in the Behaviorist," in *Theories of Cognitive Consistency*, ed. R. P. Abelson et al., pp. 246–56. Chicago: Rand McNally.

————. 1968b. "Attitudes as Self-descriptions: Another Look at the Attitude-Behavior Link," in *Psychological Foundations of Attitudes*, ed. A. G. Greenwald et al., pp. 197–215. New York: Academic Press.

————. 1968c. "The Epistemological Status of Interpersonal Stimulations: A Reply to Jones, Linder, Kiesler, Zanna, and Brehm," *Journal of Experimental Social Psychology*, 4, 270–74.

BIDERMAN, A. D., and H. ZIMMER, eds. 1961. *The Manipulation of Human Behavior*. New York: Wiley.

BREER, P. E., and E. A. LOCKE. 1965. *Task Experience as a Source of Attitudes*. Homewood, Ill.: Dorsey Press.

BREHM, J. W. 1962. "Motivational Effects of Cognitive Dissonance," in *The Nebraska Symposium on Motivation*, vol. 10, ed. M. Jones, pp. 51–83. Lincoln: University of Nebraska Press.

————. 1965. "Comment on 'Counter-norm Attitudes Induced by Consonant vs. Dissonant Conditions of Role-Playing,'" *Journal of Experimental Research in Personality*, 1, 61–64.

————. 1966. *A Theory of Psychological Reactance*. New York: Academic Press.

———— and A. R. Cohen. 1962. *Explorations in Cognitive Dissonance*. New York: Wiley.

BROCK, T. C. 1968a. "Relative Efficacy of Volition and Justification in Arousing Dissonance," *Journal of Personality*, 36, 49–66.

————. 1968b. "Implications of Commodity Theory for Value Change," in *Psychological Foundations of Attitudes*, ed. A. G. Greenwald et al., pp. 243–75. New York: Academic Press.

BROWN, R. 1965. *Social Psychology*. New York: Free Press, Macmillan.

CARLSMITH, J. M., B. E. COLLINS, and R. L. HELMREICH. 1966. "Studies in Forced Compliance: 1. The Effect of Pressure for Compliance on Attitude Change Produced by Face-to-Face Role-Playing and Anonymous Essay-Writing," *Journal of Personality and Social Psychology*, 4, 1–13.

CARTWRIGHT, D., and F. HARARY. 1965. "Structural Balance: A Generalization of Heider's Theory," *Psychological Review*, 63, 277–92.

CHAPANIS, N. P., and A. CHAPANIS. 1964. "Cognitive Dissonance: Five Years Later," *Psychological Bulletin*, 61, 1–22.

COHEN, A. R. 1962. "An Experiment on Small Rewards for Discrepant Compliance in Attitude Change," in J. W. Brehm and A. R. Cohen, *Explorations in Cognitive Dissonance*, pp. 73–78. New York: Wiley.

COLLINS, B. E. 1969. "The Effect of Monetary Inducements on the Amount of Attitude Change Produced by Forced Compliance," in *Role-Playing, Reward, and Atitude Change,* ed. A. C. Elms. New York: Van Nostrand–Reinhold.

COOPER, J. L. EISENBERG, J. ROBERT, and B. S. DOHRENWEND. 1967. "The Effect of Experimenter Expectancy and Preparatory Effort on Belief in the Probable Occurrence of Future Events," *Journal of Social Psychology,* 71, 221–26.

DEUTSCH, M., and R. M. KRAUSS. 1965. *Theories in Social Psychology.* New York: Basic Books.

DOOB, L. W. 1947. "The Behavior of Attitudes," *Psychological Review,* 54, 135–56.

FEATHER, N. T. 1967. "A Structural Balance Approach to the Analysis of Communication Effects," in *Advances in Experimental Social Psychology,* ed. L. Berkowitz, vol. 3, pp. 100–65. New York: Academic Press.

FELDMAN, S. 1966a. "Motivational Aspects of Attitudinal Elements and Their Place in Cognitive Interaction," in *Cognitive Consistency,* ed. S. Feldman, pp. 75–108. New York: Academic Press.

————, ed. 1966b. *Cognitive Consistency: Motivational Antecedents and Behavioral Consequents.* New York: Academic Press.

FERSTER, C. B., and B. F. SKINNER. 1957. *Schedules of Reinforcement.* New York: Appleton-Century-Crofts.

FESTINGER, L. 1954. "A Theory of Social Comparison Processes," *Human Relations,* 7, 117–40.

————. 1957. *A Theory of Cognitive Dissonance.* Evanston, Ill.: Row, Peterson.

————, ed. 1964. *Conflict, Decision, and Dissonance.* Stanford, Calif.: Stanford University Press.

————. 1968. "Foreword," in *Psychological Foundations of Attitudes,* ed. A. G. Greenwald et al., p. vii. New York: Academic Press.

———— and J. M. CARLSMITH. 1959. "Cognitive Consequences of Forced Compliance," *Journal of Abnormal and Social Psycholoy,* 58, 203–10.

FISHBEIN, M. 1966. "The Relationships Between Beliefs, Attitudes, and Behavior," in *Cognitive Consistency,* ed. S. Feldman, pp. 199–223. New York: Academic Press.

————, ed. 1967. *Readings in Attitude Theory and Measurement.* New York: Wiley.

———— and B. H. RAVEN. 1962. "The AB Scales: An Operational Definition of Belief and Attitude," *Human Relations,* 15, 35–44.

FREEDMAN, J. L. 1963. "Attitudinal Effects of Inadequate Justification," *Journal of Personality,* 31, 371–85.

FROMKIN, H. L. 1968. "Reinforcement and Effort Expenditure: Predictions of 'Reinforcement Theory' vs. Predictions of Dissonance Theory," *Journal of Personality and Social Psychology,* 9, 347–52.

GREENWALD, A. G. 1968. "Cognitive Learning, Cognitive Response to Persuasion, and Attitude Change," in *Psychological Foundations of Attitudes,* ed. A. G. Greenwald et al., pp. 147–70. New York: Academic Press.

————, T. C. BROCK, and T. M. OSTROM, eds. 1968. *Psychological Foundations of Attitudes.* New York: Academic Press.

HAFNER, E. M., and S. PRESSWOOD. 1965. "Strong Inference and Weak Interactions," *Science,* 149, 503–10.

HEIDER, F. 1946. "Attitudes and Cognitive Organization," *Journal of Psychology*, 21, 107–12.

————. 1958. *The Psychology of Interpersonal Relations.* New York: Wiley.

HELSON, H. 1959. "Adaptation-Level Theory," in *Psychology: A Study of a Science*, ed. S. Koch, vol. 1, pp. 565–621. New York: McGraw-Hill.

————. 1964. *Adaptation-Level Theory: An Experimental and Systematic Approach to Behavior.* New York: Harper & Row.

————. 1966. "Some Problems in Motivation from the Point of View of the Theory of Adaptation Level," in *The Nebraska Symposium on Motivation*, vol. 14, ed. D. Levine, pp. 137–82. Lincoln: University of Nebraska Press.

HOLMES, J. G., and L. H. STRICKLAND. 1970. "Choice Freedom and Confirmation of Incentive Expectancy as Determinants of Attitude Change," *Journal of Personality and Social Psychology*, 14, 39–45.

HOVLAND, C. I., I. L. JANIS, and H. H. KELLEY. 1953. *Communication and Persuasion.* New Haven: Yale University Press.

————, W. MANDELL, E. H. CAMPBELL, T. BROCK, A. S. LUCHINS, A. R. COHEN, W. J. McGUIRE, I. L. JANIS, R. L. FEIERABEND, and N. H. ANDERSON. 1957. *The Order of Presentation in Persuasion.* New Haven: Yale University Press.

INSKO, C. A. 1967. *Theories of Attitude Change.* New York: Appleton-Century-Crofts.

JANIS, I. L., and B. T. KING. 1954. "The Influence of Role-Playing on Opinion Change," *Journal of Abnormal and Social Psychology*, 49, 211–18.

———— and L. MANN. 1968. "A Conflict-Theory Approach to Attitude Change and Decision-Making," in *Psychological Foundations of Attitudes*, ed. A. G. Greenwald et al., pp. 327–60. New York: Academic Press.

JONES, R. A., D. E. LINDER, C. A. KIESLER, M. ZANNA, and J. W. BREHM. 1968. "Internal States or External Stimuli: Observers' Attitude Judgments and the Dissonance-Theory–Self-persuasion Controversy," *Journal of Experimental Social Psychology*, 4, 247–69.

KARLINS, M., and H. I. ABELSON. 1970. *Persuasion*, 2nd ed. New York: Springer.

KATZ, D. 1960. "The Functional Approach to the Study of Attitudes," *Public Opinion Quarterly*, 24, 163–204.

————. 1968. "Consistency for What? The Functional Approach," in *Theories of Cognitive Consistency*, ed. R. P. Abelson et al., pp. 179–91. Chicago: Rand McNally.

———— and E. STOTLAND. 1959. "A Preliminary Statement to a Theory of Attitude Structure and Change," in *Psychology*, ed. S. Koch, vol. 3, pp. 423–75. New York: McGraw-Hill.

KELMAN, H. C. 1953. "Attitude Change as a Function of Response Restriction," *Human Relations*, 6, 185–214.

————. 1958. "Compliance, Identification, and Internalization: Three Processes of Attitude Change," *Journal of Conflict Resolution*, 2, 51–60.

————. 1961. "Processes of Opinion Change," *Public Opinion Quarterly*, 25, 57–78.

KIESLER, C. A., B. E. COLLINS, and N. MILLER. 1969. *Attitude Change: A Critical Analysis of Theoretical Approaches.* New York: Wiley.

KOSLIN, B. L. 1967. "Laboratory Experiments and Attitude Theory," in *Attitude, Ego Involvement, and Change,* ed. C. W. Sherif and M. Sherif, pp. 76–87. New York: Wiley.

———— and R. PARGAMENT. 1969. "Effects of Attitude on the Discrimination of Opinion Statements," *Journal of Experimental Social Psychology,* 5, 244–64.

KRECH, D., R. S. CRUTCHFIELD, and E. L. BALLACHEY. 1962. *The Individual in Society.* New York: McGraw-Hill.

LAWRENCE, D. H., and L. FESTINGER. 1962. *Deterrents and Reinforcement.* Stanford, Calif.: Stanford University Press.

LEWIN, K. 1935. *A Dynamic Theory of Personality: Selected Papers.* New York: McGraw-Hill.

————. 1938. *The Conceptual Representation and the Measurement of Psychological Forces.* Durham, N.C.: Duke University Press.

LINDER, D. E., J. COOPER, and E. E. JONES. 1967. "Decision Freedom as a Determinant of the Role of Incentive Magnitude in Attitude Change," *Journal of Personality and Social Psychology,* 6, 245–54.

McGUIRE, W. J. 1960. "A Syllogistic Analysis of Cognitive Relationships," in *Attitude Organization and Change,* ed. C. I. Hovland and M. J. Rosenberg, pp. 65–111. New Haven: Yale University Press.

————. 1964. "Inducing Resistance to Persuasion: Some Contemporary Approaches," in *Advances in Experimental Social Psychology,* ed. L. Berkowitz, vol. 1, pp. 191–229. New York: Academic Press.

————. 1966. "The Current Status of Cognitive Consistency Theories," in *Cognitive Consistency,* ed. S. Feldman, pp. 1–46. New York: Academic Press.

MANCUSO, J. C., ed. 1970. *Readings for a Cognitive Theory of Personality.* New York: Holt, Rinehart, & Winston.

MILLER, N. E. 1944. "Experimental Studies of Conflict," in *Personality and the Behavior Disorders,* ed. J. McV. Hunt, pp. 431–65. New York: Ronald Press.

MYERS, A. E. 1963. "Some Connotations of Cognitive Dissonance Theory," *Psychological Reports,* 13, 807–12.

NEL, E., R. HELMREICH, and E. ARONSON. 1969. "Opinion Change in the Advocate as a Function of the Persuasibility of His Audience: A Clarification of the Meaning of Dissonance," *Journal of Personality and Social Psychology,* 12, 117–24.

NEWCOMB, T. M. 1953. "An Approach to the Study of Communicative Acts," *Psychological Review,* 60, 393–404.

————. 1961. *The Acquaintance Process.* New York: Holt, Rinehart & Winston.

OSGOOD, C. E., G. J. SUCI, and P. H. TANNENBAUM. 1957. *The Measurement of Meaning.* Urbana: University of Illinois Press.

———— and P. H. Tannenbaum. 1955. "The Principle of Congruity in the Prediction of Attitude Change," *Psychological Review,* 62, 42–55.

OSTROM, T. M. 1968. "The Emergence of Attitude Theory: 1930–1950," in *Psychological Foundations of Attitudes,* ed. A. G. Greenwald et al., pp. 1–32. New York: Academic Press.

———— and H. S. Upshaw. 1968. "Psychological Perspective and Attitude Change," in *Psychological Foundations of Attitudes,* ed. A. G. Greenwald et al., pp. 217–42. New York: Academic Press.

Pepitone, A. 1966. "Some Conceptual and Empirical Problems of Consistency Models," in *Cognitive Consistency,* ed. S. Feldman, pp. 257–97. New York: Academic Press.

Pilisuk, M. 1962. "Cognitive Balance and Self-relevant Attitudes," *Journal of Abnormal and Social Psychology,* 65, 95–103.

Platt, J. R. 1964. "Strong Inference," *Science,* 146, 347–53.

Raven, B. H. 1965. "Social Influence and Power," in *Current Studies in Social Psychology,* ed. I. D. Steiner and M. Fishbein, pp. 371–82. New York: Holt, Rinehard & Winston.

Rokeach, M. 1968. *Beliefs, Attitudes, and Values.* San Francisco: Jossey-Bass.

Rosenberg, M. J. 1956. "Cognitive Structure and Attitudinal Affect," *Journal of Abnormal and Social Psychology,* 53, 367–72.

————. 1960a. "An Analysis of Affective-Cognitive Consistency," in *Attitude Organization and Change,* ed. C. I. Hovland and M. J. Rosenberg, pp. 15–64. New Haven: Yale University Press.

————. 1960b. "Cognitive Reorganization in Response to the Hypnotic Reversal of Attitudinal Affect," *Journal of Personality,* 28, 39–63.

————. 1965. "When Dissonance Fails: On Eliminating Evaluation Apprehension from Attitude Measurement," *Journal of Personality and Social Psychology,* 1, 28–42.

————. 1966. "Some Limits of Dissonance: Toward a Differentiated View of Counterattitudinal Advocacy," in *Cognitive Consistency,* ed. S. Feldman, pp. 135–70. New York: Academic Press.

————. 1968. "Counterattitudinal Behavior and Attitude Change," Introduction to Section F of *Theories of Cognitive Consistency,* ed. R. P. Abelson et al., p. 801. Chicago: Rand McNally.

———— and R. P. Abelson. 1960. "An Analysis of Cognitive Balancing," in *Attitude Organization and Change,* ed. C. I. Hovland and M. J. Rosenberg, pp. 112–63. New Haven: Yale University Press.

Rosenberg, S. 1968. "Mathematical Models of Social Behavior," in *Handbook of Social Psychology,* ed. G. Lindzey and E. Aronson, 2nd ed., pp. 179–244. New York: Addison-Wesley.

Rosenthal, R., and R. L. Rosnow, eds. 1969. *Artifact in Behavioral Research.* New York: Academic Press.

Rosnow, R. L., and E. J. Robinson, eds. 1967. *Experiments in Persuasion.* New York: Academic Press.

Sarnoff, I. 1960. "Psychoanalytic Theory and Social Attitudes," *Public Opinion Quarterly,* 24, 251–79.

———— and D. Katz. 1954. "The Motivational Bases of Attitude Change," *Journal of Abnormal and Social Psychology,* 49, 115–24.

Schein, E. H. 1961. *Coercive Persuasion.* New York: Norton.

Schroder, H. M. and P. Suedfeld, eds. 1971. *Personality Theory and Information Processing.* New York: Ronald Press.

Sears, D. O. 1968. "The Paradox of De Facto Selective Exposure Without Preferences for Supportive Information," in *Theories of Cognitive Consistency,* ed. R. P. Abelson et al., pp. 777–87. Chicago: Rand McNally.

SECHREST, L. 1969. "Nonreactive Assessment of Attitudes," in *Naturalistic Viewpoints in Psychological Research*, ed. E. P. Williams and H. L. Raush, pp. 147–61. New York: Holt, Rinehart & Winston.

SHERIF, C. W., M. SHERIF, and R. E. NEBERGALL. 1965. *Attitude and Attitude Change: The Social Judgment-Involvement Approach*. Philadelphia: Saunders.

SHERIF, M., and C. I. HOVLAND. 1961. *Social Judgment: Assimilation and Contrast Effects in Communication and Attitude Change*. New Haven: Yale University Press.

SILVERMAN, I. 1964. "In Defense of Dissonance Theory: Reply to Chapanis and Chapanis," *Psychological Bulletin*, 62, 205–9.

SINGER, J. E. 1966. "Motivation for Consistency," in *Cognitive Consistency*, ed. S. Feldman, pp. 47–73. New York: Academic Press.

SKINNER, B. F. 1956. "A Case History in Scientific Method," *American Psychologist*, 11, 221–33.

SMITH, E. E. 1961. "The Power of Dissonance Techniques to Change Attitudes," *Public Opinion Quarterly*, 25, 626–39.

SMITH, M. B., J. S. BRUNER, and R. W. WHITE. 1956. *Opinions and Personality*. New York: Wiley.

STAATS, A., and C. STAATS. 1958. "Attitudes Established by Classical Conditioning," *Journal of Abnormal and Social Psychology*, 57, 37–40.

STEVENS, S. S. 1966. "A Metric for the Social Consensus," *Science*, 151, 530–41.

SUEDFELD, P. 1966. *Social Processes*. Dubuque, Iowa: William C. Brown.

TANNENBAUM, P. H. 1967. "The Congruity Principle Revisited: Studies in the Reduction, Induction, and Generalization of Persuasion," in *Advances in Experimental Social Psychology*, ed. L. Berkowitz, vol. 3, pp. 271–320. New York: Academic Press.

TRIANDIS, H. C. 1964. "Exploratory Factor Analyses of the Behavioral Components of Social Attitudes," *Journal of Abnormal and Social Psychology*, 68, 420–30.

WEISS, R. F. 1963. "Defection from Social Movements and Subsequent Recruitment to New Movements," *Sociometry*, 26, 1–20.

———. 1967. "A Reinforcement Learning Model of Persuasive Communication," paper presented at a symposium, "Alternatives to Consistency Theory in the Study of Attitude Change," at the meeting of the American Psychological Association.

———. 1968. "An Extension of Hullian Learning Theory to Persuasive Communication," in *Psychological Foundations of Attitudes*, ed. A. G. Greenwald et al., pp. 109–45. New York: Academic Press.

ZAJONC, R. B. 1960. "The Concepts of Balance, Congruity, and Dissonance," *Public Opinion Quarterly*, 24, 280–96.

ZASTROW, C. H. 1969. "The Theory of Cognitive Dissonance," *Psychological Record*, 19, 391–99.

ZIMBARDO, P. G. 1965. "The Effect of Effort and Improvisation on Self-persuasion Produced by Role-Playing," *Journal of Experimental Social Psychology*, 1, 103–20.

———, ed. 1969. *The Cognitive Control of Motivation: Theoretical Analysis and Experimental Research*. Glenview, Ill.: Scott, Foresman.

2 The Concepts of Balance, Congruity, and Dissonance

ROBERT B. ZAJONC

Robert B. Zajonc is Professor of Psychology and Program Director at the Research Center for Group Dynamics at the University of Michigan. He is well known among social psychologists for a willingness to propose bold and stimulating hypotheses in a variety of areas, and for his ability to demonstrate support for these hypotheses through diverse methods. His work on the presence of others as a determinant of performance level and his studies of the attitudinal effects of stimulus familiarity are good examples of both characteristics. The article that follows is one of the best general overviews of the consistency theories.

Common to the concepts of balance, congruity, and dissonance is the notion that thoughts, beliefs, attitudes, and be-

From *Public Opinion Quarterly*, 24 (1960): 280–96; reprinted by permission of the author and the publisher.

havior tend to organize themselves in meaningful and sensible ways. Members of the White Citizens Council do not ordinarily contribute to NAACP. Adherents of the New Deal seldom support Republican candidates. Christian Scientists do not enroll in medical schools. And people who live in glass houses apparently do not throw stones. In this respect the concept of consistency underscores and presumes human *rationality*. It holds that behavior and attitudes are not only consistent to the objective observer, but that individuals try to appear consistent to themselves. It assumes that inconsistency is a noxious state setting up pressures to eliminate it or reduce it. But in the *ways* that consistency in human behavior and attitudes is achieved we see rather often a striking lack of rationality. A heavy smoker cannot readily accept evidence relating cancer to smoking;[2] a socialist, told that Hoover's endorsement of certain political slogans agreed perfectly with his own, calls him a "typical hypocrite and a liar."[3] Allport illustrates this irrationality in the following conversation:

MR. X: The trouble with Jews is that they only take care of their own group.

MR. Y: But the record of the Community Chest shows that they give more generously than non-Jews.

MR. X: That shows that they are always trying to buy favor and intrude in Christian affairs. They think of nothing but money; that is why there are so many Jewish bankers.

MR. Y: But a recent study shows that the per cent of Jews in banking is proportionally much smaller than the per cent of non-Jews.

MR. X: That's just it. They don't go in for respectable business. They would rather run night clubs.[4]

Thus, while the concept of consistency acknowledges man's rationality, observation of the means of its achievement simultaneously unveils his irrationality. The psychoanalytic notion of rationalization is a literal example of a concept which assumes both rationality and irrationality—it holds, namely, that man strives to understand and justify painful experiences and to make them sensible and rational, but he employs completely irrational methods to achieve this end.

The concepts of consistency are not novel. Nor are they indigenous to the study of attitudes, behavior, or personality. These concepts have appeared in various forms in almost all sciences. It has been argued by some that it is the existence of consistencies in the universe that made science possible, and by others that consistencies in the universe are a proof of divine power.[5] There is, of course, a question of whether consistencies are "real" or mere products of ingenious abstraction and conceptualization. For it would be entirely possible to categorize natural phenomena in such a haphazard way that instead of order, unity, and consistency, one would see a picture of utter chaos. If we were to eliminate one of the spatial dimensions from the conception of the physical world, the consistencies we now know and the consistencies which allow us to make reliable predictions would be vastly depleted.

The concept of consistency in man is, then, a special case of the concept of universal consistency. The fascination with this concept led some psychologists to rather extreme positions. Franke, for instance, wrote, ". . . the unity of a person can be traced in each instant of his life. There is nothing in character that contradicts itself. If a person who is known to us seems to be incongruous with himself that is only an indication of the inadequacy and superficiality of our previous observations."[6] This sort of hypothesis is, of course, incapable of either verification or disproof and therefore has no significant consequences.

Empirical investigations employing the concepts of consistency have been carried out for many years. Not until recently, however, has there been a programmatic and systematic effort to explore with precision and detail their particular consequences for behavior and attitudes. The greatest impetus to the study of attitudinal consistency was given recently by Festinger and his students. In addition to those already named, other related contributions in this area are those of Newcomb, who introduced the concept of "strain toward symmetry,"[7] and of Cartwright and

Harary, who expressed the notions of balance and symmetry in a mathematical form.[8] These notions all assume inconsistency to be a painful or at least psychologically uncomfortable state, but they differ in the generality of application. The most restrictive and specific is the principle of congruity, since it restricts itself to the problems of the effects of information about objects and events on the attitudes toward the source of information. The most general is the notion of cognitive dissonance, since it considers consistency among any cognitions. In between are the notions of balance and symmetry, which consider attitudes toward people and objects in relation to one another, either within one person's cognitive structure, as in the case of Heider's theory of balance, or among a given group of individuals, as in the case of Newcomb's strain toward symmetry. It is the purpose of this paper to survey these concepts and to consider their implications for theory and research on attitudes.

THE CONCEPTS OF BALANCE AND STRAIN TOWARD SYMMETRY

The earliest formalization of consistency is attributed to Heider,[9] who was concerned with the way relations among persons involving some impersonal entity are cognitively experienced by the individual. The consistencies in which Heider was interested were those to be found in the ways people view their relations with other people and with the environment. The analysis was limited to two persons, labeled P and O, with P as the focus of the analysis and with O representing some other person, and to one impersonal entity, which could be a physical object, an idea, an event, or the like, labeled X. The object of Heider's inquiry was to discover how relations among P, O, and X are organized in P's cognitive structure, and whether there exist recurrent and systematic tendencies in the way these relations are experienced. Two types of relation, liking (L) and so-called U, or unit, relations (such as possession, cause, similarity, and the like) were distinguished. On the basis of incidental observations and intuitive judgment, probably, Heider proposed that the person's (P's) cognitive structure representing relations among P, O, and X are either what he termed "balanced" or "unbalanced." In particular, he proposed, "In the case of three entities, a balanced state exists if all three relations are positive in all respects or if two are negative and one positive." Thus a balanced state is obtained when, for instance, P likes O, P likes X, and O likes X; or when P likes O, P dislikes X, and O dislikes X; or when P dislikes O, P likes X, and O dislikes X (see Figure 2.1). It should be noted that within Heider's conception a relation may be either positive or negative; degrees of liking cannot be represented. The fundamental assumption of balance theory is that an unbalanced state produces tension and generates forces to restore balance. This hypothesis was tested by Jordan.[10] He presented subjects with hypothetical situations involving two persons and an impersonal entity to rate for "pleasantness." Half the situations were by Heider's definition balanced and half unbalanced. Jordan's data showed somewhat higher unpleasantness ratings for the unbalanced than the balanced situations.

Cartwright and Harary[11] have cast Heider's formulation in graph-theoretical terms and derived some interesting consequences beyond those stated by Heider. Heider's concept allows either a balanced or an unbalanced state. Cartwright and Harary have constructed a more general definition of balance, with balance treated as a matter of degree, ranging from 0 to 1. Further-

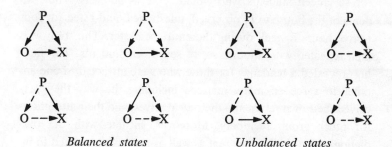

Balanced states   *Unbalanced states*

FIGURE 2.1: *Examples of balanced and unbalanced states according to Heider's definition of balance. Solid lines represent positive, and broken lines negative, relations.*

more, their formulation of balance theory extended the notion to any number of entities, and an experiment by Morrissette[12] similar in design to that of Jordan obtained evidence for Cartwright and Harary's derivations.

A notion very similar to balance was advanced by Newcomb in 1953.[13] In addition to substituting A for P, and B for O, Newcomb took Heider's notion of balance out of one person's head and applied it to communication among people. Newcomb postulates a "strain toward symmetry" which leads to a communality of attitudes of two people (A and B) oriented toward an object (X). The strain toward symmetry influences communication between A and B so as to bring their attitudes toward X into congruence. Newcomb cites a study in which a questionnaire was administered to college students in 1951 following the dismissal of General MacArthur by President Truman. Data were obtained on students' attitudes toward Truman's decision and their perception of the attitudes of their closest friends. Of the pro-Truman subjects 48 said that their closest friends favored Truman and none that their closest friends were opposed to his decision. Of the anti-Truman subjects only 2 said that their friends were generally pro-Truman and 34 said they were anti-Truman. In a longitudinal study, considerably more convincing evidence was obtained in support of the strain-toward-symmetry hypothesis. In 1954 Newcomb set up a house at the University of Michigan which offered free rent for one semester for seventeen students who would serve as subjects. The residents of the house were observed, questioned, and rated for four to five hours a week during the entire semester. The study was then repeated with another set of seventeen students. The findings revealed a tendency for those who were attracted to one another to agree on many matters, including the way they perceived their own selves and their ideal selves, and their attractions for other group members. Moreover, in line with the prediction, these similarities, real as well as perceived, seemed to increase over time.[14]

Newcomb also cites the work of Festinger and his associates on social communication[15] in support of his hypothesis. Festinger's studies on communication have clearly shown that the tendency to influence other group members toward one's own opinion increases with the degree of attraction. More recently Burdick and Burnes reported two experiments in which measures of skin resistance (GSR) were obtained as an index of emotional reaction in the presence of balanced and unbalanced situations.[16] They observed significant differences in skin resistance depending on whether the subjects agreed or disagreed with a "well-liked experimenter." In the second experiment Burdick and Burnes found that subjects who liked the experimenter tended to change their opinions toward greater agreement with his, and those who disliked him, toward greater disagreement. There are, of course, many other studies to show that the attitude toward the communicator determines his persuasive effectiveness. Hovland and his co-workers have demonstrated these effects in several studies.[17] They have also shown, however, that these effects are fleeting; that is, the attitude change produced by the communication seems to dissipate over time. Their interpretation is that over time subjects tend to dissociate the source from the message and are therefore subsequently less influenced by the prestige of the communicator. This proposition was substantiated by Kelman and Hovland,[18] who produced attitude changes with a prestigeful communicator and retested subjects after a four-week interval with and without reminding the subjects about the communicator. The results showed that the permanence of the attitude change depended on the association with the source.

In general, the consequences of balance theories have up to now been rather limited. Except for Newcomb's longitudinal study, the experimental situations dealt mostly with subjects who responded to hypothetical situations, and direct evidence is scarce. The Burdick and Burnes experiment is the only one bearing more directly on the assumption that imbalance or asymmetry produces tension. Cartwright and Harary's mathematization of the concept of balance should, however, lead to important empirical and theoretical developments. One difficulty is that there really has not been a serious experimental attempt to *disprove* the theory. It is conceivable that some situations defined by the theory as unbalanced may in fact remain stable and produce no significant pressures toward balance. Festinger once inquired in a jocular mood if it followed from balance theory that since he likes chicken, and since chickens like chicken feed, he must also like chicken feed or else experience the tension of imbalance. While this counterexample is, of course, not to be taken seriously, it does point to some difficulties in the concepts of balance. [It is not clear from Heider's theory of balance and Newcomb's theory of symmetry what predictions are to be made when attraction of both P and O toward X exists but when the origin and nature of these attractions are different.] In other words, suppose both P and O like X but for different reasons and in entirely different ways, as was the case with Festinger and the chickens. Are the consequences of balance theory the same then as in the case where P and O like X for the same reasons and in the same way? It is also not clear, incidentally, what the consequences are when the relation between P and O is cooperative and when it is competitive. Two men vying for the hand of the same fair maiden might experience tension whether they are close friends or deadly enemies.

In a yet unpublished study conducted by Harburg and Price at the University of Michigan, students were asked to name two of their best friends. When those named were of opposite sexes, subjects reported they would feel uneasy if the two friends liked one another. In a subsequent experiment subjects were asked whether they desired their good friend to like, be neutral to, or dislike one of their strongly disliked acquaintances, and whether they desired the disliked acquaintance to like or dislike the friend. It will be recalled that in either case a balanced state obtains only if the two persons are negatively related to one another. However, Harburg and Price found that 39 per cent desired their friend to be liked by the disliked acquaintenance, and only 24 per cent to be disliked. Moreover, faced with the alternative that the disliked acquaintance dislikes their friend, 55 per cent as opposed to 25 per cent expressed uneasiness. These results are quite inconsistent with balance theory. Although one may want one's friends to dislike one's enemies, one may not want the enemies to dislike one's friends. The reason for the latter may be simply a concern for the friends' welfare.

OSGOOD AND TANNENBAUM'S PRINCIPLE OF CONGRUITY

The principle of congruity, which is in fact a special case of balance, was advanced by Osgood and Tannenbaum in 1955.[19] It deals specifically with the problem of *direction* of attitude change. The authors assume that "judgmental frames of reference tend toward maximal simplicity." Thus, since extreme "black-and-white," "all-or-nothing" judgments are simpler than refined ones, valuations tend to move toward extremes, or, in the words of the authors, there is "a continuing pressure toward polarization." Together with the notion of maximization of simplicity is the assumption of identity as being less complex than the discrimination of fine differences. Therefore, related "concepts" will tend to be evaluated in a similar manner. Given these assumptions, the principle of congruity holds that when change in evaluation or attitude occurs it always occurs in the direction of increased congruity with the prevailing frame of reference. The paradigm of congruity is that of an individual who is confronted with an assertion regarding a particular matter about which he believes and feels in a certain way, made by a person toward whom he also has some attitude. Given that Eisenhower is evaluated positively and freedom of the press also positively, and given that Eisenhower (+) comes out in favor of freedom of the press (+), congruity is said to exist. But given that the *Daily Worker* is evaluated negatively, and given that the *Daily Worker* (−) comes out in favor of freedom of the press (+), incongruity is said to exist. Examples of congruity and incongruity are shown in Figure 2.2. The diagram shows the attitudes of a given individual toward the source and the object of the as-

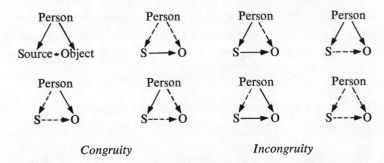

Congruity   *Incongruity*

FIGURE 2.2: *Examples of congruity and incongruity. Heavy lines represent assertions, light lines attitudes. Solid heavy lines represent assertions which imply a positive attitude on the part of the source, and broken heavy lines negative attitudes. Solid light lines represent positive, and broken light lines negative, attitudes.*

sertion. The assertions represented by heavy lines imply either positive or negative attitudes of the source toward the object. It is clear from a comparison of Figures 2.1 and 2.2 that in terms of their formal properties, the definitions of balance and congruity are identical. Thus, incongruity is said to exist when the attitudes toward the source and the object are similar and the assertion is negative, or when they are dissimilar and the assertion is positive. In comparison, unbalanced states are defined as having either one or all negative relations, which is of course equivalent to the above. To the extent that the person's attitudes are congruent with those implied in the assertion, a stable state exists. When the attitudes toward the person and the assertion are incongruent, there will be a tendency to change the attitudes toward the person and the object of the assertion in the direction of increased congruity. Tannenbaum obtained measures on 405 college students regarding their attitudes toward labor leaders, the *Chicago Tribune,* and Senator Robert Taft as sources, and toward legalized gambling, abstract art, and accelerated college programs as objects. Some time after the attitude scores were obtained, the subjects were presented with "highly realistic" newspaper clippings involving assertions made by the various sources regarding the concepts. In general, when the original attitudes toward the source and the concept were both positive and the assertion presented in the newspaper clippings was also positive, no significant attitude changes were observed in the results. When the original attitudes toward the source and the concept were negative and the assertion was positive, again no changes were obtained. As predicted, however, when a positively valued source was seen as making a positive assertion about a negatively valued concept, the attitude toward the source became less favorable, and toward the concept more favorable. Conversely, when a negatively valued source was seen as making a positive assertion about a positively valued concept, attitudes toward the source became more favorable and toward the concept less favorable. The entire gamut of predicted changes was confirmed in Tannenbaum's data; it is summarized in the accompanying table, in which the direction of change is represented by either a plus or a minus sign, and the extent of change by either one or two such signs.

A further derivation of the congruity principle is that incongruity does not invariably produce attitude change, but that it may at times lead to incredulity on the part of the individual. When confronted by an assertion which stands in an incongruous

TABLE 2.1: *Change of Attitude Toward the Source and the Object When Positive and Negative Assertions Are Made by the Source*

Original Attitude Toward the Source	Positive Assertion About an Object Toward Which the Attitude Is		Negative Assertion About an Object Toward Which the Attitude Is	
	Positive	Negative	Positive	Negative
	CHANGE OF ATTITUDE TOWARD THE OBJECT			
Positive	+	− −	− −	+
Negative	+ +	−	−	+ +
	CHANGE OF ATTITUDE TOWARD THE OBJECT			
Positive	+	+ +	− −	−
Negative	− −	−	+	+ +

relation to the person who made it, there will be a tendency not to believe that the person made the assertion, thus reducing incongruity.

There is a good deal of evidence supporting Osgood and Tannenbaum's principle of congruity. As early as 1921, H. T. Moore had subjects judge statements for their grammar, ethical infringements for their seriousness, and resolutions of the dominant seventh chord for their dissonance.[20] After two and one-half months the subjects returned and were presented with judgments of "experts." This experimental manipulation resulted in 62 per cent reversals of judgments on grammar, 50 per cent of ethical judgments, and 43 per cent of musical judgments. And in 1935 in a study on a similar problem of prestige suggestion, Sherif let subjects rank sixteen authors for their literary merit.[21] Subsequently, the subjects were given sixteen passages presumably written by the various authors previously ranked. The subjects were asked to rank-order the passages for literary merit. Although in actuality *all* the passages were written by Robert Louis Stevenson, the subjects were able to rank the passages. Moreover, the correlations between the merit of the author and the merit of the passage ranged from between .33 to .53. These correlations are not very dramatic, yet they do represent some impact of attitude toward the source on attitude toward the passage.

With respect to incredulity, an interesting experiment was conducted recently by Jones and Kohler in which subjects learned statements which either supported their attitudes or were in disagreement with them.[22] Some of the statements were plausible and some implausible. The results were rather striking. Subjects whose attitudes favored segregation learned plausible pro-segregation statements and implausible anti-segregation statements much more rapidly than plausible anti-segregation and implausible pro-segregation statements. The reverse was of course true for subjects whose attitudes favored desegregation.

While the principle of congruity presents no new ideas, it has a great advantage over the earlier attempts in its precision. Osgood and Tannenbaum have formulated the principle of congruity in quantitative terms allowing for precise predictions regarding the extent and direction of attitude change—predictions which in their studies were fairly well confirmed. While balance theory allows merely a dichotomy of attitudes, either positive or negative, the principle of congruity allows refined measurements using Osgood's method of the semantic differential.[23] Moreover, while it is not clear from Heider's statement of balance in just what direction changes will occur when an unbalanced state exists, such predictions can be made on the basis of the congruity principle.

FESTINGER'S THEORY OF COGNITIVE DISSONANCE

Perhaps the largest systematic body of data is that collected in the realm of Festinger's dissonance theory. The statement of the dissonance principle is simple. It holds that two elements of knowledge ". . . are in dissonant relation if, considering these two alone, the obverse of one element would follow from the other."[24] It further holds that dissonance ". . . being psychologically uncomfortable, will motivate the person to try to reduce dissonance and achieve consonance" and ". . . in addition to trying to reduce it, the person will actively avoid situations and information which would likely increase the dissonance."[25] A number of rather interesting and provocative consequences follow from Festinger's dissonance hypothesis.

First, it is predicted that all decisions or choices result in dissonance to the extent that the alternative not chosen contains positive features which make it attractive also, and the alternative chosen contains features which might have resulted in rejecting it. Hence after making a choice people seek evidence to confirm their decision and so reduce dissonance. . . . Ehrlich [found] that new car owners noticed and read ads about the cars they had recently purchased more than ads about other cars.[26]

Post-decision dissonance was also shown to result in a change of attractiveness of the alternative involved in a decision. Brehm had female subjects rate eight appliances for desirability.[27] Subsequently, the subjects were given a choice between two of the eight products, given the chosen product, and after some interpolated activity (consisting of reading research reports about four of the appliances) were asked to rate the products again. Half the subjects were given a choice between products which they rated in a similar manner, and half between products on which the ratings differed. Thus in the first case higher dissonance was to be expected than in the second. The prediction from dissonance theory that there should be an increase in the attractiveness of the chosen alternative and decrease in the attractiveness of the rejected alternative was on the whole confirmed. Moreover, the further implication was also confirmed that the pressure to reduce dissonance (which was accomplished in the above experiment by changes in attractiveness of the alternatives) varies directly with the extent of dissonance.

Another body of data accounted for by the dissonance hypothesis deals with situations in which the person is forced (either by reward or punishment) to express an opinion publicly or make a public judgment or statement which is contrary to his own opinions and beliefs. In cases where the person actually makes such a judgment or expresses an opinion contrary to his own as a result of a promised reward or threat, dissonance exists between the knowledge of the overt behavior of the person and his privately held beliefs. Festinger also argues that in the case of noncompliance dissonance will exist between the knowledge of overt behavior and the anticipation of reward and punishment.

An example of how dissonance theory accounts for forced-compliance data is given by Brehm.[28] Brehm offered prizes to eighth-graders for eating disliked vegetables and obtained measures of how well the children liked the vegetables. Children who ate the vegetables increased their liking for them. Of course, one might argue that a simpler explanation of the results is that the attractiveness of the prize generalized to the vegetable, or that, even more simply, the vegetables increased in utility because a reward came with them. However, this argument would also lead one to predict that the increment in attraction under such conditions is a *direct* function of the magnitude of the reward. Dissonance theory makes the opposite prediction, and therefore a test of the validity of the two explanations is possible. Data collected by Festinger and Carlsmith[29] and by Aronson and Mills[30] support the dissonance point of view. In Festinger and Carlsmith's experiment subjects were offered either $20 or $1 for telling someone that an experience which had actually been quite boring had been rather enjoyable and interesting. When measures of the subjects' private opinions about their actual enjoyment of the task were taken, those who were to be paid only $1 for the false testimony showed considerably higher scores than those who were to be paid $20. Aronson and Mills, on the other hand, tested the effects of negative incentive. They invited college women to join a group requiring them to go through a process of initiation. For some women the initiation was quite severe, for others it was mild. The prediction from dissonance theory that those who had to undergo severe initiation would increase their attraction for the group more than those having no initiation or mild initiation was borne out.

A third set of consequences of the theory of dissonance deals with exposure to information. Since dissonance occurs between cognitive elements, and since information may lead to change in these elements, the principle of dissonance should have a close bearing on the individual's commerce with information. In particular, the assumption that dissonance is a psychologically uncomfortable state leads to the prediction that individuals will seek out information reducing dissonance and avoid information increasing it. The study on automobile-advertising readership described above is a demonstration of this hypothesis.[31] In another study Mills, Aronson, and Robinson gave college students a choice between an objective and an essay examination.[32] Following the decision, the subjects were given articles about examinations presumably written by experts, and they were asked if they would like to read them. In addition, in order to vary the intensity of dissonance, half the subjects were told that the examination counted 70 per cent toward the final grade, and half that it counted only 5 per cent. The data were obtained in the form of rankings of the articles for preference. While there was a clear preference for reading articles containing positive information about the alternative chosen, no significant selective effects were found when the articles presented arguments against the given type of examination. Also, the authors failed to demonstrate effects relating selectivity in exposure to information to the magnitude of dissonance, in that no significant differences were found between subjects for whom the examination was quite important (70 per cent of the final grade) and those for whom it was relatively unimportant (5 per cent of the final grade).

Festinger was able to account for many other results by means of the dissonance principle, and in general his theory is rather successful in organizing a diverse body of empirical knowledge by means of a limited number of fairly reasonable assumptions. Moreover, from these reasonable assumptions dissonance theory generated several nontrivial and nonobvious consequences. The negative relationship between the magnitude of incentive and attraction of the object of false testimony is not at all obvious. Also not obvious is the prediction of an increase in proselytizing for a mystical belief following an event that clearly contradicts it. Festinger, Riecken, and Schachter studied a group of "Seekers" —people who presumably received a message from outer space informing them of an incipient major flood.[33] When the flood failed to materialize on the critical date, instead of quietly withdrawing from the public scene, as one would expect, the "Seekers" summoned press representatives, gave extended interviews, and invited the public to visit them and be informed of the details of the whole affair. [In a very recent study by Brehm, a "nonobvious" derivation from dissonance theory was tested.[34] Brehm predicted that when forced to engage in an unpleasant activity, an individual's liking for this activity will increase more when he receives information essentially berating the activity than when he receives information promoting it.] The results tended to support Brehm's prediction. Since negative information is said to increase dissonance, and since increased dissonance

ROBERT B. ZAJONC : 79

leads to an increased tendency to reduce it, and since the only means of dissonance reduction was increasing the attractiveness of the activity, such an increase would in fact be expected.

CONCLUSIONS

The theories and empirical work dealing with consistencies are mainly concerned with intra-individual phenomena, be it with relationships between one attitude and another, between attitudes and values, or information, or perception, or behavior, or the like. One exception is Newcomb's concept of "strain toward symmetry." Here the concern is primarily with the interplay of forces among individuals which results in uniformities or consistencies among them. There is no question that the concepts of consistency, and especially the theory of cognitive dissonance, account for many varied attitudinal phenomena. Of course, the various formulations of consistency do not pretend, nor are they able, to account completely for the phenomena they examine. Principles of consistency, like all other principles, are prefaced by the *ceteris paribus* preamble. Thus, when other factors are held constant, then the principles of consistency should be able to explain behavior and attitudes completely. But the question to be raised here is just what factors must be held constant and how important and significant, relative to consistency, are they.

Suppose a man feels hostile toward the British and also dislikes cricket. One might be tempted to conclude that if one of his attitudes were different he would experience the discomfort of incongruity. But there are probably many people whose attitudes toward the British and cricket are incongruent, although the exact proportions are not known and are hardly worth serious inquiry. But if such an inquiry were undertaken it would probably disclose that attitudes depend largely on the conditions under which they have been acquired. For one thing, it would show that the attitudes depend at least to some extent on the relationship of the attitude object to the individual's needs and fears, and that these may be stronger than forces toward balance. There are in this world things to be avoided and feared. A child bitten by a dog will not develop favorable attitudes toward dogs. And no matter how much he likes Popeye you can't make him like spinach, although according to balance theory he should.

The relationship between attitudes and values or needs has been explored, for instance, in *The Authoritarian Personality,* which appeared in 1950.[35] The authors of this work hypothesized a close relationship between attitudes and values on the one hand and personality on the other. They assumed that the ". . . convictions of an individual often form a broad and coherent pattern, as if bound together by a mentality or spirit." They further assumed that ". . . opinions, attitudes, and values depend on human needs and since personality is essentially an organization of needs, then personality may be regarded as a determinant of ideological preference." Thus the *Authoritarian Personality* approach also stresses consistency, but while the concepts of congruity, balance, and dissonance are satisfied with assuming a general tendency toward consistency, the *Authoritarian Personality* theory goes further in that it holds that the dynamic of consistency is to be found in personality, and it is personality which gives consistency meaning and direction. Attitudes and values are thus seen to be consistent among themselves and with one another because they are both consistent with the basic personality needs, and they are consistent with needs because they are determined by them.

The very ambitious research deriving from the *Authoritarian Personality* formulation encountered many difficulties and, mainly because of serious methodological and theoretical shortcomings, has gradually lost its popularity. However, some aspects of this general approach have been salvaged by others. Rosenberg, for instance, has shown that attitudes are intimately related to the capacity of the attitude object to be instrumental to the attainment of the individual's values.[36] Carlson went a step further and has shown that, if the perceived instrumentality of the object with respect to a person's values and needs is changed, the attitude itself may be modified.[37] These studies, while not assuming a general consistency principle, illustrate a special instance of consistency, namely that between attitudes and utility, or instrumentality of attitude objects, with respect to the person's values and needs.

The concepts of consistency bear a striking historical similarity to the concept of vacuum. According to an excellent account by Conant,[38] for centuries the principle that nature abhors a vacuum served to account for various phenomena, such as the action of pumps, behavior of liquids in joined vessels, suction, and the like. The strength of everyday evidence was so overwhelming that the principle was seldom questioned. However, it was known that one cannot draw water to a height of more than 34 feet. The simplest solution of this problem was to reformulate the principle to read that "nature abhors a vacuum below 34 feet." This modified version of *horror vacui* again was satisfactory for the phenomena it dealt with, until it was discovered that "nature abhors a vacuum below 34 feet only when we deal with water." As Torricelli has shown, when it comes to mercury, "nature abhors a vacuum below 30 inches." Displeased with the crudity of a principle which must accommodate numerous exceptions, Torricelli formulated the notion that it was the pressure of air acting upon the surface of the liquid which was responsible for the height to which one could draw liquid by the action of pumps. The 34-foot limit represented the weight of water which the air pressure on the surface of earth could maintain, and the 30-inch limit represented the weight of mercury that air pressure could maintain. This was an entirely different and revolutionary concept, and its consequences had drastic impact on physics. Human nature, on the other hand, is said to abhor inconsistency. For the time being the principle is quite adequate, since it accounts systematically for many phenomena, some of which have never been explained and all of which have never been explained by one principle. But already today there are exceptions to consistency and balance. Some people who spend a good portion of their earnings on insurance also gamble. The first action presumably is intended to protect them from risks, the other to expose them to risks. Almost everybody enjoys a magician. And the magician only creates dissonance—you see before you an event which you know to be impossible on the basis of previous knowledge—the obverse of what you see follows from what you know. If the art of magic is essentially the art of producing dissonance, and if human nature abhors dissonance, why is the art of magic still flourishing? If decisions are necessarily followed by dissonance, and if nature abhors dissonance, why are decisions ever made? Although it is true that those decisions which would ordinarily lead to great dissonance take a very long time to make, they are made anyway. And it is also true that human nature does not abhor dissonance absolutely, as nature abhors a vacuum. Human nature merely avoids dissonance, and it would follow from dissonance theory that decisions whose instrumental consequences would not be worth the dissonance to follow would never be made. There are thus far no data to support this hypothesis, nor data to disprove it.

According to Conant, *horror vacui* served an important purpose besides explaining and organizing some aspects of physical knowledge. Without it the discomfort of "exceptions to the rule" would never have been felt, and the important developments in theory might have been delayed considerably. If a formulation has then a virtue in being wrong, the theories of consistency do have this virtue. They do organize a large body of knowledge. Also, they point out exceptions, and thereby they demand a new formulation. It will not suffice simply to reformulate them so as to accommodate the exceptions. I doubt if Festinger would be satisfied with a modification of his dissonance principle which would read that dissonance, being psychologically uncomfortable, leads a person to actively avoid situations and information would would be likely to increase the dissonance, except when there is an opportunity to watch a magician. Also, simply to disprove the theories by counterexamples would not in itself constitute an important contribution. We would merely lose explanations of phenomena which had been explained. And it is doubtful that the theories of consistency could be rejected simply *because* of counterexamples. Only a theory which accounts for all the data that the consistency principles now account for, for all the exceptions to those principles, and for all the phenomena which these principles should now but do not consider, is capable of replacing them. It is only a matter of time until such a development takes place.

N O T E S

1. The concepts of balance, congruity, and dissonance are due to Heider, Osgood and Tannenbaum, and Festinger, respectively (F. Heider, "Attitudes and Cognitive Organization," *Journal of Psychology,* 21 (1946): 107–12; C. E. Osgood and P. H. Tannenbaum, "The Principle of Congruity in the Prediction of Attitude Change," *Psychological Review,* 62 (1955): 42–55; L. Festinger, *A Theory of Cognitive Dissonance* [Evanston, Ill.: Row, Peterson, 1957]). For purposes of simplicity we will subsume these concepts under the label of consistency.
2. Festinger, *op. cit.,* pp. 153–156.
3. H. B. Lewis, "Studies in the Principles of Judgments and Attitudes: IV, The Operation of 'Prestige Suggestion,' " *Journal of Social Psychology,* 14 (1941): 229–56.
4. G. W. Allport, *The Nature of Prejudice* (Cambridge, Mass.: Addison-Wesley, 1954).
5. W. P. Montague, *Belief Unbound* (New Haven: Yale University Press, 1930), pp. 70–73.
6. R. Franke, "Gang und Character," *Beihefte, Zeitschrift für angewandte Psychologie,* no. 58 (1931), p. 45.
7. T. M. Newcomb, "An Approach to the Study of Communicative Acts," *Psychological Review,* 60 (1953): 393–404.
8. D. Cartwright and F. Harary, "Structural Balance: A Generalization of Heider's Theory," *Psychological Review,* 63 (1956): 277–93.
9. Heider, *op. cit.*
10. N. Jordan, "Behavioral Forces That Are a Function of Attitudes and of Cognitive Organization," *Human Relations,* 6 (1953): 273–87.
11. Cartwright and Harary, *op. cit.*
12. J. Morrissette, "An Experimental Study of the Theory of Structural Balance," *Human Relations,* 11 (1958): 239–54.
13. Newcomb, *op. cit.*
14. T. M. Newcomb, "The Prediction of Interpersonal Attraction," *American Psychologist,* 11 (1956): 575–86.

15. L. Festinger, K. Back, S. Schachter, H. H. Kelley, and J. Thibaut, *Theory and Experiment in Social Communication* (Ann Arbor: University of Michigan, Institute for Social Research, 1950).
16. H. A. Burdick and A. J. Burnes, "A Test of 'Strain toward Symmetry' Theories," *Journal of Abnormal and Social Psychology*, 57 (1958): 367–69.
17. C. I. Hovland, I. L. Janis, and H. H. Kelley, *Communication and Persuasion: Psychological Studies of Opinion Change* (New Haven: Yale University Press, 1953).
18. H. C. Kelman and C. I. Hovland, " 'Reinstatement' of the Communicator in Delayed Measurement of Opinion Change," *Journal of Abnormal and Social Psychology*, 48 (1953): 327–35.
19. Osgood and Tannenbaum, *op. cit.*
20. H. T. Moore, "The Comparative Influence of Majority and Expert Opinion," *American Journal of Psychology*, 32 (1921): 16–20.
21. M. Sherif, "An Experimental Study of Stereotypes," *Journal of Abnormal and Social Psychology*, 29 (1935): 371–75.
22. E. E. Jones and R. Kohler, "The Effects of Plausibility on the Learning of Controversial Statements," *Journal of Abnormal and Social Psychology*, 57 (1958): 315–20.
23. C. E. Osgood, "The Nature and Measurement of Meaning," *Psychological Bulletin*, 49 (1952): 197–237.
24. Festinger, *op. cit.*, p. 13.
25. *Ibid.*, p. 3.
26. D. Ehrlich, I. Guttman, P. Schönbach, and J. Mills, "Post-decision Exposure to Relevant Information," *Journal of Abnormal and Social Psychology*, 54 (1957): 98–102.
27. J. Brehm, "Post-decision Changes in the Desirability of Alternatives," *Journal of Abnormal and Social Psychology*, 52 (1956): 384–89.
28. J. Brehm, "Increasing Cognitive Dissonance by a *Fait Accompli*," *Journal of Abnormal and Social Psychology*, 58 (1959): 379–82.
29. L. Festinger and J. M. Carlsmith, "Cognitive Consequences of Forced Compliance," *Journal of Abnormal and Social Psychology*, 58 (1959): 203–10.
30. E. Aronson and J. Mills, "The Effect of Severity of Initiation on Liking for a Group," *Journal of Abnormal and Social Psychology*, 59 (1959): 177–81.
31. Ehrlich *et al.*, *op. cit.*
32. J. Mills, E. Aronson, and H. Robinson, "Selectivity in Exposure to Information," *Journal of Abnormal and Social Psychology*, 59 (1959): 250–53.
33. L. Festinger, J. Riecken, and S. Schachter, *When Prophecy Fails* (Minneapolis: University of Minnesota Press, 1956).
34. J. W. Brehm, "Attitudinal Consequences of Commitment to Unpleasant Behavior," *Journal of Abnormal and Social Psychology*, 60 (1960): 379–83.
35. T. W. Adorno, E. Frenkel-Brunswik, D. J. Levinson, and R. N. Sanford, *The Authoritarian Personality* (New York: Harper, 1950).
36. M. J. Rosenberg, "Cognitive Structure and Attitudinal Affect," *Journal of Abnormal and Social Psychology*, 53 (1956): 367–72.

37. E. R. Carlson, "Attitude Change Through Modification of Attitude Structure," *Journal of Abnormal and Social Psychology,* 52 (1956): 256–61.
38. James B. Conant, *On Understanding Science* (New Haven: Yale University Press, 1947).

3

Symbolic Psycho-logic: A Model of Attitudinal Cognition

ROBERT P. ABELSON
MILTON J. ROSENBERG

Robert P. Abelson *is currently Professor of Psychology at Yale University. His notable contributions to the study of attitudes have been followed by studies of the computer simulation of human emotion and cognition and of language usage.*

Milton J. Rosenberg, *Professor of Psychology at the University of Chicago, is one of the most eminent of the attitude theorists. As a member of Carl I. Hovland's famous Yale group, he contributed to much of the basic knowledge in the field. More recently he has produced not only valuable original formulations, but also highly insightful critiques. His writings are not only substantively important, but—especially in such*

From *Behavioral Science*, 3 (1958):1–13; reprinted by permission.

open formats as book chapters—easy and fun to read.

The following article presents a consistency theory of unusual clarity and rigor. The difference between logic and psycho-logic has been emphasized by later workers in many areas, but the implications and the formulae of psycho-logic are spelled out most completely in this paper.

Several lines of theoretical and research interest have gradually been converging upon the study of "cognitive structure," especially in the area of social attitudes. Attitudes, by the definitions of Smith, Bruner, and White (18), Peak (15), Rosenberg (17), Green (7) and many others, involve both affective and cognitive components. These components interact intimately with one another, so that cognitions about attitudinal objects are not felt to be meaningfully analyzable without consideration of affective forces. Theorists are reluctant even to consider cognitive units of an attitude apart from other cognitive units, preferring to treat cognition as "structured" into meaningful wholes (13, 19). Krech and Crutchfield (12, p. 152) define attitude globally as "an enduring organization of motivational, emotional, perceptual and cognitive processes with respect to some aspect of the individual's world." They state (p. 108), "Each of our perceptions does not lead 'a life of its own' but is embedded in an organization of other perceptions—the whole making up a specific cognitive structure." Smith, Bruner, and White (18, p. 286), in discussing attitude measurement, caution, "Recent advances in the theory and technique of attitude measurement . . . have yet to take this complexity [of opinions] into account. Characteristically, they have conceived of attitudes as a matter of pro-ness and con-ness. . . . We would question whether it is reasonable to expect them to generate the dimensions required for an adequate description of opinion. [An adequate description] comes rather from intensive explorations. . . ." Asch (2) is another author who has employed a holistic concept of attitude structure. He seeks to explain certain attitude change phenomena in terms of the "restructuring" of the attitudinal object (3). Rokeach (16) treats structure as an individual difference variable of cognitive style, defining one extreme, dogmatism, as "a relatively closed cognitive organization of beliefs and disbeliefs about reality . . . which . . . provides a framework for patterns of intolerance and qualified tolerance toward others."

This Gestalt emphasis, motivated by the desire to construct an accurate model of the phenomenal organization of attitudes, has underscored the difficulties inherent in attempts to deal analytically with a set of cognitive units or elements. Nevertheless, if psychologists are to talk about "cognitive structure," they must do something about it; there must be a correspondence between theory and some sort of research operation. At least two important recent theoretical developments, Festinger's (6) "dissonance theory," and Heider's (10) "theory of cognitive balance," deal conceptually with the effects of organizing forces and affective forces upon cognitive elements. Both theories are concerned with changes in cognitive structure. Festinger's theory deals mainly with inconsistencies between belief and action, and attempts to specify certain circumstances under which there will be more or less change in belief as an outgrowth of cognitive "dissonance," due to such inconsistencies. The research operations which are used to test Festinger's theory are not addressed to the details of cognitive structure, but rather to single-response predictions derivative from the theory. Heider's theory is addressed to structural details of cognition, but there has been no research operation available to investigate these details with particular attitude contents. On the other hand, the recently proposed methodological devices of Rosenberg (17) and Abelson (1) are not completely anchored in a general theory of attitudes. A fresh approach to the measurement of cognitive structure is clearly called for.

This paper proposes one such approach. We have drawn some inspiration from Cartwright and Harary's (5) objective system for the examination of "structural balance," from Heider's (10) ideas on cognitive balance, and are also intellectually indebted to Zajonc (20), who has suggested clever procedural devices in eliciting cognitive material. Otherwise, the system to be proposed is our own, albeit with a strong historical tether. The paper is divided into two parts: the "Psychological Model" and the "Mathematical System."

The Psychological Model

Cognitive Elements

Human thought, for all its complexity and nuance, must involve some cognitive representation of "things," concrete and abstract. These things or concepts are the *elements* of our system. Though it does not seem absolutely necessary, we shall for convenience assume that individuals can attach some sort of verbal labels to the elements of their thinking. We will refer, then, to cognitive elements by verbal labels.

We may distinguish three broad classes of elements: Actors, Means (Actions, Instrumentalities), and Ends (Outcomes, Values). These classes are not completely exhaustive nor mutually exclusive. We propose this classification merely to suggest the variety of possible cognitive elements. To exemplify each class, consider the illustrative issue: "Having an honor system at Yale." The following elements were among those frequently elicited from Yale students in a pilot study.

Actors: myself, the Faculty, the Administration, the Student Body, a certain minority of students, the honest student. . . .

Means: the honor system, other honor systems, the present examination system, cheating, reporting those who cheat, social pressure from other students. . . .

Ends: the feeling of being trusted, mature moral standards, loyalty to friends, the university's reputation, having well-run examinations. . . .

Note that all elements are expressed here substantively to reflect their "thing-like" character.

Cognitive Relations

Of all the conceivable relations between cognitive elements, we choose to consider only four: *positive, negative, null,* and *ambivalent*. These will be denoted *p, n, o,* and *a*. (See also, "Mathematical System"). We again conveniently assume that cognitive materials of a relational sort can be verbally labeled. Some typical examples of relations between elements follow:

		positive (p)	negative (n)	null (o)
Actor vs.	Actor	likes; supports	dislikes, fights	is indifferent to
	Means	uses; advocates	opposes; undermines	is not responsible for
	End	possesses; aims for	inhibits; aims against	is indifferent to
Means vs.	Actor	helps; promotes	hinders; insults	does not affect
	Means	is equivalent to	is alternative to; counteracts	is unrelated to
	End	brings about	prevents	does not lead to
End vs.	Actor	serves; is vital to	is inimical to	does not interest
	Means	justifies	obviates	cannot ensue from
	End	is consistent with	is incompatible with	is unconnected to

Ambivalent relations (*a*) are defined as conjunctions of positive and negative relations; they are psychologically secondary or "derived," and have been omitted from the above list.

Note that relations are expressed here as verbs.

Certain omissions from the above scheme may occur to the reader. Relations like "is next in line to," "is north of," etc., are certainly not included. Other phrases which imply relationship without specifying its sign, e.g., "depends upon," "is connected with," etc., are difficult to classify. Furthermore, notions of time sense, moral imperative, and conditionality or probability, e.g., "might have acted upon," "probably will help," "ought to seek," etc., are not dealt with explicitly. Time sense and conditionality are beyond the scope of the present treatment. We deal here only with cognitions of the psychological present, and temporarily set aside the past, conditional past, future, and conditional future. As for the other exceptions to the scheme, note that their phrasing tends to be affectless. Dispassionate descriptions of, say, the mating habits of flamingoes or the operation of a nuclear reactor or the economic situation in Viet Nam would probably contain many relations impossible to classify. But such descriptions are reportorial, not attitudinal. When cognition is invested with affect, when the Actors, Means, and Ends are responded to emotionally, then the relations become classifiable in terms of the present system. Our intent is to be able to code all relations occurring in attitudinal cognitions into these four broad categories.

Cognitive Units or Sentences

Cognitive units are built out of pairs of elements, connected by a relation. That is, the basic "sentences" of attitudinal cognition are of the form ArB, where A and B are elements and r is a relation. Many sentences which at first seem more complicated than the simple ArB unit may be reduced to such a unit by broadening the definition of an element. For example, consider the sentence, "Nasser (A) insists on (p) all Suez tolls (B) belonging to (p) Egypt (C)." (Here p denotes a positive relation.) This sentence, symbolically, is $Ap(BpC)$. But regard (BpC) as a new element D, the broader conception "all Suez tolls belonging to Egypt." Then we have simply ApD.

In this way, we reduce our catalogue of basic sentences to four:

$$ApB$$
$$AnB$$
$$AoB$$
$$AaB$$

The Conceptual Arena: The Structure Matrix

For the convenience of both theory and operation, we conceive of an attitude as being defined over a certain delimited though perhaps large *conceptual arena.* We restrict attention, in other words, to those elements which are (phenomenally) relevant to the given issue or attitude object.

Operationally, what one can do is this. Following Zajonc (20), we ask the subject to list all the words or short phrases that come to mind as he mulls over a given topic, such as "Having an Honor System at Yale" or "The State Department Ban on Reporters Going to Red China." Subjects will typically write several phrases in rapid-fire order, then pause, give one or two more, and finally stop. These words or phrases are not always "noun-like," but by simple instructions to the subject, they can be reworded satisfactorily and be treated subsequently as the cognitive elements. This procedure yields the conceptual arena idiosyncratic to each subject.[1]

After the arena is defined, the relations between pairs of elements may be mapped. We conceptualize a matrix setting forth the relations between each element and every other. This matrix we denote the *structure matrix, R* (see the "Mathematical System"). As an illustration of a structure matrix, consider the following:

Structure Matrix: Topic: Having an Honor System at Yale

	Ego	Honest student	Reporting cheaters	Feeling trusted	Cheating by few	Honor system
Ego (the subject himself)	p	p	n	p	n	o
The honest student	p	p	n	p	o	p
Reporting cheaters	n	n	p	o	n	p
Feeling trusted	p	p	o	p	o	p
Cheating by a few	n	o	n	o	p	n
An honor system	o	p	p	p	n	p

The entries in this matrix were elicited by instructing a subject to fill in the *middles* of sentences linking his elements (the six listed). He wrote these "open-middled" sentences:

The honest student *feels very reluctant about* reporting cheaters.
The honest student *possesses* the feeling of being trusted.

The honor system *is fine for* the honest student.
The honor system *promotes* the feeling of being trusted.
Cheating by a few *is cut down by* reporting cheaters.
The honor system *is harmed by* cheating by a few.
The honor system *involves* reporting cheaters.

The verb forms in these sentences were coded[2] into the relations *p* and *n* shown in the matrix. In addition, the subject himself was asked whether he felt favorable, neutral, or unfavorable toward each element. His responses are shown in the first row (column) of the matrix.

All relations between elements and themselves are taken to be positive. Also, relations are considered to be symmetric; i.e., if A*r*B, then B*r*A. Our preliminary work does not suggest a pressing need to revise these assumptions.

The structure matrix is our basic description of attitudinal cognition. One may wish to superimpose further refinements upon the structure such as the intensity of different relations, the confidence with which they are held, time perspective, and so on. In this paper, we answer only the simplest question, "In what way can the structure matrix be used to characterize the fundamental structural varieties of attitudinal cognition, apart from specific content?"

Thinking: Psycho-logic

Individual cognition units may originate in various ways—through exposure to written information, through social pressure, emotional need, thinking, etc. Once originated, these units may be manipulated in thought.

We propose a set of rules by which an individual imputes or discovers new symbolic sentences by combining two old sentences with an element in common. We hypothesize that *these rules apply only when the individual thinks about the topic,* or "rehearses the arguments" (11, p. 129).

Rule 1. A*p*B and B*p*C implies A*p*C.
Rule 2. A*p*B and B*n*C implies A*n*C.
Rule 3. A*n*B and B*n*C implies A*p*C.

Rule 4. A*o*B and B*r*C implies nothing about the relation between A and C, irrespective of *r*.

Rule 5. If A*p*C and A*n*C are both implied, or if one is held initially and the other implied, then A*a*C. This is the definition of the ambivalent relation.

Rule 6. A*a*C and C*p*D implies A*a*D.

Rule 7. A*a*C and C*n*D implies A*a*D.

Rule 8. A*a*C and C*a*D implies A*a*D.

Each rule above has several equivalent forms not listed, arising from the symmetry assumption A*r*B = B*r*A.

Though we have given formal status to these rules,[3] note that the verbal corollaries are not necessarily logical at all. Exemplify Rule 3 by the sentences:

India (A) opposes *(n)* U.S. Far Eastern policy (B).
U.S. Far Eastern policy (B) is directed against *(n)* Communism (C).
Therefore, India (A), is in favor of (*p*) Communism (C).

Such "reasoning" would mortify a logician, yet it can be found in much this form inside of millions of heads. Thus we speak of the formal system as *psycho-logic* rather than as *logic*.

We assume that thinking about a topic *must be motivated before it will occur*. Some possible motivating conditions[4] would be these:

1. Pressure to reach a decision on the topic.

2. Socially derived needs to appear informed on the topic, to converse well about it, to win over others, etc. Anticipation of the relevant social situations would motivate thinking.

3. Relevance of the topic to needs, conflicts, and persisting preoccupations. Activation of such processes would generate pressure to think.

4. A general "cognitive style" of the individual such that thinking per se is satisfying. For such individuals, mere mention of the topic might motivate thinking.

Suppose that a given individual is motivated to think about a given topic. He already possesses certain relevant cognitive units.

Using psycho-logic, he imputes new units. These new units may or may not be compatible with his existing units. Referring back to the India-China example, if the individual had originally thought, "India (A) resists the influence of (n) Communism (C)," then we would be confronted with the coexistence of ApC and AnC. By Rule 5, this is expressed AaC, the ambivalent relation, which might translate back into words thus: The relationship between India (A) and Red China (C) is very confusing (a). On the other hand, had he originally held ApC, then the imputed sentence ApC would reinforce rather than contradict his original view.

Balance and Imbalance

Certain structure matrices are characterized by the interesting property that no amount of thinking (i.e., imputing of new relations according to the rules above) leads the individual into any inconsistency (i.e., ambivalent relation). The cognitive structures represented by such matrices are said to be *balanced*. When the structure matrix is such that one or more ambivalent relations will be discovered in thinking, the structure is said to be *imbalanced*. (Our statement of the mathematical condition for cognitive balance is given in the "Mathematical System.") In common-sense terms, a balanced cognitive structure represents a "black and white" attitude. The individual views some elements as good and the other elements as bad. All relations among "good elements" are positive (or null), all relations among "bad elements" are positive (or null), and all relations between good and bad elements are negative (or null).

Redressing Imbalance

Heider (10), Festinger (6), Osgood and Tannenbaum (14), and others have postulated that individuals strive to reduce or redress cognitive imbalance, or "dissonance." This is probably especially true for attitudinal cognitions. It is important to note, however, that potential imbalance will remain undiscovered by an individual unless he is motivated to think about the topic and in fact does so. Assuming these necessary preconditions, suppose that an individual does come upon a cognitive inconsistency in his attitude. What can he do about it? Three things:

1. Change one or more of the relations.

2. Redefine, "differentiate," or "isolate" one or more elements.

3. Stop thinking.

A simple example will illustrate the first two methods. The third method is self-explanatory. Take the three elements, E, C, G: Ego (a Yale student), Having Co-eds at Yale, and Getting Good Grades. The subject might tell us:

"I'm for having co-eds at Yale." (EpC)

"I want good grades." (EpG)

"Having co-eds at Yale would undoubtedly interfere with getting good grades." (CnG)

This attitudinal cognition

$$R = \begin{array}{c c c c} & E & C & G \\ E & p & p & p \\ C & p & p & n \\ G & p & n & p \end{array}$$

is imbalanced. Never having been forced to take a consistent stand on the issue, however, our subject may readily tolerate (or even be unaware of) this imbalance. Now suppose that the issue is hotly debated and our subject thinks. The imbalance becomes apparent and he seeks a balance-producing resolution.

Method 1. He alters any one of the three relations, by abandoning the desire for good grades, by opposing the admission of co-eds, or by rationalizing to the effect that "Co-eds do not really interfere with getting good grades (in fact, they enhance the chances, etc.)."

Method 2. (The following is one of various possibilities.) He differentiates the concept "Getting good grades" into "Getting

A's" and "Getting C's" and then reasons that while co-eds may interfere with getting A's, they don't interfere with getting C's, and what he really wants is not to get A's but to get C's.

It is assumed that under sufficient pressure to continue thinking, the individual will try Methods 1 and 2, presumably seeking a relatively effortless means to achieve balance. If these attempts fail, because certain relations are resistant to change and certain elements are difficult to redefine, the individual may resort to Method 3 which is to stop thinking. If, however, strong pressures, internal or external, do not permit him to stop thinking, he will re-examine the topic, seeking a more complex utilization of either or both of the first two methods. And so on. With extremely strong pressure to continue thinking, some cognitive units will in all probability ultimately yield to one attack or another.[5] With weak pressure and a structure that is highly resistant to change, the individual will most likely stop thinking, and his attitudinal structure will revert to its state before he started thinking.

In other words, we envision an extensive hierarchy of cognitive solutions to the problem of reducing imbalance. Experimental prediction of outcome is extremely difficult under these circumstances, and represents a considerable challenge. The next section presents a crude preliminary step toward meeting the challenge.

Experimental Prediction of Cognitive Changes

Our present machinery is not refined enough to permit predictions with respect to Method 2 above, "redefining the elements." It would appear feasible, however, to restrict experimentally the availability of this alternative (the arguments of Asch [3] to the contrary) and focus upon Method 1.

The question we pose for ourselves is this: "Given an imbalanced structure with highly stably defined elements, can we predict which particular set of relations in the whole conceptual arena will be changed in order to achieve balance?"

The mathematical system presented later in detail is helpful in providing what we hope will be an approximate answer. In that system, the *complexity of imbalance* of a structure is defined as the *minimum number of changes of relations necessary to achieve balance*.[7] The system also implies a way of identifying which particular changes constitute the minimum set, or, when there are alternative minimal sets, identifies all of them. In addition, the "next to minimal" sets of changes can be identified, and so on.

Working under the highly tentative heuristic assumption that all relations are equally resistant to change, the least effortful balancing operation on an imbalanced structure is the one that requires the fewest changed relations. A predicted set of changes can easily be generated under this assumption.

The steps involved in the analysis are:

1. Write down the structure matrix.

2. Find the row (column) with the largest plurality of n's over p's, exclusive of the p in the main diagonal of the matrix. Change all n's to p's and p's to n's, in both the row and the corresponding column (leaving the diagonal entry p unchanged). Ignore the o entries.

3. Repeat the previous step on a new row (column).

4. Continue the change operations on selected rows and columns until the number of n's in the matrix cannot be further reduced.[8]

This irreducible minimum number defines the complexity of imbalance. Duplication due to symmetry is avoided by counting n's on one side of the diagonal only. The entries where the n's appear identify the minimal set. If the minimum number can be attained in more than one way, the sets so identified are alternative "solutions." If the minimum number is zero, then the structure is balanced. The entire procedure is based upon Theorem 13 of the "Mathematical System."

The method will now be illustrated with the Yale student's structure on "Having an honor system at Yale," presented in an earlier section.

His structure matrix was:

	1. Ego	2. Honest student	3. Reporting cheaters	4. Feeling trusted	5. Cheating by few	6. Honor system
1. Ego	p	p	n	p	n	o
2. The honest student	p	p	n	p	o	p
3. Reporting cheaters	n	n	p	o	n	p
4. Feeling trusted	p	p	o	p	o	p
5. Cheating by a few	n	o	p~~n~~	o	p	n
6. An honor system	o	p	p	p	n	p

Row 5 contains three n's and one p. We then carry out the change operation on Row 5 and Column 5, carrying p into n (except in the diagonal) and n into p. The result is:

	1.	2.	3.	4.	5.	6.
1.	p	p	n	p	p	o
2.	p	p	n	p	o	p
3.	n	n	p	o	p	p
4.	p	p	o	p	o	p
5.	p	o	p	o	p	p
6.	o	p	p	p	p	p

Both remaining n's lie in Row 3. Three p's also lie in this row, but one of them is the unchanging diagonal element, so that essentially it is two n's versus two p's. The change operation on Row 3 and Column 3 would yield

	1.	2.	3.	4.	5.	6.
1.	p	p	p	p	p	o
2.	p	p	p	p	o	p
3.	p	p	p	o	n	n
4.	p	p	o	p	o	p
5.	p	o	n	o	p	p
6.	o	p	n	p	p	p

The number of n's here is also two. It is evident that the number of n's cannot be further reduced by the change operation. It is also evident upon further inspection that no other set of change operations will yield as few as two n's. Thus the structure matrix is of complexity *two* and there are two alternate minimal solutions to the balancing problem.

The first solution tells us that had the subject's initial relations between elements 3 and 1, and 3 and 2 not been as they were, there would not have been any imbalance. In other words, achieving balance requires changing the relations between elements 3 and 1, and elements 3 and 2. Looking back at his original structure matrix, this means that were he to *favor* reporting cheaters, or at least not be opposed, and also regard honest students as favoring or not opposing reporting cheaters, his structure would be balanced. The "good elements" would be *Ego, The honest student, Reporting cheaters, Feeling trusted,* and *The honor system,* while *Cheating by a few* would be a "bad element." In short, "We honest students would all feel trusted in an honor system. A few cheaters might violate the system, but they should be reported."

The second solution tells us that the subject must change the relations between elements 3 and 5, and elements 3 and 6 to achieve balance. In other words, were he to view *Reporting cheaters* as not identified with the honor system, and as in any case ineffective in cutting down *Cheating by a few* his structure would be balanced. *Ego, The honest student, Feeling trusted,* and *The honor system* would be "good elements," and *Reporting cheaters* and *Cheating by a few,* "bad elements." A hypothetical quote would read, "We honest students would all feel trusted in an honor system. A few cheaters might violate the system, but I wouldn't feel right about reporting them and it probably wouldn't work anyway. There are a few lousy guys who will always try to foul things up."

We make no claim that this subject would necessarily make one or the other of these changes in striving for a balanced structure. We only claim that if the strengths of all relations are equal, the above changes would be preferred for their simplicity.

We are now working on various means for empirical measurement of the strength of relations. Incorporation of the strength variable in the model will represent an important refinement.

THE MATHEMATICAL SYSTEM

The mathematical system is designed specifically for dealing analytically with the structure of attitudinal cognitions. There is some exercise of invention in suiting definitions and devices to the problem at hand; otherwise, the system is a self-contained axiomatic treatment of a standard mathematical nature. Many of the results parallel those of Harary (8, 9) although his mathematical treatment differs from the present one.

Consider a set E of four "relations": $p, n, o,$ and a (the positive, negative, null, and ambivalent relations of the Psychological Model) with the following properties under the fundamental operations of addition and multiplication:

[1] $r + o = r$
[2] $r + r = r$ for all $r \in E$
[3] $r + a = a$
[4] $p + n = a$
[5] $r \cdot p = r$ for all $r \in E$
[6] $r \cdot o = o$
[7] $r \cdot a = a$ for $r = p, n,$ or a
[8] $n \cdot n = p$

Each operation is taken to be commutative, so that

[9] $r_1 + r_2 = r_2 + r_1$ for all $r_1, r_2 \in E$
[10] $r_1 \cdot r_2 = r_2 \cdot r_1$

These fundamental definitions may readily be scanned in the following addition and multiplication tables (tables 3.1 and 3.2).

It will be noted that the inverse operations, subtraction and division, are not uniquely defined for all pairs of elements. For example, the equation $p + x = p$ cannot be uniquely solved for x. A similar situation holds for the equations $a \cdot x$

TABLE 3.1: *Addition Table for Relations*

+	p	n	o	a
p	p	a	p	a
n	a	n	n	a
o	p	n	o	a
a	a	a	a	a

TABLE 3.2: *Multiplication Table for Relations*

•	p	n	o	a
p	p	n	o	a
n	n	p	o	a
o	o	o	o	o
a	a	a	o	a

$= a$ and $o \cdot x = o$. However, the associative and distributive properties of multiplication and addition hold in this system.

[11] $(r_1 + r_2) + r_3 = r_1 + (r_2 + r_3)$
[12] $(r_1 \cdot r_2) \cdot r_3 = r_1 \cdot (r_2 \cdot r_3)$ } for all $r_1, r_2, r_3 \in E$
[13] $r_1 \cdot (r_2 + r_3) = r_1 \cdot r_2 + r_1 \cdot r_3$

Now consider an $N \times N$ matrix R with elements r_{ij} ($i = 1, 2, \cdots N; j = 1, 2 \cdots N$) such that:

[R1] all $r_{ij} = p, n,$ or o
[R2] $r_{ii} = p$ for all i
[R3] $r_{ij} = r_{ji}$ for all i and j.

These stipulations define a *structure matrix*. Denote the class of all $N \times N$ structure matrices R by $R^{(N)}$, or when the context clearly refers to any arbitrary fixed N, simply R.

Define the pseudo-determinant[9] $\dagger R \dagger$ of a martix R as

[14] $$\dagger R \dagger = \sum_{\text{all } \phi} \prod_{i=1}^{N} r_{i\phi_i}$$

where ϕ is a permutation on the integers $i = 1, 2, \cdots N$, and ϕ_i is the integer into which i is carried by the permutation. The rules of addition and multiplication are as given previously. Otherwise, this idiosyncratic definition corresponds to the usual definition of a determinant (4) except that no algebraic signs are attached to the individual products involved in the summation. They are all positive, so to speak. The prefix "pseudo-" is intended to warn of this distinction from an ordinary determinant.

The pseudo-determinant provides the basis for an interesting partition of the class R of all structure matrices. Note that specification [R2] for R-matrices requires all elements on the main diagonal to be p. Thus the term in $\dagger R\dagger$ corresponding to all $\phi_i = i$ must be the product $(p \cdot p \cdots p) = p$, regardless of the nature of the off-diagonal elements of a given R. Given that at least one term in the summation in [14] equals p, it readily follows from Table 1 and condition [11] that

[15] $\dagger R\dagger = p$ or a, for all $R \subset R$

The former is true if and only if *no* term in the summation [14] equals n.

Definition

If $\dagger R\dagger = p$, then R is said to be *balanced*. If $\dagger R\dagger = a$, then R is said to be *imbalanced*.

The definition in these terms is completely equivalent to the definition of balance in the psychological model and to the definition of "structural balance" given by Cartwright and Harary (5). Proof of this equivalence is straightforward but space-consuming and will be omitted here. The heart of the matter is the equivalence between permutations in the pseudo-determinant and "cycles" of cognitive elements.

Definition

R_0 is the class of all balanced R-matrices.
R_a is the class of all imbalanced R-matrices.

Clearly the union $\mathbf{R}_0 \cup \mathbf{R}_a = \mathbf{R}$.

A further partition of the class $\mathbf{R}_a$ is possible, giving rise to an index of the complexity or degree of imbalance in any given imbalanced R.

To accomplish this, it is convenient to define a class $\mathbf{T}$ of square *transformation matrices* T with elements T_{ij}, such that:

[*T*1] All t_{ij} = the element s ("sameness") or the element c ("change")

[*T*2] $t_{ii} = s$ for all i.

[*T*3] $t_{ij} = t_{ji}$ for all i and j.

The specifications [*T*1–3] are parallel to the specifications [*R*1–3], and indeed, the elements s and c will be defined in such a way as to parallel the elements p and n.

Multiplication is the main operation in which the elements s and c enter, as follows:

[16] $\quad s \cdot s = s$

[17] $\quad s \cdot c = c \cdot s = c$

[18] $\quad c \cdot c = s$

[19] $\quad s \cdot r = r$, for $r = p$, n, or o

[20] $\quad c \cdot p = n$

[21] $\quad c \cdot n = p$

[22] $\quad c \cdot o = o$

The elements s and c may readily be understood as representing "sameness" and "change" respectively. A transformation matrix T embodies a set of changes which may be applied to a structure matrix R, in a way to be described later.

The operation of addition is also defined on c and s. It is commutative and associative.

[23] $\quad c + c = c$

[24] $\quad s + s = s$

[25] $\quad c + s = a$

[26] $\quad a + c = a$

[27] $\quad a + s = a$

The addition of c or s to p, n, or o is not defined.

The pseudo-determinant of T is defined as it was for R in equation [14].

$$[28] \quad \dagger T \dagger \ = \ \sum_{\text{all } \phi} \prod_{i=i}^{N} t_{i\phi_i}$$

There are only two possibilities for the value of $\dagger T\dagger$, just as there were for $\dagger R\dagger$ by equation [15].

$$[29] \quad \dagger T\dagger = s \text{ or } a, \text{ for all } T \subset \mathsf{T}$$

The former is true if and only if *all* terms in the summation [28] equal s.

Definition

If $\dagger T\dagger = s$, then T is said to be *passive*. If $\dagger T\dagger = a$, then T is said to be *active*.

Denote by T_0 the class of all passive T-matrices and by T_a the class of all active T-matrices. Clearly the union $\mathsf{T}_0 \cup \mathsf{T}_a = \mathsf{T}$.

Theorem 1 (The "Interchange Condition")

A matrix T is passive if and only if, for all h, i, j, k,
$$t_{hj} t_{ik} = t_{hk} t_{ij}.$$

PROOF

To prove sufficiency, we use the definition [28]. Consider the term $\prod_{i=1}^{N} t_{i\phi_i}$ in the summation, corresponding to some permutation ϕ. If no interchange of a pair of column subscripts alters the value of a product, then it must follow that no permutation of N column subscripts alters the product. In particular, the permutation ϕ^{-1} would not. But ϕ^{-1} carries $\prod_{i=1}^{N} t_{i\phi_i}$ onto $\prod_{i=1}^{N} t_{ii}$, which equals s by [T2]. Therefore $\prod_{i=1}^{N}$

$t_i\phi_i$ necessarily equals s. This being true for all terms in the summation, thus $\dagger T\dagger = s$, and T is passive.

To prove that any violation of the "interchange condition" $t_{hj}t_{ik} = t_{hk}t_{ij}$ necessarily implies T nonpassive, suppose that at least one set h, i, j, k were found with $t_{hj}t_{ik} = c \cdot t_{hk}t_{ij}$. (Every case of violation of the interchange condition must be express-able in this way, since elements of T can only equal s or c.) Now consider any term Π_1 of [28] in which $t_{hj}t_{ik}$ appears. Let the product of the remaining elements in the term be denoted Π_0, that is, $\Pi_1 = t_{hj}t_{ik}\Pi_0$. By definition of the pseudo-deter-minant, the product Π_0 also appears in another term, namely $\Pi_2 = t_{hk}t_{ij}\Pi_0$. Whatever the value of Π_0, it follows that $\Pi_1 = c \cdot \Pi_2$, whence $\dagger T\dagger = a$, since not all terms in [28] equal s.

Theorem 2

The interchange condition of Theorem 1 is satisfied if and only if, for each pair h and i of rows in T, either

  (i) $t_{hj} = c \cdot t_{ij}$ for all j, or

  (ii) $t_{hj} = s \cdot t_{ij}$ for all j.

Rows satisfying (i) we shall call *antagonistic*, and satisfying (ii), *compatible*.

PROOF

Any columns j and k of two antagonistic rows, h and i, would by [i] display

$$t_{hj} = ct_{ij}$$
$$t_{hk} = ct_{ik}$$

Whence $\qquad t_{hj}(ct_{ik}) = t_{hk}(ct_{ij}),$

or $\qquad c(t_{hj}t_{ik}) = c(t_{hk}t_{ij}).$

Thus $\qquad t_{hj}t_{ik} = t_{hk}t_{ij},$

the interchange condition. A similar derivation holds for com-patible rows, with s appearing wherever c does above.

For the proof of necessity, note that a pair of rows which is neither antagonistic nor compatible will violate the interchange condition, since then some j and k will exist for which

$$t_{hj} = ct_{ij}$$
$$t_{hk} = st_{ik}$$
and
$$t_{hj}t_{ik} = ct_{hk}t_{ij}.$$

COROLLARY 1

A T-matrix is passive if and only if every pair of rows is either antagonistic or compatible.

COROLLARY 2

A T-matrix is passive if and only if its rows can be partitioned into two subsets, $\bar{\alpha}$ and $\bar{\alpha}$, such that all pairs of rows in α are compatible, all pairs in α are compatible, and all pairs with one member in each subset are antagonistic.

Next we proceed to define a special operation of one T-matrix on another.

Definition

The *application* $TU = W$, where $T, U \subset \mathsf{T}$ are matrices of the same order (N), is defined simply by

$$w_{ij} = t_{ij}u_{ij} \text{ for all } i, j.$$

The definition immediately implies $W \subset \mathsf{T}$, since the conditions [$T1$–3] must be satisfied by the elements w_{ij} of W. In other words:

Theorem 3

The class $\mathsf{T}^{(N)}$ is closed under the operation of application. The following theorems may be proved with dispatch.

Theorem 4

Application is commutative.

$$TU = UT, \text{ with } T, U \subset \mathsf{T}^{(N)}$$

Theorem 5

Application is associative.

$$(TU)V = T(UV), \text{ with } T, U, V \subset \mathsf{T}^{(N)}$$

Definition

The *identity transformation* $S \subset \mathsf{T}$ is given by the matrix with all $t_{ij} = s$. (Note that $S \subset \mathsf{T}_0$; that is, the identity transformation is a passive transformation.) Clearly $ST = T$ for all $T \subset \mathsf{T}$, by virtue of [16] and [17].

Theorem 6

Every $T \subset \mathsf{T}$ is self-inverse, i.e.,

$$T \cdot T = S$$

This follows immediately from the definition of application and rules [16] and [18].

Theorem 7

The class $\mathsf{T}_0^{(N)}$ is closed under application.

PROOF

If $T \subset \mathsf{T}_0^{(N)}$, then by theorem 1

$$t_{hj}t_{ik} = t_{hk}t_{ij} \text{ for all } h, i, j, k.$$

If $U \subset \mathsf{T}_0{}^{(N)}$, then

$$u_{hj}u_{ik} = u_{hk}u_{ij} \text{ for all } h, i, j, k.$$

Then for $W = TU$, we will have for all h, i, j, k

$$
\begin{aligned}
w_{hj}w_{ik} &= (t_{hj}u_{hj})(t_{ik}u_{ik}) \\
&= (t_{hj}t_{ik})(u_{hj}u_{ik}) \\
&= (t_{hk}t_{ij})(u_{hk}u_{ij}) \\
&= (t_{hk}u_{hk})(t_{ij}u_{ij}) \\
&= w_{hk}w_{ij} ,
\end{aligned}
$$

and thus $W \subset \mathsf{T}_0{}^{(N)}$.

Definition

Let $_iT^*$, the "allegiance transform on i," denote the T-matrix with

(i) $t_{ij} = t_{ji} = c$ for a given i and all $j \neq i$.

(ii) all other elements $= s$.

By Corollary 1 of Theorem 2, $_iT^* \subset \mathsf{T}_0$, since the above definition implies that row i is antagonistic to all other rows, while any two rows $g \neq i$ and $h \neq i$ are compatible. From this and Theorem 7, we infer:

Theorem 8

An application of the form

$$U = \prod_{i\epsilon\alpha} {}_iT^*,$$

where α is any subset of the integers 1 to N, implies $U \subset \mathsf{T}_0$.

COROLLARY 1

All $U \subset \mathsf{T}_0$ formed as above must satisfy Corollary 2 of Theorem 2. The subset α above and the subset α of the previous corollary are in fact one and the same. This may be shown by a straightforward albeit clumsy tracing through of the elements u_{hk} of U for the separate cases $(h, k \epsilon \alpha)$, $(h, k \epsilon \overline{\alpha})$, $(h \epsilon \alpha, k \epsilon \overline{\alpha})$, $(h \epsilon \overline{\alpha}, k \epsilon \alpha)$.

Now, since specification of various partitions α generates an exhaustive catalogue of passive T-matrices by Corollary 2 of Theorem 2, and since a passive T-matrix with any given partition α may in fact be constructed by successive application on matrices of the form T^*, we have the important

Theorem 9

All passive T-matrices can be constructed by applications of the form

$$\prod_{i\epsilon\alpha} {}_iT^*$$

Rewording this, we may say that the *set of allegiance transforms T^* is a "basis" for the class* T_0.

Returning to the analysis of R-matrices, we establish the

Definition

The application $TR = Q$, where $T \subset \mathsf{T}^{(N)}$, $R \subset \mathsf{R}^{(N)}$ is given by

$$q_{ij} = t_{ij} \cdot r_{ij} \text{ for all } i, j$$

This directly implies $Q \subset \mathsf{R}^{(N)}$, by the rules [R1–3] and [19–22].

The application of a transformation matrix thus carries one structure matrix into another. This is an important tool, since it enables the analysis of R-matrices to proceed in terms of analysis of their transforms, which is often simpler.

Theorem 10

$(TU)R = T(UR)$, with $T, U \subset \mathsf{T}^{(N)}$ and $R \subset \mathsf{R}^{(N)}$.

Proof follows immediately from the above definition.

Let us examine what happens when a passive T is applied to a balanced R.

Theorem 11

A transformation $T \subset \mathsf{T}_0$ applied to an $R \subset \mathsf{R}_0$ yields some $Q \subset \mathsf{R}_0$. That is, *passive transforms of balanced R-matrices are balanced.* (Recall from the psychological model that balanced R-matrices represent "black and white" attitudes. A passive transform will change one or more elements from "black" to "white," or "white" to "black," but leave the state of balance undisturbed.)

PROOF

The pseudo-determinant of Q is

$$Q = \sum_{\text{all } \phi} \prod_{i=1}^{N} q_i \phi_i$$

$$= \sum_{\text{all } \phi} \prod_{i=1}^{N} (t_i \phi_i \cdot r_i \phi_i)$$

$$= \sum_{\text{all } \phi} \left\{ \prod_{i=1}^{N} t_i \phi_i \right\} \left\{ \prod_{i=1}^{N} r_i \phi_i \right\},$$

since all t and r elements commute. But the former product is s for all ϕ when $T \subset \mathsf{T}_0$, and the latter product is p for some ϕ and possibly o for others, though it is never n when $R \subset \mathsf{R}_0$ (see the remarks following conditions [29] and [15]).

Therefore

$$\dagger Q \dagger = p, \text{ and } Q \subset \mathsf{R}_0.$$

Next, consider the case of imbalanced R-matrices. Given some $R \subset \mathsf{R}_a$, it is always possible to find at least one $X \subset \mathsf{T}$ such that $XR = Q \subset \mathsf{R}_0$. In particular, one could choose $X \subset \mathsf{T}$ with the property that $x_{ij} = c$ wherever $r_{ij} = n$, and s otherwise. Then all entries in Q would be either p or o and clearly $\dagger Q \dagger = p$, ergo $Q \subset \mathsf{R}_0$. Now consider applications of the form *(WX)R*, with $W \subset \mathsf{T}_0$ (and thus $WX = V \subset \mathsf{T}$, by Theorem 3).

$$(WX)R \;=\; W(XR) \;=\; WQ \;=\; \text{some } Q' \subset \mathsf{R}_0 \,,$$

using Theorems 10 and 11. The construction WX enables the formation of many transforms carrying a given imbalanced R into a balanced one, once the special transform X is established. The various transforms $V = WX$ differ from each other in the number of c-entries they contain, suggesting a

Definition

The *complexity* of an imbalanced R-matrix is the integer m, determined as follows:

  (i) Construct $X \subset \mathsf{T}$ with $x_{ij} = c$ whenever $r_{ij} = n$ and s otherwise.

  (ii) Form all possible applications $V = WX$, with $W \subset \mathsf{T}_0$.

  (iii) Count the number of c-entries in each V, dividing by two to avoid duplication due to symmetry.

  (iv) Denote by m the *minimum* count thus determined.

The complexity of imbalance, then, is the *minimum number of changes necessary to produce balance.*

Denote the class of all $R \subset \mathsf{R}_a$ with complexity m by R_m. This provides the partition, promised earlier, of the class R_a into R_1, R_2, R_3, etc.

Theorem 12

A transformation $T \subset \mathsf{T}_0$ applied to an $R \subset \mathsf{R}_m$ yields some $P \subset \mathsf{R}_m$. That is, *complexity of imbalance is invariant under a passive transformation.*

PROOF

The complexity of R, denoted say m_1, is defined on the class of matrices WX, where $W \subset \mathsf{T}_0$ and X is such that $XR = Q \subset \mathsf{R}_0$.

Now consider the complexity m_2 of the transform $P = TR$.

We establish an analogue Y of the previous X by choosing $Y = XT$. Then,

$$YP = (XT)(TR) = XSR = XR = Q \subset \mathsf{R}_0.$$

Thus m_2 is defined on the class of matrices WY, with $W \subset \mathsf{T}_0$. But $WY = WXT = (WT)X$.

Now we have m_1 defined on WX, and m_2 defined on $(WT)X$. But since the only requirement on W is that it be a member of the class T_0, and since by Theorem 7 the application (WT) must be a member of T_0 inasmuch as $T \subset \mathsf{T}_0$, it follows that the class of (WT) is identical to the class of W. (They both correspond to T_0.) Therefore the class of all WX is identical to the class of all $(WT)X$, and $m_1 = m_2$.

Theorem 13

Complexity of imbalance is invariant under all "allegiance" transformations of the form

$$\prod_{i \in \alpha} {}_i T^*.$$

This follows immediately from Theorems 9 and 12.

The operational simplifying procedure recommended in the psychological model for determining complexity of imbalance is a consequence of this theorem. "Changes of allegiance" do not alter the complexity of imbalance, so that one may reverse p's and n's in any successive set of rows and columns until the complexity of imbalance is apparent.

Many other theorems may be derived from this system. However, limitations of space make it imperative to conclude here.

We state one final result, without proof.

Theorem 14

The maximum complexity possible for an $N \times N$ R-matrix is

$$m_{\max}.(N) = \frac{N^2 - 2N + \delta}{4} \qquad \delta = \begin{cases} 1 \text{ if } n \text{ odd} \\ 0 \text{ if } n \text{ even} \end{cases}$$

NOTES

1. For some experimental purposes, it is more convenient to define a common conceptual arena for a group of subjects. Some topics yield low overlap between subjects, but other topics possess sufficient overlap so that it is worthwhile to construct a group arena encompassing the most generally salient elements.

2. In order to circumvent the coding problem, one may require the subject to choose his verb forms from a precoded list. This version is presently being attempted. Full details of the entire procedure will be set forth elsewhere.

3. The entire set of rules may be organized into one with the aid of Tables 1 and 2 of The "Mathematical System." Letting R denote the structure matrix, derived or imputed sentences may be found from the matrix multiplication of R by itself. The powers R^2, R^3, etc. yield imputations which are successively more removed from the original sentences.

4. The potency of these various motivating conditions could be subjected to empirical test, using before and after measures of cognitive structure and experimental manipulation of motivating conditions in-between. One such experiment has in fact been carried out by Zajonc (20), using a different theoretical context. See his discussion of "cognitive tuning."

5. So-called "conversion experiences" may be representative of the extreme case: very extensive cognitive changes are characteristic of this phenomenon.

6. One may provoke imbalance experimentally by strong persuasive communication aimed at a given cognitive unit. We are presently launching an experiment of this type.

7. Cartwright and Harary (5) have proposed a different index for degree of structural imbalance. The present index is simpler to compute, and has also the appealing feature that it refers to the dynamic property of change in structure. Harary, in a personal communication, has indicated that he has recently and independently hit upon an index equivalent to the present one. He calls it the "line index of balance." A "line" in his terminology is a relation in our terminology. His "line index of balance" is the minimal number of lines (relations) whose negation yields balance. He points out that negation in the sense of changed sign and negation in the sense of deletion or elimination are equivalent insofar as balancing is concerned. Where we say "change of relation," this may be taken to mean change from p to either n or o, and change from n to either p or o.

8. A certain amount of trial-and-error may be required before reaching a final decision. This decision is not automatic; the change operation is sometimes useful on a row and column with a plurality of p's over n's—a temporary *increase* in the number of n's can lead to an ultimate further reduction in the minimum number of n's.

9. Often referred to as the "permanent."

REFERENCES

1. ABELSON, R. P. 1954. "A Technique and A Model for Multi-dimensional Attitude Scaling," *Public Opinion Quarterly*, 18, 405–18.
2. ASCH, S. E. 1952. *Social Psychology*. New York: Prentice-Hall.
3. ASCH, S. E., H. BLOCK, and M. HERTZMAN. 1938. "Studies in the Principles of Judgments and Attitudes: I. Two Basic Principles of Judgment," *Journal of Psychology*, 5, 219–51.
4. BIRKHOFF, G. and S. MACLANE. 1947. *A Survey of Modern Algebra*. New York: Macmillan.
5. CARTWRIGHT, D., and F. HARARY. 1956. "Structural Balance: A Generalization of Heider's Theory," *Psychological Review*, 63, 277–93.
6. FESTINGER, L. 1957. *Theory of Cognitive Dissonance*. Evanston, Ill.: Row, Peterson.
7. GREEN, B. F. 1954. "Attitude Measurement," in *Handbook of Social Psychology*, ed. G. Lindzey. Cambridge: Addison-Wesley.
8. HARARY, F. 1953–54. "On the Notion of Balance of a Signed Graph," *Michigan Mathematics Journal*, 2, 143–46.
9. ———. "A Line Index for Structural Balance." (In process of publication.)
10. HEIDER, F. 1946. "Attitudes and Cognitive Organization," *Journal of Psychology*, 21, 107–12.
11. HOVLAND, C. L., I. L. JANIS, and H. H. KELLEY. 1953. *Communication and Persuasion*. New Haven: Yale University Press.
12. KRECH, D., and R. CRUTCHFIELD. 1948. *Theory and Problems of Social Psychology*. New York: McGraw-Hill.
13. LEWIN, K. 1951. *Field Theory in Social Science*. New York: Harper.
14. OSGOOD, C. E., and P. H. TANNENBAUM. 1955. "The Principle of Congruity in the Prediction of Attitude Change," *Psychological Review*, 62, 42–55.
15. PEAK, H. 1955. "Attitude and Motivation," in *Nebraska Symposium on Motivation*, ed. M. Jones. Lincoln: University of Nebraska Press.
16. ROKEACH, M. 1954. "The Nature and Meaning of Dogmatism," *Psychological Review*, 61, 194–204.
17. ROSENBERG, M. 1956. "Cognitive Structure and Attitudinal Affect," *Journal of Abnormal and Social Psychology*, 53, 367–72.
18. SMITH, M. B., J. S. BRUNER, and R. W. WHITE. 1956. *Opinions and Personality*. New York: Wiley.
19. TOLMAN, E. C. 1932. *Purposive Behavior in Animals and Men*. New York: Century.
20. ZAJONC, R. B. 1954. "Structure of Cognitive Field," unpublished doctoral dissertation, University of Michigan.

4 Cognitive Dissonance: Five Years Later

NATALIA P. CHAPANIS
ALPHONSE CHAPANIS

Natalia P. Chapanis *and* Alphonse Chapanis *are members of the faculty of The Johns Hopkins University. Their major interests are, respectively, the interplay of perception and personality (including learning to read) and the application of psychology to the design of man-machine systems. Since neither has concentrated on attitude research, or even on social psychology, they were an unexpected source of the most devastating, the most general, and ultimately the best-known attack on cognitive dissonance theory. Specific aspects of the critique have themselves been attacked; but there is no doubt that it has been a beneficial influence, both in pointing out the failings of previous*

From *Psychological Bulletin*, 61 (1964): 1–22, copyright 1964 by the American Psychological Association. Reprinted by permission.

This article is based on material prepared by the senior author while she was employed at the Tavistock Institute of Human Relations, London, England. It appeared originally as Tavistock Document No. 626, "Cognitive Dissonance: A Dissenting Voice," dated June 1961. That work was part of a research program

116

work and in motivating the defenders of dissonance theory to improve their efforts (see the subsection entitled "Criticisms and Alternatives" under the heading "Cognitive Dissonance Theory" in Chapter 1).

Social psychologists have been trying for many years to predict the conditions under which attitudes and opinions are changed. In general their attempts have not been conspicuously successful. One of the first major breakthroughs in this area came when Leon Festinger (1957) published his book on *A Theory of Cognitive Dissonance*. In this book the author presented a simple conceptual scheme by which he could predict with precision the outcomes of certain social situations. To support his theory, Festinger marshaled data from an impressive variety of field and experimental studies. In addition, he and other workers have since then conducted a number of studies designed to test specific derivations of the theory. What can we say about all this literature?

Cognitive dissonance theory has already been reviewed by Bruner (1957), Asch (1958), Osgood (1960), and Zajonc (1960). These writers, however, have been primarily concerned with a critical evaluation of the conceptual system employed in dissonance theory. And, whatever they might think of the theory, most workers (except perhaps Asch) have been impressed by the scope, relevance, and ingenuity of the experimental evidence gathered in its support.

There is an engaging simplicity about Festinger's dissonance formulations. No matter how complex the social situation, Fes-

financed by S. H. Benson, Limited, and carried out by the Tavistock Institute. The extensive expansion and revision of the original document undertaken with the collaboration of the junior author was supported in part by Contract Nonr 248(55) between the Office of Naval Research and the Johns Hopkins University. We are pleased to acknowledge the assistance provided us by both organizations. The views expressed in this article are, however, those of the authors. Neither S. H. Benson, Limited, nor the Office of Naval Research is responsible for any of the statements contained in it.

We are greatly indebted to the staff of the Tavistock Institute, and particularly to Frederick E. Emery, for many helpful comments, guidance, and encouragement throughout the preparation of the original document. Grateful appreciation is also extended to our many American colleagues—too numerous to name individually—who read various versions of this article and offered helpful comments and encouragement.

tinger assumes that it is possible to represent the meaning which the situation has for an individual by a series of elementary *cognitions*—statements that an individual might make describing his "knowledge, opinions or beliefs" (Festinger, 1957, p. 3). Moreover, a simple inventory of a group of related cognitions is sufficient to reveal whether or not they are consistent. The theory assumes further that people prefer consistency among their cognitions and that they will initiate change in order to preserve this consistency. So far these ideas are not new. They had been promulgated as early as 1946 by Heider with his concept of balance and imbalance. The magic of Festinger's theory, however, seems to lie in the ease with which imponderably complex social situations are reduced to simple statements, most often just two such statements. This having been done, a simple inspection for rational consistency is enough to predict whether or not change will occur. Such uncomplicated rationality seems especially welcome after having been told for years that our attitudes and resulting behavior are strongly dependent on motivational, emotional, affective, and perceptual processes (e.g., Krech & Crutchfield, 1948; Rosenberg, 1960).

Five years have elapsed since the publication of Festinger's book, and this seems to be an appropriate time to pause for a close look at the evidence in support of the theory. For no matter how appealing a theory might be, in the final analysis it is the evidence that counts. This paper, therefore, will be concerned with a review of experiments on cognitive dissonance in humans from two points of view. First we shall consider whether an experimenter really did what he said he did. Then later we shall consider whether the experimenter really got the results he said he did.

CONTROVERSIAL EXPERIMENTAL MANIPULATIONS

As we all know, good experimental work always involves manipulating conditions in such a way that we may ascribe changes we observe in our dependent variables to the manipulations we carried out on the independent variables. In actual practice we rarely define these manipulations in careful operational terms. When a pellet drops into a cup in front of a hungry rat we call it a reward, or reinforcement; when a wire transmits an electric shock to a person we call it punishment, or stress; and so on. Moreover, we do not, in general, quarrel with our fellow experimenter's interpretation of the situation. After all, he was there, he ought to know what it was about. However, when we deal with experiments on cognitive dissonance we have a very special problem on our hands.

Experimental Dissonance

Simply stated, cognitive dissonance theory is concerned with what happens when the cognitions of a person are discrepant. The basic premise is that discrepant cognitions create tension which the individual strives to reduce by making his cognitions more consistent. This tension is called cognitive dissonance, and the drive towards consistency, dissonance reduction. "When two or more cognitive elements are psychologically inconsistent, dissonance is created. Dissonance is defined as psychological tension having drive characteristics" so that when dissonance arises the individual attempts to reduce it (Zimbardo, 1960, p. 86).

For our purposes at the moment the most important thing to note about the theory is that dissonance is an intervening variable whose antecedents are the private internal cognitions of a person. To test a theory like this, it is up to the experimenter to create various degrees of dissonance by introducing various discrepant cognitions within an individual. Whenever contradictory statements or syllogisms or opinions are used, there is not likely to be much controversy about the fact that they must lead to discrepant internal cognitions, and so, by definition, to dissonance. Indeed, studies on cognitive dissonance of this type have yielded results which are well established, clear-cut, and consistent. But for the experiments under review here, the situation is rarely as simple as this. The Festinger group is primarily concerned with applying their dissonance formulation to predict complex social events. In order to do this experimentally, they use elaborate instructions and intricate relationships between experimenter and *S* to introduce discrepant cognitions and therefore to produce dissonance. Under such conditions, how can we be sure that the experimental situation has been successful in creating dissonance and dissonance alone?

In the face of such difficulties, it is always a good policy to ask the *S* himself about the situation, either directly or indirectly. It should be possible, for instance, to find out how the *S*s perceived each of the experimental manipulations. One could also determine whether *S*s perceived the situation as conflictful and, if so, to what extent. This kind of information is crucial to the theory of cognitive dissonance because all its predictions are based on the assumption that a state of differing, incompatible cognitions has been produced within the *S*. Unfortunately, evidence of this kind from the *S*s themselves is not always available in the studies under review here. As a result, it is up to the reader to decide whether the experimental manipulations had the effect which the authors claim.

The other side of the coin, equally important, is that we must also assure ourselves that the experimental manipulations did not at the same time produce other internal states or cognitions within the *S* which could contaminate or even account for the findings. In fact, certain "nonobvious" derivations of some of these experiments may perhaps become a little more obvious when the experiments are reinterpreted to take other factors into consideration.

It is worthwhile spending a few moments on these nonobvious derivations. If we disregard the intermediate steps and simply consider the independent and dependent variables, it is possible to describe the essential aspects of some of these derivations by saying that they follow a *pain principle*. Reduced to essentials, some of Festinger's derivations say that the more rewarding a situation, the more negative is the effect; and contrariwise, the more painful a situation, the more positive is the effect. This is clearly illustrated by the following quotation from Festinger (1961): "Rats and people come to love the things for which they have suffered." However, if we carefully examine the kinds of experiments which are supposed to test these derivations, we find that, in general, the situation contains both painful and re-warding conditions, but that the manipulation is interpreted in terms of only one of these. It should be apparent that if a situa-tion is both rewarding *and* painful, and the dependent variable shows a positive effect, it is not legitimate to attribute it solely to the painful variable, or vice versa. To use a statistician's termi-nology, the variables are confounded.

Our most general criticism, then, is that some dissonance ex-periments have been designed in such a way that it is impossible to draw any definite conclusions from them.

Examples

The best way of illustrating these points is to describe an ex-perimental procedure and then to analyze it from two points of view: Did the experimenter really produce the discrepant cogni-tions he said he did? Did the experimental manipulations pro-duce other cognitions that could contaminate or account for his findings?

RELIEF OR DISSONANCE?

Let us take this experiment: College women volunteered to participate in a series of group discussions on the psychology of sex. They were seen individually by the experimenter before being allowed to join an "on-going group." Some of the girls were told they would have to pass an embarrassment test to see if they were tough enough to stand the group discussion. They were free to withdraw at this point, and one S did so. Girls in the severe embarrassment group had to read out loud in the presence of the male experimenter some vivid descriptions of sexual activ-ity and a list of obscene sex words. Another group of girls—the mild embarrassment group—read some mild sexual material. All of these girls were told that they were successful in passing the embarrassment test. Each *S* then listened as a silent member to a simulated, supposedly on-going group discussion, which was actually a standard tape recording of a rather dull and banal discussion about the sexual behavior of animals. A control group listened only to the simulated group discussion. All groups then made ratings about this discussion, its participants, and their own interest in future discussions. The ratings made by the severe embarrassment group were, on the average, somewhat more favorable than those made by the other two groups.

What was this experiment about? Was it to demonstrate the effect of feelings of relief when people discover that a task (the group discussion) is not as painfully embarrassing as the embarrassment test led them to believe? No. Was it to demonstrate the effect of success in a difficult test (passing the embarrassment test) on task evaluation? No. Was it to demonstrate the displacement of vicarious sexual pleasure from a discomfiting but sexually arousing situation to a more socially acceptable one? No. The experimenters called it "The Effect of Severity of Initiation on Liking for a Group" (Aronson and Mills, 1959); that is, the more painful the initiation, the more the *S*s like the group. They predict the outcome for the severe embarrassment group in the following way: In successfully passing the embarrassment test these girls "held the cognition that they had undergone a painful experience" in order to join a group; the discussion, however, was so dull and uninteresting that they realized the unpleasant initiation procedure was not worth it. This produced dissonance, since "negative cognitions about the discussion . . . were dissonant with the cognition that they had undergone a painful experience." One of the ways they could reduce this dissonance was by reevaluating the group discussion as more interesting than it really was.

All this may be so, but in order to accept the authors' explanation we must be sure the girls really did hold these discrepant cognitions, and no others. We have to be sure, for instance, that they felt no relief when they found the group discussion banal instead of embarrassing, that success in passing a difficult test (the embarrassment test) did not alter their evaluation of the task, that the sexual material did not evoke any vicarious pleasure or expectation of pleasure in the future, and that the group discussion was so dull that the girls would have regretted participating. There is no way of checking directly on the first three conditions, although other experimental evidence suggests that their effect is not negligible. However, to check on the fourth factor we have the data from the control group showing that the group discussion was, in fact, more interesting than not (it received an average rating of 10 on a 0–15 scale.). It is, therefore, difficult to believe that the girls regretted participating. To sum up, since the design of this experiment does not exclude the possibility that pleasurable cognitions were introduced by the sequence of events, and since, in addition, the existence of "painful" cognitions was not demonstrated, we cannot accept the authors' interpretation without serious reservations.

It is interesting to speculate what would have happened if the girls had been "initiated" into the group by the use of a more generally accepted painful procedure, such as using electric shock. Somehow it seems doubtful that this group would appreciate the group discussion more than the control group, unless —and here is the crucial point—the conditions were so manipulated that Ss experienced a feeling of successful accomplishment in overcoming the painful obstacle. [It seems to us that if there is anything to the relationship between severity of initiation and liking for the group, it lies in this feeling of successful accomplishment.] The more severe the test, the stronger is the pleasurable feeling of success in overcoming the obstacle. There is no need to postulate a drive due to dissonance if a *pleasure principle* can account for the results quite successfully.

The same feeling of successful accomplishment may, incidentally, be the relevant variable involved in some of the "effort" experiments done by the Festinger group (e.g., Cohen, 1959). It seems reasonable to expect that in such experiments the higher the degree of perceived effort, the greater the feeling of successful accomplishment in performing a task. Thus, *effort* would be confounded with *feeling of success*. Note, however, that success is pleasant, whereas effort is painful. Here is a situation which could be both rewarding and painful, but dissonance workers see it only as painful. (Two other effort experiments will be analyzed in greater detail later in this section.)

REWARD OR INCREDULITY?

Let us look at another experiment, this time by Festinger and Carlsmith (1959): Out of several possibilities, Ss chose to take part in a 2-hour experiment falsely labeled as an experiment on "measures of performance." The Ss were tested individually and were given a "very boring" and repetitive task for about one hour. At the end of the hour each S was given a false explanation about the purpose of the experiment. He was told that it was an experiment to test the effect of expectation on task performance. Some Ss were then asked if they would mind acting in a deception for the next couple of minutes, since the person regularly employed for this was away. The Ss of one group were hired for $1.00 each, those of another group for $20.00 each, to tell the next incoming S how enjoyable and interesting the experiment had been (ostensibly the expectation variable). Each S was also told he might be called on to do this again. Some Ss refused to be hired. A control group of Ss was not asked to take part in any deception. Subsequently, all Ss (control and hired Ss) were seen by a neutral interviewer, supposedly as part of the psychology department's program of evaluating experiments. During the interview, Ss were asked to rate the experiment along four dimensions. The only significant difference between the three groups was in terms of enjoyment. The control group rated the experiment as just a little on the dull side, the $1.00 group thought it was somewhat enjoyable, and the $20.00 group was neutral. The mean ratings for the control and $20.00 groups were not significantly different from each other nor from the neutral point.

What was this experiment about? The authors call it "Cognitive Consequences of Forced Compliance." They make the prediction that "the larger the reward given to the *S*" the smaller the dissonance and therefore "the smaller the subsequent opinion change," and "furthermore . . . the observed opinion change should be greatest when the pressure used to elicit the overt behavior is just sufficient to do it." As an aside we should point out that, inasmuch as these statements clearly refer to a maximum and so by inference to some sort of a curvilinear or nonmonotonic relationship, it would have been better if more reward categories had been used. In addition, two more control groups—a *deception-but-no-reward* group, and a *reward-but-no-deception* group—should have been included to separate out the effects of reward and deception. However, our primary concern at the moment is not with such technical matters of experimental design.

Let us examine instead the meaning of the descriptive term "forced compliance." According to Festinger (1957), it means "public compliance without private acceptance [p. 87]." The reward *S*s, it is true, complied publicly with the instructions in that they described a boring task as enjoyable to another *S*. Notice, however, that even the control group rated the task as only slightly boring. This suggests that the false explanation placed the task in a wider context and may have led to "private acceptance" of the whole situation by both control and reward *S*s. We could also question the choice of the word "forced." Forced implies a lack of freedom, but it is extremely difficult to predict how an *S* perceives his freedom of choice even when this variable is experimentally manipulated (e.g., Brehm & Cohen, 1959*a*). All we can say is that the term "forced compliance" is not a good description of the events in this experiment.

What seems to be even more important, however, is that the experiment could be more appropriately entitled "The Effect of a Plausible and Implausible Reward on Task Evaluation." As far as we can tell, *S*s were not asked to describe their reactions to the size of the reward. Nevertheless, $20.00 is a lot of money for an undergraduate even when it represents a whole day's work.

When it is offered for something that must be much less than 30 minutes work, it is difficult to imagine a student accepting the money without becoming wary and alert to possible tricks. In fact, more than 16% of the original Ss in the $20.00 group had to be discarded because they voiced suspicions, or refused to be hired. Under such circumstances, it seems likely that those who were retained might have hedged or been evasive about their evaluation of the experiment. The mean rating for the $20.00 groups was $-.05$ on a scale that ranged from -5.00 (dislike) to 5.00 (like), that is, the mean rating was at the neutral point. As other workers (e.g., Edwards, 1946) have suggested, a rating at the zero or neutral point may be ambiguous, ambivalent, or indifferent in meaning and may simply represent an evasion. The authors' data, unfortunately, do not permit us to determine whether individual Ss did in fact respond this way. In any event, if we assume that $1.00 is a plausible, but $20.00 an implausible, reward, then the results fall neatly into the pattern of all previous and more extensive experiments on the effect of credulity on pressures to conformity (Fisher & Lubin, 1958).

To sum up, the design of this experiment does not allow us (*a*) to check whether discrepant cognitions were in fact produced, and (*b*) to rule out alternative explanations.

Incidentally, the authors of other related studies (Brehm, 1960; Brehm & Lipsher, 1959; Cohen, Terry, & Jones, 1959) have difficulty in accounting for all of their results according to dissonance theory predictions. These difficulties disappear if we use a plausibility explanation. The argument would proceed along these lines: If an individual is subjected to many pressures towards change from a number of sources, (*a*) each pressure will act on the individual, and (*b*) their effect will be cumulative. For instance, we may increase pressure on an individual by limiting his freedom of choice, by giving him acceptable rewards, by presenting him with statements that strongly support a position discrepant to his own, by increasing the size of the discrepancy, and so on. Each of these alone will produce a greater and greater opinion change until—and this is the critical part of the argument—the situation becomes implausible, at which point the *S* will ignore the pressures and show no change. It also seems reasonable to suppose that a combination of *any* of these factors will act cumulatively to produce the implausible effect.

We can express this situation in statistical terminology. For example, if we have a two-factor experiment with two levels of pressure towards opinion change in each variable, we would expect to find that the two main effects are significant. Moreover, we would predict that the interaction would also be significant primarily because the combination of both "high pressures" would be implausible and so produce the least opinion change. In general, this is the pattern of results obtained by the dissonance workers in experiments of this type.

MEALTIME TROUBLES

Another example of an untested interpretation occurs in the Brehm (1959) experiment on the effect of a *fait accompli* in which boys were offered a prize if they ate a portion of a disliked vegetable. While eating it, some *S*s were casually told that a letter would be sent to their parents informing them of their participation in the experiment and of the vegetable they ate. Those boys who indicated they had trouble about eating the vegetable at home (i.e., it was more often served than eaten) subsequently changed their rating of the disliked vegetable towards a more favorable one. What did the letter mean to these boys? According to the author it meant that the "the *S*s would have to eat more" of the vegetable at home. But this is a guess, not based on any evidence in the experiment. Furthermore, in an extension of the same procedure at the same school with equivalent *S*s from the same classes, direct manipulation of the commitment to further eating "failed to produce an overall effect on liking [Brehm, 1960, p. 382]." Under the circumstances, we find it difficult to accept the author's contention that the *fait accompli* increased cognitive dissonance by increasing the commitment to eating. There is little doubt that mentioning the letter changed the ratings, but only for boys who had mealtime troubles. The key to the problem most likely lies in the expectation these boys had about the effect of the letter on their parents and on themselves. However, the design of the experiment does not allow us to find out what this expectation was.

CONFOUNDED EFFORT

In a recent experiment, Aronson (1961) tried to separate the effects of secondary reinforcement from dissonance in a rewarding situation. "Reinforcement theory suggests that stimuli associated with reward gain in attractiveness; dissonance theory suggests that stimuli associated with 'no reward' gain in attractiveness . . . if a person has expended effort in an attempt to attain the reward [p. 375]." Aronson argues that since the effect of secondary reinforcement is constant, nonrewarded objects should become more attractive as the effort to obtain them increases.

In order to test this hypothesis, Ss fished for cans to obtain a reward ($.25) inside one-third of the cans. The rewarded cans were of one color, the nonrewarded ones of another, but the Ss could not determine which they had snared until the cans had actually been pulled out. One group of Ss—the low-effort group—was told that their task was not tedious. They had the relatively easy task of fishing out a can with a magnet, a task which took them, on the average, only 14 seconds per can. Another group of Ss—the high-effort group—was told that their task was extremely tedious. They had the relatively difficult task of fishing out a can with a hook, which took them, on the average, 52 seconds per can. All Ss continued fishing for the reward money until 16 unrewarded cans had been pulled out. The Ss rated the relative attractiveness of the two colors before and after carrying out the task. The results show that in the low-effort condition, the attractiveness of the color on the rewarded cans increased (a secondary reinforcement effect), but in the high-effort condition no change was observed. All of this was interpreted as substantiating the cognitive dissonance predictions.

Aronson explains the lack of change in the high-effort condition by saying that the effects of dissonance and secondary reinforcement are equal but opposite in direction, and so cancel each other. However, if we look more carefully at the experimental manipulation of effort, we see that the low-effort condition is actually a reward rate of $.25 about every 42 seconds, and the high-effort condition is actually a reward rate of $.25 about every 156 seconds. In other words, the low-effort group is, at the same time, a high-reward-rate group, and the high-effort group, a low-reward-rate group. The difference obtained between the two groups could then be simply the result of the difference in reward rates, and the lack of change in the high-effort group, the result of their low reward rate.

To summarize, Aronson tried to demonstrate the effect of effort in a rewarding situation. However, the design of the experiment confounds effort with reward rate. As a result, no unambiguous conclusions can be drawn as to the effect of effort.

There is yet another experiment on effort in which confounding occurs. Yaryan and Festinger (1961) tried to show the effect of "preparatory effort" on belief in a future event. The Ss volunteered to participate in an experiment labeled "Techniques of Study" which was supposed to investigate the techniques, hunches, and hypotheses that students use to study for exams. The Ss were told that only half of them would take part in the complete experiment, which involved taking an IQ test. All Ss were given an information sheet on which there were definitions essential to this supposed IQ test. In the high-effort condition, Ss were told to study the sheet and memorize the definitions. In the low-effort condition, Ss were told to glance over the definitions briefly. The latter were also told that they would have access to the sheet later if they were to take IQ test. Each S was then asked to express his estimate of the probability that he would take the IQ test. The results show that Ss in the high-effort group thought it was more probable that they would take the test.

The authors (Yaryan & Festinger, 1961) explain the results in the following way: Exerting "a great deal of effort" is inconsistent with the cognition that one may not take the test, so Ss in the high-effort group should believe "more strongly in the likelihood of the occurrence of the event [p. 606]." This might very well be the case, but in this experiment the variable of effort is confounded with the presence of other predictors for the event. All *S*s had been told that this was an experiment on the techniques of study, but the only group which *did* any studying was the high-effort group. In addition, the studying that was done was highly relevant for the IQ test. Under the circumstances, it does not seem at all surprising that *S*s in this group took these additional cues to mean that they were assigned to the complete experiment and to the IQ test. As it stands now, the Yaryan and Festinger experiment does not separate the effect of effort from that of additional cues.

RELIABILITY IS NOT VALIDITY

As we have seen, most cognitive dissonance formulations are concerned with what happens after a person makes a decision. One of the earliest experiments designed specifically to investigate this problem was the gambling experiment described by Festinger (1957, p. 164) and successfully replicated by Cohen, Brehm, and Latané (1959) with minor variations in procedure. The agreement between these two studies has done much to enhance the belief in the validity of cognitive dissonance formulations (e.g., Riecken, 1960, p. 489).

The experimental procedure in these two studies was relatively simple. Each *S* played a card game with the experimenter for variable money stakes. Before beginning the game each *S* was informed of the rules of the game, and on the basis of this information chose one of two sides on which to play. He was told that he could change sides once during the game, but that it would cost him money. He was led to expect that he would play 30 games. At the end of 12 games, play was interrupted and *S* was given a probability graph to study. The graph, a different one for each side, gave the (false) information that the chosen side was the losing one. The dependent variables were the time spent in studying the graph and the number of people who changed sides. Results were analyzed in terms of a weighted average of the amount of money won or lost. The pattern of results obtained is very complex and would require at least a fourth-order parabola to describe it. Nevertheless, the various ups-and-downs were interpreted as supporting the dissonance theory predictions for postdecision, information-seeking processes.

Two things strike us about the dissonance theory interpretation of this experiment. First, Festinger is not consistent in his dissonance formulations. Let us look at the way in which the results are interpreted. The money winners spent a moderate amount of time studying the graph. Festinger considers this the result of dissonance produced by the information in the graph which purported to show that these winners were actually on the losing side. If we accept this line of reasoning, it should follow that the losers would have no such dissonance (the graph confirmed their losses), and would therefore spend little time on the graph. This was not so. Festinger (1957), however, has three other dissonance explanations to account for the complex behavior of the losers. He argues, first of all, that loss of money is itself dissonance producing and the bigger the loss, the bigger the dissonance. The small losers spent as much time as they did in the "hope that the graph would tell them they were actually on the correct side [p. 171]." If this explanation is correct, the bigger losers should have spent an even longer time searching the graph —but they did not. Festinger explains this away by saying that the bigger losers would avoid the graph "if the graph were perceived as yielding information which would probably increase the dissonance which already existed [p. 172]." If this explanation is correct, the biggest losers should have spent the least amount of time on the graph—but they did not. To explain this behavior Festinger postulates yet another hypothesis. For the biggest losers "the easiest way to eliminate the dissonance would be to increase it temporarily to a point when it was greater than the resistance to change of the behavior," that is, they would study the graph, then switch sides. If this explanation is true, then we would expect that all of the biggest losers, and only the biggest losers, would switch sides—but this was not so. It should be noted that these four dissonance hypotheses are inconsistent with each other, since they predict effects in different directions. Moreover, there is no a priori way of determining the degree to which each particular hypothesis applies to the groups. This whole matter can be summarized in another way: If the pattern of results had been exactly the reverse, these same explanations would apply just as well.

This brings us to the second point. The most important criticism of this gambling experiment is that it is not so much an experiment on the dissonance-reducing effects of information in postdecision processes, as it is an experiment on "information seeking in predecision processes" (suggested by F. E. Emery). The *S*s had been told that they could change sides and they were actually given an opportunity to do so when they were handed the graph. Festinger (1957) and Cohen et al. (1959) reported that many *S*s, both winners and losers, announced their decision to switch sides at this time. What was not reported, however, was the number of *S*s who looked at the graph in order to reach a decision whether or not it would be more profitable to change sides. In other words, *S*s looked at the graph not to reduce dissonance, but to look for information to help them decide whether they should change sides. With this interpretation, the pattern of results becomes more obvious and reasonable. For example, in one of the two conditions of the Cohen et al. replication those *S*s who neither won nor lost any money spent the most time looking at the graph. This finding is entirely inexplicable in dissonance terms, even with an imaginative use of all four of Festinger's hypotheses. However, if we consider this experiment to be concerned with predecision processes, then we see that these *S*s had gained the least amount of information from the actual play of the game and were, therefore, trying to extract as much information as possible from the graph before reaching a decision.

Taking all of these factors into consideration, we are forced to conclude that Festinger's interpretations, however ingenious, are unnecessarily elaborate and unjustified. Moreover, the successful replication of the experiment suggests—not that the cognitive dissonance formulations are valid—but only that the results of experiments of this type are reproducible.

Subsequent experiments on selected aspects of information-seeking in postdecision processes have done nothing to clarify the situation. Adams (1961) and Maccoby, Maccoby, Romney, and Adams (1961) showed that people tend to seek information which agrees with their viewpoint, but Rosen (1961) obtained results which show that people tend to seek information which disagrees with their viewpoint. It seems more likely to us that, in general, people will often seek new information, whether it be consonant or contrary. Indeed this is apparently the kind of result that Feather (1962) obtained. To be sure, when prejudice or some other highly motivated state is involved, people are selective in their perceptions and avoid contrary material. But under these conditions it is the motive itself, and not dissonance, that seems to be crucial.

Interpretation of Manipulations

Perhaps the illustrations cited above will suffice to show that the experiments adduced to support the theory of cognitive dissonance involve highly complex manipulations. The effects of these manipulations are open to alternative explanations which have generally not been dealt with adequately by the authors. We can diagram this in the following way: Let us suppose that the complex experimental manipulations produce the cognitions 1, 2, 3, 4 . . . n in the S, as illustrated on the left side of Figure 4.1. Two of these cognitions (Cognitions 1 and 2) are chosen by the experimenter as being the relevant discrepant cognitions producing dissonance. Any observed change in the dependent variable is then attributed to that dissonance. But, as we see by examining the whole of Figure 4.1, this may not necessarily be the case. Any one cognition, or any combination of cognitions, could have been responsible for the change in the dependent variable. There is no way of ascertaining which, because the effects of all these cognitions have been confounded.

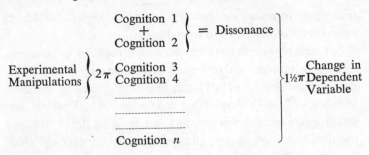

FIGURE 4.1: *The type of confounding frequently found in experiments on cognitive dissonance*

It is possible to design experiments so that these effects are not confounded. As a step in this direction we recommend first of all that the experimental manipulations be simplified. It is difficult to agree about differences in cognitions when the instructions, task, and procedure differ in many ways for control and experimental groups. Our second recommendation is that additional control groups be included in the design of these experiments to deal with the irreducible differences in experimental manipulation. Our third recommendation is that a little more attention be given to discovering the possible cognitions that an *S* might have about the situation, particularly those which might be contrary to dissonance theory. Only under such carefully controlled conditions can we begin to talk about unequivocal evidence in support of cognitive dissonance theory.

CONTROVERSIAL TREATMENTS OF THE DATA

So much for experimental manipulations. Now to see if the experimenter really got the results he says he did. Our most serious criticisms of the experiments cited in support of dissonance theory fall under the heading of methodological inadequacies in the analyses of results. Of these inadequacies the most important is the rejection of cases, not only because it is so fundamental a flaw, but also because the supporters of dissonance theory so often do it.

Rejection of Cases

If an experimenter is interested in the performance of only a certain group of *S*s, it is legitimate for him to select these *S*s before beginning the experiment, or sometimes even after the experiment, before the results are analyzed. However, when *S*s are selectively discarded after the data of an experiment have been collected, tabulated, and sometimes even analyzed, it leaves the reader with a feeling of uneasiness. The uneasy feeling grows if the *S*s are discarded because their results are said to be "unreliable," or if the experimenter gives inconsistent reasons—or no reasons at all—for their rejection. But let us look at the experiments themselves.

UNRELIABLE SUBJECTS

Brehm and Cohen (1959*b*) asked sixth-grade children to indicate how much they liked several different toys before and after they had chosen one for themselves. The choice of the gift and the postchoice rating were made a week after the prechoice rating. The authors hypothesized that there would be an increase in the evaluation of the chosen article, and a decrease in the evaluation of the nonchosen article, the greater the dissimilarity among the toys, and the greater the number of alternatives from which to choose. In general these predictions were upheld. But of the original sample of 203 children *only 72* were used in the analysis. In the authors' (Brehm and Cohen, 1959b) words, the reasons for the reduction were as follows:

First, the choice alternatives for each *S* had to be liked, but not so much that an increase in liking would be impossible. Second, one alternative had to be initially more liked than any other so that its choice could be expected. Increased ratings of the chosen item are thus not likely to be simply a result of normal (and random) changes in actual liking from the first questionnaire to the second. *In addition, Ss who failed to choose the alternative initially marked as most liked were excluded because they gave unreliable or invalid ratings.* Finally, in order to ensure that initially less liked alternatives were seriously considered as possible, initial ratings of these alternatives could not be much lower than the most liked alternative [p. 375; italics added].

Note first that the exact limits of all these requirements were determined only after inspection of the data, despite the fact that each *S* had been given a prearranged choice based on his initial ratings. However, let us look more carefully at the italicized item —the exclusion of *S*s because of unreliability. If *S*s give unreliable results, it is usual to assume that the measuring instrument itself is unreliable; indeed, the authors themselves admit this when they mention "the low reliability of our measure of liking." However, discarding selected *S*s does nothing to improve the reliability of an instrument.

Discarding *S*s who did not choose the alternative initially marked as most liked may in fact falsely reduce the computed error variance, change the mean values, and so enhance the possibility of obtaining a significant difference in rating. To illustrate, the upper half of Figure 4.2 shows the ratings for two toys, X and Y, which satisfy the conditions specified by Brehm and Cohen: they are both liked, one is liked more than the other, but the difference is not great. Now let us assume that the ratings are subject to errors of measurement and that they vary randomly from time to time. Let us further assume that the expressed rating, the liking, at any one moment in time, is perfectly correlated with choice.

The situation a week later is shown in the bottom half of Figure 4.2. The ratings for X are now distributed as X', the ratings for Y, as Y'. Now the *S*s are asked to make a choice. Let us assume the null hypothesis, that is, the actual process of choosing a gift does not alter the liking or rating of a toy. Since the choice and the postchoice rating occur so close together in time, we can also assume that no random change occurs from just before the choice to just after it. If, as Brehm and Cohen did, we discard all those *S*s who chose Y rather than X, this means that we eliminate from the shaded area in the bottom half of Figure 4.2 all

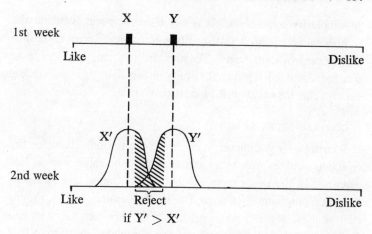

FIGURE 4.2: *This illustration shows how the rejection of Ss from the shaded area may have introduced a statistical artifact into the experiment by Brehm and Cohen (1959b).*

those cases in which $Y'>X'$. Such a process can only reduce the variance of both distributions of differences in ratings (that is, $X'-X$ and $Y'-Y$), and automatically increase the mean difference between them. Moreover, this selection procedure will automatically produce precisely the effect which the authors predicted, namely, that the mean rating for the chosen toy increases, while the rating for the nonchosen toy decreases. Furthermore, these effects will be greatest in the group from which most such Ss were discarded. Most of these discards came from the "four alternatives condition,"* and the change in rating is actually greatest for this condition.

In a footnote (p. 376) the authors (Brehm & Cohen, 1959b) state they carried out similar computations on their "unselected population," that is, on the entire sample of 203 Ss. Although the sensitivity of the statistical test is now nearly twice as great (because of the increase in N from 27 to 203), they find no effect due to the number of alternatives (one of the two predictions made). Tests of the other prediction "yield support" for the

* J. Brehm, personal communication, 1961.

"dissimilarity hypothesis." It is not clear, however, whether the authors mean by this a statistically significant difference, or simply a nonsignificant trend. To sum up, it seems reasonable to conclude that the significant results obtained in this and similar experiments may very well be statistical artifacts.

CONTRADICTORY REASONS

Sometimes it is difficult to reconcile the reasons given for the rejection of cases with other statements by the same author. For example, in the experiment on "Attitude Change and Justification for Compliance" (Cohen, Brehm, & Fleming, 1958), the initial analysis showed no significant difference between the two justification groups. The authors then eliminated more than half of the *S*s (47 out of 92), carried out a second analysis on the remainder, and concluded that "the difference in amount of change is significant by one-tailed *t* test at .07 level." Relatively more *S*s whose opinion did not change were eliminated from the low-justification condition (35 out of 63). Not surprisingly, the new mean for the low-justification condition turned out to be greater than for the high-justification condition.

Part of the reasoning for this selection of cases was as follows (Cohen et al., 1958): "since extremity of position inhibits attitude change . . . it seems reasonable to eliminate the extremes [p. 277]." A year later, however, Cohen (1959) made this statement: "If the individual . . . engages in some behavior with regard to the contrary communication . . . then the greater the discrepancy [extremity of position], the greater the opinion change [p. 387]."

In their original article, Cohen et al. state that their results should be interpreted cautiously, but, unfortunately, they do not follow their own advice. Whenever these authors refer to their findings in later articles (e.g.; Brehm, 1960; Cohen, 1960), they quote their results as substantiating cognitive dissonance theory without any of these cautionary reminders.

WHAT IS GOING ON?

An example of sample reduction for obscure reasons occurs in an experiment on the readership of "own car" and "other car" advertisements by new and old car owners (Ehrlich, Guttman, Schonbach, & Mills, 1957). A group of 65 new car owners was randomly chosen from a list of recent auto registrants. The car advertisements read by this group were compared with those read by a group of 60 old car owners chosen from a telephone directory. The raw data for these analyses were the percentages of car advertisements noticed and read in a selection of magazines and newspapers which the owners had previously indicated they read regularly. The cognitive dissonance theory predictions were that new car owners would most often read advertisements about their own make of car and avoid reading those of competing makes. In general, these predictions were upheld for the data presented.

The principal difficulty with this experiment is that cases were successively rejected in various stages of the analysis so that when one finally arrives at the critical statistical test it is virtually impossible to determine what the remaining data mean. Let us see if we can trace the authors' steps in this process. The authors first present a table showing the mean percentage of advertisements noticed and mean percentage of advertisements read of those noticed for each of the categories "own," "considered," and "other car." They (Ehrlich et al., 1957) state in a note accompanying the table that: "The N's are reduced because in some cases no advertisements of a particular kind appeared in the issues shown or none of those which appeared were noticed. They are further reduced because not all respondents named cars as 'seriously considered' [p. 99]." The first and third reasons impose a limit on the number of Ss whose results could be used. The largest reduction due to these two limitations was in the category "considered car" for old car owners, where the N of 60 was reduced to 31.

The second reason given in the quotation above means that an owner who did not notice any advertisement in a particular category was discarded from the table of "advertisements read" for that category. For example, if an owner noticed (or noticed and read) an ad about another car but did not notice any advertisements about his own car, he was included under the category of "other car," but excluded from the category of "own car" in computing the mean percentage of "advertisements read of those noticed." Up to one-third of the remaining cases were eliminated from the various categories for this reason.

The next point at which still more cases are rejected is in the computation of several sign tests of significance. We are told that the Ns are reduced because not all comparisons were possible. What this means is that significance tests were computed only on those owners who *noticed at least one advertisement in each of the pairs of categories compared*. Finally, those owners who read an equal percentage of advertisements in each of the two categories were also discarded.

Taking all of the above factors into account we find that as much as 82% of the original sample was discarded in certain categories!

The sign tests mentioned above were used only for making certain pairs of comparisons. For overall tests of their hypotheses the authors resorted to chi square and give terminal chi square values, with their associated probabilities, alongside the tables for the sign tests. The article itself does not say upon what Ns, or what groupings, the chi squares were computed, but correspondence* reveals that the chi square tests were made on the same Ss as were used in computing the sign tests.

At best this entire situation may be described as unclear. In the first place, it is difficult to know how to interpret significance tests based on such highly selected data. Furthermore, in computing chi squares for the same Ss as were used in the sign tests, it appears that the authors discarded some data (the ties) which should properly have been included. If we have been able to thread our way correctly through the authors' manipulations of the data, we find that the chi squares, computed for all the relevant data, are less significant than reported by the authors, and, in two of three cases, change a nominally significant value to a nonsignificant one. In any event, there can be no doubt that the authors' (Ehrlich et al., 1957) summary statement "It was found that new car owners read advertisements of their own car more

* J. Mills, personal communication, 1962.

often than . . ." needs considerable qualification. With so much selection of Ss and with such intricate manipulations of the data, some of it never fully explained, one can hardly describe the results as *public,* or the findings as necessarily significant.

MANIPULATION NOT SUCCESSFUL

Still another type of rejection we find in these studies is the elimination of entire groups of Ss. If one variant of the manipulation fails to show an effect, it is not legitimate to discard all the Ss in that group from the analysis. The analysis should properly be carried out on all the data and the interpretations should be based on the complete analysis. Brehm (1960), for example, used reports on the vitamin and mineral content of vegetables to try to influence the attitudes of Ss after they had eaten a disliked vegetable. One group of Ss received the vitamin report, the other group the mineral report. Since the mineral report "failed to affect" the dependent variable, "the results for these subjects [were] omitted from this report [Brehm, 1960, footnote, p. 380]." One consequence of rejecting an entire group is that we do not know if there is a significant interaction between type of report and the other variables. Until this is established, it is misleading to consider a segment of the results as significant. In addition, the author nowhere states that his findings are specific to one type of report only. His summary is in terms of "communications about food value."

REALLOCATION INSTEAD OF REJECTION

An interesting variant of the rejection of Ss occurs in the Raven and Fishbein (1961) study on the effect of "Acceptance of Punishment and Change in Belief." Groups of Ss were run under two conditions, "shock" and "no-shock." There were 13 females and 13 males in each of these two conditions. The results show that there was no overall difference between the shock and no-shock groups. However, when the results were tabulated separately for the two sexes, it appeared that the female Ss in the shock group changed in the predicted direction, but that the male Ss did not. Here is how the authors (Raven & Fishbein, 1961) dealt with the situation: "Overall analysis of variance and interaction was not significant. Assuming that male shock Ss were part of a common population with the non-shock subjects, with respect to dissonance, an analysis of variance was conducted which showed the female shock subjects to be significantly different from the others [p. 415]." In other words, the authors disposed of the Ss who did not conform to their prediction, not by rejecting them, but by reallocating them to another group, the no-shock group. If females in the shock group really are significantly different from all the others, this should show up in a significant interaction. It does not.

Rejection of cases is poor procedure, but reallocation of Ss from experimental to control group, across the independent variable, violates the whole concept of controlled experimentation.

DANGER OF REJECTING SUBJECTS

A theme common to many of these rejections is that the unselected sample "does not permit of an adequate test" of the dissonance hypothesis. We are told:

In a social influence situation there are a number of potential channels of dissonance reduction, such as changing one's own opinion, changing the opinion of the communicator, making the communicator noncomparable to oneself, seeking further support for one's position, dissociating the source from the content of the communication, and distorting the meaning of the communication [dissonance theory position ably summarized by Zimbardo, 1960, p. 86].

Such a theoretical formulation is indeed all-encompassing and it provides a rationale which certain other dissonance theory workers have used for rejecting cases. The reasoning goes like this: If some Ss do not follow the specific predictions in a particular experiment (for instance, if they fail to show any opinion change) then those Ss are probably reducing their dissonance through some other channel or else they had little dissonance to begin with. If either of these conditions holds, it is legitimate to exclude these Ss from the analysis since they could not possibly be used to test the particular hypothesis in the experiment. An inspection of results is considered sufficient to determine whether Ss are, or are not, to be excluded. Unfortunately, this line of reasoning contains one fundamental flaw: *it does not allow the possibility that the null hypothesis may be correct.* The experimenter, in effect, is asserting that his dissonance prediction is correct and that Ss who do not conform to the prediction should be excluded from the analysis. This is a foolproof method of guaranteeing positive results.

Some people may feel that no matter how questionable the selection procedure, it must still mean something if it leads to significant results. This point of view, however, cannot be reconciled with the following fact of life: it is always possible to obtain a significant difference between two columns of figures in a table of random numbers provided we use the appropriate scheme for rejecting certain of those numbers. For all we know, selecting Ss so as "to permit an adequate test of the hypothesis" may have had precisely this effect. A significance test on selected Ss may therefore be completely worthless.

We strongly recommend that Ss not be discarded from the sample *after* data collection and inspection of the results. Nor is it methodologically sound to reject Ss whose results do not conform to the prediction on the grounds that they have no dissonance, or that they must be reducing it some other way. If there are any theoretical grounds for suspecting that some Ss will not show the predicted dissonance-reduction effect, the characteristics of such Ss, or the conditions, should be specifiable in advance. It should then be possible to do an analysis on all Ss by dividing them into two groups, those predicted to show dissonance reduction, and those predicted not to show it. If such a thing as dissonance reduction exists, it is theoretically and practically important to know the precise conditions under which it does and does not occur.

A summary of experiments in which *S*s are rejected is given in Table 4.1.

TABLE 4.1: *List of Experiments from Which Subjects Were Discarded After Data Collection*

Experiment	Total *N*	Discarded (%)	Reasons given
Brehm (1956)	225	35	To permit adequate test of hypothesis 1. Unreliable *S*s 2. Conditions not fulfilled
Brehm (1960)	85[a]	38[a]	One manipulated condition not significant
Brehm & Cohen (1959*b*)	203	65	To permit adequate test of hypothesis 1. Ceiling effect for high scorers 2. Adequate separation of choice points for dissonance to occur 3. Unreliable *S*s
Brehm & Lipsher (1959)	114	10–14	None
Cohen, Brehm, & Fleming (1958)	92	51	To permit adequate test of hypothesis 1. Extremity of attitude inhibits attitude change
Ehrlich et al. (1957)	125	17–82	1. Material missing 2. Advertisements not noticed 3. Not all comparisons possible 4. Ties
Mills (1958)	643	30	To permit adequate test of hypothesis 1. Ceiling effect for high scorers 2. Honest improvers have no dissonance

[a] Estimated.

Refusals

The previous section has been concerned with sampling bias due to the deliberate rejection of cases by the experimenter. There is another type of sampling bias, equally important but much more subtle, that occurs when Ss reject themselves from the study by refusing to participate.

In a recent review of cognitive dissonance experiments, Cohen (1960) concluded with what he considered was a "depressing" and "Orwellian" statement: "It could be said that when the individual feels that he has most freedom of choice, when his volition and responsibility are most engaged, he is then most vulnerable to the effects of persuasive communications and to all sorts of controlled inducements from the world at large [p. 318]." This statement follows hard on the heels of "The more negative the person is toward a communication or communicator, the more he can be expected to change his attitudes in the direction of the communication or communicator." These are indeed sweeping generalizations, particularly since they are based on the results of experiments in which from 4% (Cohen, Terry, & Jones, 1959) to as many as 46% (Rabbie, Brehm, & Cohen, 1959) of the total number of Ss refused to participate. Moreover, there is evidence in these studies that the Ss who refused to participate were actually those who had both the greatest freedom of choice and the strongest (most negative) views on the attitude in question. What actually appears to have happened is that those Ss with the strongest (most negative) views were so *in*vulnerable to the effects of persuasive communications that they exercised their freedom of choice by walking out on the experimenter or refusing to comply in other ways. To take the results of the remaining more vulnerable Ss and extrapolate from them to the population in general seems unjustified.

Inadequate Design and Analysis

It is rare to find in this area a study that has been adequately designed and analyzed. In fact, it is almost as though dissonance theorists have a bias against neat, factorial designs with adequate *N*s, capable of thorough analysis either parametrically or non-parametrically. The majority of their experiments are some variant of the 2 × 2 factorial with unequal, nonproportional, and generally small *N*s in each cell. These restrictions make it impossible for the authors to carry out ordinary analyses of variance. Instead we find them making use of a hodgepodge of *t* tests and a statistic which they refer to as an "interaction *t*" (Walker & Lev, 1953, pp. 159–160).

Making a number of ordinary *t* tests on the same set of data, without a prior overall test of the null hypothesis, can be misleading. The principal difficulty is that in making such multiple comparisons the experimenter is allowing himself a number of opportunities to find an event (significance) which normally occurs infrequently. As a result, the usual *t* tables underestimate the true probabilities; that is, the probabilities obtained suggest a level of significance which is higher than warranted. Another way of saying it is that if, out of several subgroups, one finds one or two *t*s significant, he is, in effect, capitalizing on chance (e.g., Sakoda, Cohen, & Beall, 1954). A further complication arises if the interaction is significant, since this introduces the usual difficulties about interpreting the main effects (e.g., Lindquist, 1953, p. 209). Some of the special statistical problems involved in the "postmortem" testing of comparisons were, of course, being discussed in the psychological literature well before dissonance theory appeared on the scene (e.g., McHugh & Ellis, 1955); but for an excellent discussion of the basic issues involved in making multiple comparisons, see the article by Ryan (1959). None of these problems is ever faced squarely by the writers in this field. As a result, the authors sometimes reach conclusions that are not really warranted.

EXAMPLES

We can illustrate these remarks by referring to an analysis carried out by Brehm (1960) on two treatment variables, commitment and communication. There are three levels of commitment—control, low-eating, and high-eating—and, in addition, two types of communication—support and no support. Since the Ns for these six groups are different (they vary from 7 to 11), it is not possible to carry out an ordinary analysis of variance. With such data at least 15 t tests and 3 interaction ts are possible. Brehm gives the results of 7 such t tests (4 are nominally significant) and 2 such interaction ts (both nominally significant). How do we interpret the results? Frankly, it is impossible. Taken at its face value, the analysis is not only useless, it is misleading.

An allied set of criticisms can be leveled at the analysis carried out by Brehm and Cohen in their study of the effects of choice and chance in cognitive dissonance (1959a). The design involved two types of relative deprivation, high and low. Five sections of an introductory psychology course were used as Ss. The low- and high-deprivation conditions were experimentally manipulated and perceived as such by the Ss. The low- and high-choice conditions were, however, determined separately for each section on the basis of their medians on the perceived-choice rating scale. Separate interaction ts were calculated for each of the five sections. The Ns in each cell were very small, ranging between 3 and 10 with an average of about 7. The probability values for these 5 interaction ts showed that one was significant, two tended to significance, and two were nonsignificant (one was actually a reversal). Here again the authors' failure to compute and report the results of an overall test make it exceedingly difficult for readers to interpret their findings. Moreover, there seems to be little justification for using a different value for the cutoff point between high- and low-choice for each section. In fact, such a procedure might in itself lead to statistically significant median differences between the sections. There may indeed be a significant interaction between choice and deprivation, but the evidence for it is, at best, questionable.

In dissonance experiments there is often a marked change between the pre- and posttest measures for both control and experimental groups. This is in itself an interesting phenomenon and should be thoroughly evaluated. An analysis should be complete —large main effects should not be ignored just because dissonance theory predicts only an interaction, or vice versa.

It is not impossible to apply a rigorous methodology to this area. Dissonance theorists would have done well to emulate the example set by Kelman as far back as 1953 (a study which, incidentally, anticipates and predates most of the areas of interest for cognitive dissonance workers). All of the problems that beset research in this area, such as unequal Ns, class differences, and so on, were handled expertly by Kelman. More recently, such eclectic workers as Rosenbaum and Franc (1960) and McGuire (1960) have also been working in this area and have been using rigorous and comprehensive methods of analysis. In short, there appears to be no reason why methodology in this area cannot be sharpened.

A summary of experiments in which the analyses and statistical interpretations are doubtful is given in Table 4.2.

Straining for Significance

The final feature of the analyses that is apt to be misleading is the fact that authors tend to present results as significant and as supporting the dissonance theory prediction when the probabilities are greater than the usually accepted value of .05. Probability values between .06 and .15 (once even .50!) do not constitute striking support for any theory, particularly if it is preceded by a selection of Ss and poor analysis. It is also extremely disconcerting to find these statistically nonsignificant trends quoted authoritatively in subsequent reports and later reviews as substantiating the theory, without any qualifying statements.

OVERALL EVALUATION

Having now reviewed much of the experimental work supporting cognitive dissonance theory, we conclude that, as a body of literature, it is downright disappointing. Too many studies have failed to stand up to close scrutiny. Yet it is also obvious that the dissonance framework has a seductive allure for many social scientists, an allure not possessed by the rather similar, but symbolically more complex, interpretations by Heider (1958), Osgood and Tannenbaum (1955), or Newcomb (1953).

Paradox of Simplicity

The magical appeal of Festinger's theory arises from its extreme simplicity both in formulation and in application. But in

TABLE 4.2: *Summary of Some Experiments with Inadequate Design and Analysis*

Study	Criticism of Design and Analysis
Allyn & Festinger (1961)	No control group (repeat attitude test, no talk); interaction significance not presented
Aronson & Mills (1959)	Overall significance not presented
Brehm (1956)	Maximum $N = 225$, but regression equation based on $N = 557$ and $N = 534$
Brehm (1960)	Overall significance not presented
Brehm & Cohen (1959a)	Overall significance not presented
Cohen (1959)	No control group (repeat attitude test, no counterinformation); groups not equated on initial attitude
Cohen, Terry, & Jones (1959)	No control group (repeat attitude test, no new information); groups not equated on initial attitude
Ehrlich et al. (1957)	No control group (predecision car ad reading)
Festinger & Carlsmith (1959)	Overall significance not presented
Mills (1958)	Overall significance not presented
Mills, Aronson, & Robinson (1959)	No control group (preferences, but no decision); overall significance not presented
Rosen (1961)	No control group (preferences, but no decision)

our review we have seen that this simplicity was generally deceptive; in point of fact it often concealed a large number of confounded variables. Clearly much can be done to untangle this
confounding of variables by careful experimental design. None-
theless, there may still remain another problem more fundamental than this. In general, a cognitive dissonance interpretation of
a social situation means that the relevant social factors can be
condensed into two simple statements. To be sure, Festinger
does not say formally that a dissonance theory interpretation
works only for two discrepant statements; but it is precisely because in practice he does so limit it that the theory has had so
much acceptance. Which brings us now to the crux of the matter: *is it really possible to reduce the essentials of a complex social situation to just two phrases?* Reluctantly we must say "No."
To condense most complex social situations into two, and only
two, simple dissonant statements represents so great a level of
abstraction that the model no longer bears any reasonable re-
semblance to reality. Indeed the experimenter is left thereby with
such emasculated predictors that he must perforce resort to a
multiplicity of ad hoc hypotheses to account for unexpected findings. We see then that the most attractive feature of cognitive
dissonance theory, its simplicity, is in actual fact a self-defeating
limitation.

In conclusion, all of the considerations detailed above lead us
to concur with Asch's (1958) evaluation of the evidence for
cognitive dissonance theory, and return once more a verdict of
NOT PROVEN.

REFERENCES

ADAMS, J. S. 1961. "Reduction of Cognitive Dissonance by Seeking
    Consonant Information," *Journal of Abnormal and Social Psy-
    chology,* 62, 74–78.
ALLYN, JANE, and L. FESTINGER. 1961. "The Effectiveness of Unan-
    ticipated Persuasive Communications," *Journal of Abnormal and
    Social Psychology,* 62, 35–40.

ARONSON, E. 1961. "The Effect of Effort on the Attractiveness of Rewarded and Unrewarded Stimuli," *Journal of Abnormal and Social Psychology*, 63, 375–80.

ARONSON, E., and J. MILLS. 1959. "The Effect of Severity of Initiation on Liking for a Group," *Journal of Abnormal and Social Psychology*, 59, 177–81.

ASCH, S. E. 1958. "Review of L. Festinger, *A Theory of Cognitive Dissonance*," *Contemporary Psychology*, 3, 194–95.

BREHM, J. W. 1956. "Postdecision Changes in the Desirability of Alternatives," *Journal of Abnormal and Social Psychology*, 52, 384–89.

————. 1959. "Attitudinal Consequences of Commitment to Unpleasant Behavior," *Journal of Abnormal and Social Psychology*, 60, 379–83.

BREHM, J. W., and A. R. COHEN. 1959a. "Choice and Chance Relative Deprivation as Determinants of Cognitive Dissonance," *Journal of Abnormal and Social Psychology*, 58, 383–87.

———— and ————. 1959b. "Re-evaluation of Choice Alternatives as a Function of Their Number and Qualitative Similarity," *Journal of Abnormal and Social Psychology*, 58, 373–78.

BREHM, J. W., and D. LIPSHER. 1957. "Communicator-Communicatee Discrepancy and Perceived Communicator Trustworthiness," *Journal of Personality*, 27, 352–61.

BRUNER, J. 1957. "Discussion of Leon Festinger: The Relation Between Behavior and Cognition," in J. S. Bruner, E. Brunswik, L. Festinger, F. Heider, K. F. Muenzinger, C. E. Osgood, and D. Rapaport, *Contemporary Approaches to Cognition: A Sympoisum Held at the University of Colorado*, pp. 151–56. Cambridge: Harvard University Press.

COHEN, A. R. 1959. "Communication Discrepancy and Attitude Change: A Dissonance Theory Approach," *Journal of Personality*, 27, 386–96.

————. 1960. "Attitudinal Consequences of Induced Discrepancies Between Cognitions and Behavior," *Public Opinion Quarterly*, 24, 297–318.

COHEN, A. R., J. W. BREHM, and W. H. FLEMING. 1958. "Attitude Change and Justification for Compliance," *Journal of Abnormal and Social Psychology*, 56, 276–78.

COHEN, A. R., H. I. TERRY, and C. B. JONES. 1959. "Attitudinal Effects of Choice in Exposure to Counter-Propaganda," *Journal of Abnormal and Social Psychology*, 58, 388–91.

EDWARDS, A. L. 1946. "A Critique of 'Neutral' Items in Attitude Scales Constructed by the Method of Equal Appearing Intervals," *Psychological Review*, 53, 159–69.

EHRLICH, D., I. GUTTMAN, P. SCHONBACH, and J. MILLS. 1957. "Postdecision Exposure to Relevant Information," *Journal of Abnormal and Social Psychology*, 54, 98–102.

FEATHER, N. T. 1962. "Cigarette Smoking and Lung Cancer: A Study of Cognitive Dissonance," *Australian Journal of Psychology*, 14, 55–64.

FESTINGER, L. 1957. *A Theory of Cognitive Dissonance*. Evanston, Ill.. Row, Peterson.

————. 1961. "The Psychological Effects of Insufficient Rewards," *American Psychologist*, 16, 1–11.

FESTINGER, L., and J. M. CARLSMITH. 1959. "Cognitive Consequences of Forced Compliance," *Journal of Abnormal and Social Psychology*, 58, 203–10.

FISHER, S., and A. LUBIN. 1958. "Distance as a Determinant of Influence in a Two-Person Serial Interaction Situation," *Journal of Abnormal and Social Psychology*, 56, 230–38.

HEIDER, F. 1946. "Attitudes and Cognitive Organization," *Journal of Psychology*, 21, 107–12.

————. 1958. *The Psychology of Interpersonal Relations*. New York: Wiley.

KELMAN, H. C. 1953. "Attitude Change as a Function of Response Restriction," *Human Relations*, 6, 185–214.

KRECH, D., and R. S. CRUTCHFIELD. 1948. *Theory and Problems of Social Psychology*. New York: McGraw-Hill.

LINDQUIST, E. F. 1953. *Design and Analysis of Experiments in Psychology and Education*. Boston: Houghton Mifflin.

MACCOBY, ELEANOR E., N. MACCOBY, A. K. ROMNEY, and J. S. ADAMS, 1961. "Social Reinforcement in Attitude Change," *Journal of Abnormal and Social Psychology*, 63, 109–15.

McGUIRE, W. J. 1960. "Cognitive Consistency and Attitude Change," *Journal of Abnormal and Social Psychology*, 60, 345–53.

McHUGH, R. B. and D. S. ELLIS. 1955. "The 'Postmortem' Testing of Experimental Comparisons," *Psychological Bulletin*, 52, 425–28.

MILLS, J. 1958. "Changes in Moral Attitudes Following Temptation," *Journal of Personality*, 26, 517–31.

MILLS, J., E. ARONSON, and H. ROBINSON. 1959. "Selectivity in Exposure to Information," *Journal of Abnormal and Social Psychology*, 59, 250–53.

NEWCOMB, T. M. 1953. "An Approach to the Study of Communicative Acts," *Psychological Review*, 60, 393–404.

OSGOOD, C. E. 1960. "Cognitive Dynamics in the Conduct of Human Affairs," *Public Opinion Quarterly*, 24, 341–65.

OSGOOD, C. E., and P. H. TANNENBAUM. 1955. "The Principle of Congruity in the Prediction of Attitude Change," *Psychological Review*, 62, 42–55.

RABBIE, J. M., J. W. BREHM, and A. R. COHEN. 1959. "Verbalization and Reactions to Cognitive Dissonance," *Journal of Personality*, 27, 407–17.

RAVEN, B. H., and M. FISHBEIN. 1961. "Acceptance of Punishment and Change in Belief," *Journal of Abnormal and Social Psychology*, 63 411–16.

RIECKEN, H. W. 1960. "Social Psychology," *Annual Review of Psychology*, 11, 479–510.

ROSEN, S. 1961. "Postdecision Affinity for Incompatible Information," *Journal of Abnormal and Social Psychology*, 63, 188–90.

ROSENBAUM, M. E. and D. E. FRANC. 1960. "Opinion Change as a Function of External Commitment and Amount of Discrepancy from the Opinion of Another," *Journal of Abnormal and Social Psychology*, 61, 15–20.

ROSENBERG, M. J. 1960. "An Analysis of Affective-Cognitive Consistency," in *Attitude Organization and Change,* ed. C. I. Hovland and M. J. Rosenberg, pp. 15–64. New Haven: Yale University Press.

RYAN, T. A. 1959. "Multiple Comparisons in Psychological Research," *Psychological Bulletin,* 56, 26–47.

SAKODA, J. M., B. H. COHEN, and G. BEALL. 1954. "Test of Significance for a Series of Statistical Tests," *Psychological Bulletin,* 51, 172–75.

WALKER, HELEN M., and J. LEV. 1953. *Statistical Inference.* New York: Holt.

YARYAN, RUBY B., and L. FESTINGER. 1961. "Preparatory Action and Belief in the Probable Occurrence of Future Events," *Journal of Abnormal and Social Psychology,* 63, 603–6.

ZAJONC, R. B. 1960. "The Concepts of Balance, Congruity, and Dissonance," *Public Opinion Quarterly,* 24, 280–96.

ZIMBARDO, P. G. 1960. "Involvement and Communication Discrepancy as Determinants of Opinion Conformity, *"Journal of Abnormal and Social Psychology,* 60, 86–94.

5 In Defense of Dissonance Theory: Reply to Chapanis and Chapanis

IRWIN SILVERMAN

Irwin Silverman, *whose article rebuts some of the criticisms presented in the paper by Chapanis and Chapanis, was formerly at the State University of New York (Buffalo) and is now at the University of Florida. His research has been concerned with personality factors—particularly with the effects of personality variables on cognitive functioning—as well as with attitude change. He recently wrote a stimulating analysis of the importance of experimental artifact in the area of attitude research.*

For the most part, what Chapanis and Chapanis (1964) offer to substitute for existing interpretations of the data of dissonance research may be described as the first half of an al-

From *Psychological Bulletin*, 62 (1964): 205–9, copyright 1964 by the American Psychological Association. Reprinted by permission.

ternative explanation. They supply a novel account of the effect of the experimental manipulation upon the mediating processes of the subject, that is, they ask the question, "how can we be sure that the experimental situation has been successful in creating dissonance and dissonance alone? [p. 3]," but they do not complete the process of explanation by indicating how the intervening variable which they have invoked in lieu of dissonance accounts for the subject's response. Further, in several cases the premise on which they base their reinterpretation of the mediating variable appears highly questionable. Let us consider each of their critiques in turn.

Aronson and Mills (1959) performed an experiment whereby they varied degree of punishment, in the form of embarrassment, that the subject endured in order to participate in what was arranged to be a dull group discussion. Their findings were consistent with the prediction that the high-punishment group would tend to more greatly enhance the value of the discussion in order to resolve the greater amount of dissonance between the pain they had suffered and the reward they had obtained. Chapanis and Chapanis (1964) question whether high embarrassment did provide an experience of punishment, and maintain that "pleasurable cognitions" may have been introduced, stemming from "a feeling of successful accomplishment in overcoming a painful obstacle [p. 5]." Consider the implications of this line of reasoning. It may be extended to any experimental manipulation labeled as punishment and it insists that these be reevaluated in terms of their rewarding effects, a deduction which is generally inconsistent with the data on escape and avoidance conditioning. Even if the possibility is allowed that there is reward value in the punishment condition, there is no explanation of how this variable determines the subject's response. To this end the Chapanises (1964) leave us solely with the statement: "There is no need to postulate a drive due to dissonance if a *pleasure principle* can account for the results quite successfully [p. 5]." Bear in mind, however, that the criterion variable was not the subject's evaluation of the painful or pleasurable initiation, but the group discussion following. An alternate model would have to demonstrate how the pleasurable effects associated with the embarrassment condition were transmitted to the contiguous but independent event of the discussion. This may have interesting possibilities for some theoretician, but until these are explored, dissonance theory affords the only complete explanation.

The authors then turn to the original test by Festinger and Carlsmith (1959) of the hypothesis that size of incentive for engaging in attitude-discrepant behavior is negatively related to subsequent attitude change. Here the Chapanises consider that the high incentive ($20.00) was an "implausible reward," and thus "the results fall neatly into the pattern of all previous and more extensive experiments on the effect of credulity on pressures to conformity (Fisher & Lubin, 1958) [p. 7]."

We find, however, that the implausibility which the authors refer to in evaluating the dissonance experiment, that is, suspicion of the experimenter's motivation for giving a $20.00 incentive, is not directly comparable to the credulity variable in the studies cited by Fisher and Lubin (1958). The latter refer to the effects upon conformity of "the size of discrepancy between the subject's pre-influence judgment and the subsequent judgment originating from an influence source [p. 230]," for example, the distance between lines in an Asch-type paradigm. Decreased conformity at the higher levels of discrepancy is attributed to disbelief on the part of the subject that the influence source is giving true judgments. The only way we might link these two sets of results by a credulity explanation is by stating the principle that any suspicion of the experimenter's intentions in an influence study produces nonconformity, a proposition which may be developed into an alternative interpretation of Festinger and Carlsmith's (1959) results, if it were first corroborated.

Rosenberg (1963), in fact, has provided an explanation of the Festinger and Carlsmith findings, based in part on a credulity notion, in which it is assumed that high-incentive subjects perceive the actual purpose of the study as an investigation of their capacity to be bribed into opinion change and respond in a socially desirable manner. It should be pointed out, however, that

Brehm and Cohen (1962) anticipated a possible explanation of the Festinger and Carlsmith results in terms of suspicion of the $20.00 incentive and replicated their findings using high and low incentives of $1.00 and $.50. More recently, a student of the present author (Lependorf, 1964) obtained significantly less opinion change in a $.50 incentive group compared to a $.05 incentive group.

Further in the article the Chapanises "reinterpret" the findings of Aronson (1961) that subjects expending less effort to obtain both nonrewarding and rewarding objects would tend more to enhance the characteristics of the latter. They attempt to explain these effects by noting that the low-effort group was also a higher rate-of-reward group (though total amount of reward was the same for both). Again there is no attempt to link the intervening variable to the dependent variable, but the implication is that rate of reward is positively related to the magnitude of secondary reinforcement effects. Do the existing data substantiate this notion? The studies by Skinner and his students (cf. Ferster & Skinner, 1957) comparing the effects of continuous and periodic reinforcement conditions suggest that the opposite relationship exists.

In one case the authors do not begin to formulate an alternative explanation. In evaluating Brehm's study (1959) in which boys who had consented to eat a disliked vegetable became more positive about it when told that their parents would be informed of the event, the Chapanises note simply that "The key to the problem most likely lies in the expectation these boys had about the effect of the letter on their parents and on themselves [p. 8]." This is not inconsistent with the rationale underlying Brehm's hypothesis; however, this author offered an interpretation of the expectation which allowed him to predict the obtained effects. The critical point of the Chapanises' objection appears to be that "the design of the experiment does not allow us to find out what this expectation was [p. 8]" Need it be pointed out that the mediating variable, by definition, does not have to be operationally represented; that it functions in the hypothetico-deductive method to enable the experimenter to predict the dependent variable, which Brehm seems to have accomplished very well.

Chapanis and Chapanis spend a large part of their review on a study performed by Festinger (1957, p. 164) and replicated by Cohen, Brehm, and Latané (1959) demonstrating the relationship between magnitude of induced dissonance and avoidance of further dissonance. The crux of their critique is that Festinger offers several explanations for various aspects of the data which, taken together, could account for results in any direction. An important consideration, however, is ignored by the reviewers.

Festinger's study investigated the behavior of subjects who had chosen the side they believed advantageous in a two-person game based solely on probabilities, and who were either winning or losing. Subjects of the former group were considered to have no dissonance between their choice of side and its consequences. The others were assumed to have dissonance in amounts directly related to the amount of money lost. On the basis of these assumptions, Festinger was able to predict the precise form of the relationship, which approximated a fourth-order parabola, between amount of winnings or losings and time spent studying a graph which purported to show the actual probabilities for winning for either side. Festinger considered, however, that though the time scores for the winners, relative to the losers, were as predicted, they were higher in terms of absolute values than his deductions would lead him to expect. On this basis he proposed that an additional set of dissonant cognitions may have been introduced in this group between their performance and information contained in the graph to the effect that they were on the side with a lower probability of success. Thus, two sets of cognitive elements were assumed to be operative in this study, and each considered alone would predict an opposite pattern of relationships between the independent and dependent variables. The essential point, however, is that the relationship that was observed was hypothesized on the basis of deductions concerning one of these sets of cognitions. Deductions concerning the other were invoked, post facto, to account for an aspect of the larger effects of the manipulation which was not consistent with theoretical expectations. Further, the propositions of Festinger's post-hoc analysis meet the sole criteria for their justification; they lend themselves readily to investigation. A partial replication of the original experiment is called for in which dissonance between performance and information contained in the graph is eliminated by modifications of the latter.

In one instance alone, the Yaryan and Festinger study (1961), the Chapanises provide us with an alternative explanation of the effects of the independent variable upon the dependent variable, and it is agreed that this experiment needs to be redesigned before it may be considered support for dissonance theory.

In the second section of their review, Chapanis and Chapanis (1964) challenge what they term "methodological inadequacies in the analysis of results" of which they state, "the most important is the rejection of cases [p. 12]." The examples they cite, however, do not contain evidence of data exclusion on the basis of the dependent variable, which would certainly constitute a methodological flaw, but involve, for the most part, the acceptable and widely used procedure of preselecting subjects by some criterion that enables test of the hypothesis. The cases where these criteria are established and applied after inspection of the results for a larger sample represent a different aspect of the scientific method than the instance described above, but inasmuch as these criteria are other than the dependent variable, this may be regarded as induction rather than "methodological inadequacy." In the areas of behavior probed by dissonance theory we are a long way from making predictions with anything approaching one-to-one precision, and until this time it will be incumbent upon the researcher to try to account for data which do not fit his theory in a manner which will lead to further research. When this process involves the attempt to partial out potential sources of error variance, it will often require observation of the effects of the independent variable upon a more limited subject sample defined on the basis of the proposed error factor. Similar practices may be noted in any area of psychological research where they are equally justified and productive. Consider the various studies where interpretations were based upon the discovery that predicted relations held for one sex and not the other (e.g., Janis, 1954; Sears, Whiting, Nowlis, & Sears, 1953).

A valid objection to subject selection, whether it occurs as part of the deductive or inductive process, requires that the objector demonstrate how the selection procedure may account for the results in a manner other than that proposed by the experimenter. The Chapanises do so in just one case, the study by Brehm and Cohen (1959).

In their conclusion the Chapanises attribute the greater attention given to dissonance theory, as compared to the rather similar models proposed by Heider (1958), Osgood and Tannenbaum (1955), and Newcomb (1953), to the "generally deceptive" simplicity of the former. A more feasible explanation might be offered. All four of these models are based upon the principle of "cognitive balance" as a motivational construct. The latter three systems, however, are limited in their application to imbalance which may occur when two attitude objects, here including other persons or the self as objects, are linked in what Osgood and Tannenbaum term as assertion (unit or sentiment relation in Heider's theory). Festinger's theory accounts for this event but extends the balance principle as well to a multiplicity of apparently diverse areas of behavior. This is accomplished by the artful process of considering the cognitive mediator which is interposed in the person's response to all complex stimuli, including his own behavior.

In one respect we agree that the dissonance model must become less "simple" if it is to continue to function as a useful theoretical instrument. If we accept the statement that the value of a theory resides both in the magnitude of testable deductions generated from it and the extent and diversity of the phenomena that it can explain, then, by these criteria, dissonance theory appears to be a good theory. A good theory, however, by its own definition, cannot remain intact. Every research based upon it, by virtue of the variance in the data which is not accounted for, should lead the investigator back to the theory to revise and elaborate and thus develop new hypotheses for test. It is this interplay between induction and deduction which contributes to the progress of a science, with theory functioning as an instrument of logic in the service of extending the possibilities for acquiring data.

Many may agree that we have had an abundance of deduction from dissonance theory, that is, hypotheses based directly on Festinger's original principles, but a relative paucity of induction, that is, attempts to reconstruct and extend the theory so that it may incorporate more components of the behavior under scrutiny. For example, the study of factors determining which mode of dissonance reduction will be employed in a given situation remains largely outside the province of our conceptual schemas, though Rosenberg and Abelson (1960) offer a model directed to some aspects of this question. Psychology appears to be ready for neodissonance theory, by whatever name we choose to call it, just as it has progressed to neobehaviorism and neo-Freudianism.

REFERENCES

ARONSON, E., 1961. "The Effect of Effort on the Attractiveness of Rewarded and Unrewarded Stimuli," *Journal of Abnormal and Social Psychology,* 63, 375–80.
ARONSON, E., and J. MILLS. 1959. "The Effect of Severity of Initiation on Liking for a Group," *Journal of Abnormal and Social Psychology*, 59, 177–81.
BREHM, J. W. 1959. "Increasing Cognitive Dissonance by a *Fait Accompli*," 58, 379–82.
BREHM, J. W., and A. R. COHEN. 1959. "Re-evaluation of Choice Alternatives as a Function of Their Number and Qualitative Similarity," *Journal of Abnormal and Social Psychology,* 58, 373–78.
———— and ————. 1962. *Explorations in Cognitive Dissonance.* New York: Wiley.

CHAPANIS, NATALIA P., and A. CHAPANIS. 1964. "Cognitive Dissonance: Five Years Later," *Psychological Bulletin,* 61, 1–22.

COHEN, A. R., J. W. BREHM, and B. LATANE. 1959. "Choice of Strategy and Voluntary Exposure to Information Under Public and Private Conditions," *Journal of Personality,* 27, 63–73.

FERSTER, C. B., and B. F. SKINNER. 1957. *Schedules of Reinforcement.* New York: Appleton-Century-Crofts.

FESTINGER, L. 1957. *A Theory of Cognitive Dissonance.* Evanston, Ill.: Row, Peterson.

FESTINGER, L., and J. M. CARLSMITH. 1959. "Cognitive Consequences of Forced Compliance," *Journal of Abnormal and Social Psychology,* 58, 203–10.

FISHER, S., and A. LUBIN. "Distance as a Determinant of Influence in a Two-Person Serial Interaction Situation," *Journal of Abnormal and Social Psychology,* 56, 230–38.

HEIDER, F. 1958. *The Psychology of Interpersonal Relations.* New York: Wiley.

JANIS, I. L. 1954. "Personality Correlates of Susceptibility to Persuasion," *Journal of Personality,* 22, 504–18.

LEPENDORF, S. 1964. "The Effects of Incentive Value and Expectancy on Dissonance Resulting from Attitude-Discrepant Behavior and Disconfirmation of Expectancy." Unpublished doctoral dissertation, State University of New York at Buffalo.

NEWCOMB, T. M. 1953. "An Approach to the Study of Communicative Acts," *Psychological Review,* 60, 393–404.

OSGOOD, C. E., and P. H. TANNENBAUM. 1955. "The Principle of Congruity in the Prediction of Attitude Change," *Psychological Review,* 62, 42–55.

ROSENBERG, M. J. 1963. "An Evaluation of Models for Attitude Change," paper read at American Psychological Association, Philadelphia.

ROSENBERG, M. J., and R. P. ABELSON. 1960. "An Analysis of Cognitive Balancing," in *Attitude Organization and Change,* ed. M. J. Rosenberg et al. New Haven: Yale University Press.

SEARS, R. R., J. W. M. WHITING, V. NOWLIS, and P. S. SEARS. 1953. *Some Child-Rearing Antecedents of Aggression and Dependency in Young Children, Genetic Psychology Monographs,* no. 47., 135–234.

YARYAN, RUBY B., and L. FESTINGER. 1961. "Preparatory Action and Belief in the Probable Occurrence of Future Events," *Journal of Abnormal and Social Psychology,* 63, 603–6.

6

A Reinforcement Learning Model of Persuasive Communication

ROBERT FRANK WEISS

Robert Frank Weiss, Associate Professor at the University of Oklahoma, presents a learning theory approach to attitude change. An experimental psychologist who started out doing traditional learning experiments, Weiss has demonstrated generalization and positive transfer in applying old concepts to new and less tightly controlled situations.

The research I'm going to discuss with you today is an instance of what Neal Miller calls the extension of liberalized S-R theory. Learning-theory has been developed primarily to

Paper presented at the 1967 annual meeting of the American Psychological Association, as part of a symposium entitled "Alternatives to Consistency Theory in the Study of Attitude Change." Reprinted by permission of the author.

* Research supported by grant MH-12402 from the National Institute of Mental Health.

predict individual behavior in highly controlled experimental situations. The theory has, nevertheless, been extended, with a considerable measure of success, into more complex areas. The explanatory power of learning-theory stems, in part, from two sources. First, Hullian theory includes a number of principles which may be combined in a determinate manner. Principles which may seem relatively trivial when taken singly become powerful explanatory tools when the manner of their interaction can be specified. Secondly, Hullian theory is quantitative, with the usual advantages that attend scientific quantification.

The use of a model in theory construction typically involves the specification of a dictionary of analogies, or rules of correspondence, which relate the variables of the model to the variables of the data area to be explained and predicted. Once this is done, the relations holding among the variables of the model must, theoretically, also hold between the corresponding variables in the data area to be explained. The systematic use of learning theory as a model for attitude change makes it possible to take full advantage of the previously mentioned characteristics of learning theory: combination of principles in a determinate manner and quantitative specification. For example, there are a number of principles regarding delay of reward in instrumental conditioning, three of which may be stated informally as

1. The delay of reward gradient is decreasing and negatively accelerated in shape;
2. Delay of reward and number of trials combine multiplicatively;
3. Delay of reward and drive combine additively.

If a social variable is to be theoretically analogous to delay of reward, then we must expect that

1. This social variable gradient is decreasing and negatively accelerated in shape;
2. This social variable and number of trials combine multiplicatively;
3. This social variable and drive combine additively.

So far we've illustrated the development of an analogy between learning and social *independent* variables. The analogy does not have testable implications until analogies between learning and social *dependent* variables are also developed. Moreover, it is necessary to clearly specify *what kind of learning situation* the social conditions are analogous to; approach-avoidance conflict, instrumental reward conditioning, selective learning, etc. differ sharply in certain regards. For example, an important distinction is made in learning research between conditioning and habit reversal. We have not used a habit-reversal model, and we have therefore studied attitude *formation* in initially neutral subjects, rather than attitude *reversal*.

Much of the discussion will be at an informal level, with the more formal theoretical machinery remaining in the background. We'll begin with an instrumental reward conditioning model and proceed from there to the selective learning and classical conditioning models.

INSTRUMENTAL CONDITIONING

In terms of the empirical law of effect, an event which follows a response and increases the strength of that response on the next trial is called a reinforcer. In the instrumental conditioning of attitudes, subjects read aloud persuasive communications designed so that the subject says the opinion to be learned, followed by an opinion-supporting argument. This argument consists of information supporting the opinion, and specifically excludes repetitions of the opinion. It seems reasonable to expect that an opinion which is followed by a convincing argument will be strengthened more than an unsupported opinion. Such an argument would then function as a reinforcer of the opinion response and might perhaps exhibit other functional properties of reinforcers. One such property is the inverse relationship between delay of reinforcement and response strength, and a logical development of the paradigm outlined above indicates that delay of argument —the time interval between the opinion response and the rein-

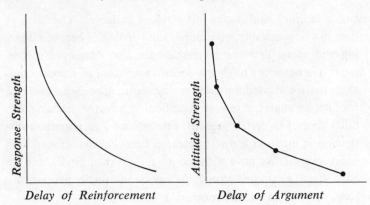

FIGURE 6.1: *Negatively accelerated decreasing effects of delay of reinforcement on speed of response in instrumental conditioning*

FIGURE 6.2: *Negatively accelerated decreasing effects of delay of argument on speed of agreement in instrumental attitude learning*

forcing argument—may be regarded as analogous to delay of reinforcement.

Figure 6.1 shows the results predicted by the Hullian theory of conditioning, and typically obtained in conditioning studies of delay of reinforcement. Figure 6.2 shows the closely analogous results obtained in our experiment on delay of argument in persuasive communication. Both delay gradients are negatively accelerated decreasing functions.

Continuing with the analogy between delay of reinforcement and delay of argument, we come to Figures 6.3 and 6.4. The diverging curves in Figure 6.3 shows how delay of reinforcement and number of conditioning trials combine multiplicatively to determine response speed. Figure 6.4 shows the same relationship between the corresponding persuasion variables, delay of argument and the number of persuasion trials, one vs. two exposures to the persuasive communication. As in conditioning, delay and trials combine multiplicatively.

In the two delay of reinforcement studies mentioned so far, as well as in the rest of these instrumental conditioning studies, the dependent variable was speed, the reciprocal of latency. In all our experiments on instrumental conditioning of attitudes, the dependent variable was speed of agreement, the reciprocal of latency of agreement. An attitude measuring apparatus assessed each subject's speed of agreement with the opinion after he had been exposed to the persuasive communication. A statement of the opinion was projected on a screen and the subject signified his agreement (if he agreed) by moving a lever toward the statement. When an opinion was projected on the screen, an electric timer automatically began to measure latency of agreement, until the lever was moved a quarter of an inch and a photobeam silently stopped the timer.

Returning to the attitude data, we see in Figure 6.4 that speed of agreement increases from one to two persuasion trials, just as speed increases with conditioning trials. We have some data using conventional attitude measures which do not show this trials effect.

If the argument is analogous to a reinforcer, then a stronger argument should be a stronger reinforcer. Figure 6.5 indicates that speed is an increasing function of drive and magnitude of

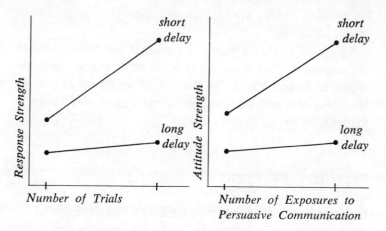

FIGURE 6.3: *Multiplicative effects of delay of reinforcement and number of instrumental conditioning trials on speed of response*

FIGURE 6.4: *Multiplicative effects of delay of argument and number of persuasion exposures on speed of agreement*

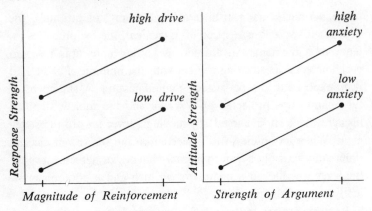

FIGURE 6.5: *Additive effects of drive and magnitude of reinforcement on speed of response*

FIGURE 6.6: *Additive effects of anxiety and strength of argument on speed of agreement*

reinforcement, and the parallel curves show how these 2 variables combine additively. Figure 6.6 shows the same relationships among the corresponding persuasion variables: Speed of agreement is an increasing function of strength of argument and Taylor Manifest Anxiety Scale scores, with these two variables combining additively.

Figure 6.8 shows the results of a study in which we confirmed the persuasion trials effect, but in which we found no significant argument strength effect. We were therefore unable to test the prediction of a multiplicative interaction such as that shown in Figure 6.7.

SELECTIVE LEARNING

(Learning theory treats selective learning as an extension of instrumental reward conditioning. Each subject learns two instrumental reward conditioned responses, which are differentially rewarded. The relative strengths of the two responses may then be assessed by presenting both alternatives simultaneously and allowing the subject to choose between them.) The dependent variable is percent choice. Typically, the number of trials for each response is controlled by forced trials in which the subject is presented with only one of the alternatives; for example, the right arm of the T maze is closed off and the subject can only go to the left. Selective learning of attitudes is treated as an extension of instrumental attitude conditioning, employing the same persuasive communications. Each subject learns two separate and unrelated instrumental reward conditioned attitudes through exposure to two persuasive communications. Each exposure to a communication constitutes a "forced trial." The relative strength of the two opinions is assessed by presenting both alternatives simultaneously, and then requiring the subject to choose between them. After exposure to the persuasive communications, subjects were tested with the previously described attitude-measuring apparatus, modified so that the two attitude statements were presented simultaneously, one on each of two screens. The subject chose the opinion with which he most agreed by moving the lever toward one of the statements.

When subjects have learned two responses, one reinforced with a short delay and the other with a long delay, the subjects

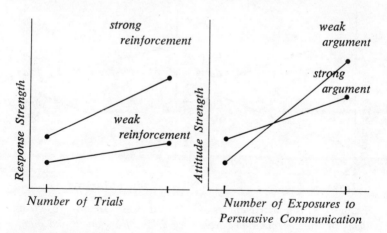

FIGURE 6.7: *Multiplicative effects of strength of reinforcement and number of trials on speed of response*

FIGURE 6.8: *Effects of strength of argument and number of persuasion exposures on speed of agreement*

will tend to choose the response which was reinforced with the shorter delay. An analogous result was found in persuasive communication. When subjects were persuaded on two opinions, one reinforced with a short delay of argument and one reinforced with a long delay, the subjects tended to choose the opinion which was persuaded with the shorter delay.

A little-known aspect of Hullian theory is that, under certain circumstances, it predicts that discrimination at *low* drive will be superior to discrimination at high drive, as shown in Figure 6.9. As Spence puts it, "The implications of the theory are that there will be an inverse relation between percent choice of short delay and drive level under conditions which keep the reaction potentials in the low range. These conditions may be specified as low initial habit strengths of the two competing responses, the early stages of selective learning and low ranges of drive level. Thus, it would be expected that a differential in favor of lower drive groups would tend to be present in the early stages of training and at low absolute levels of drive." Analogs of these conditions for keeping excitatory potentials in the low range were met in an

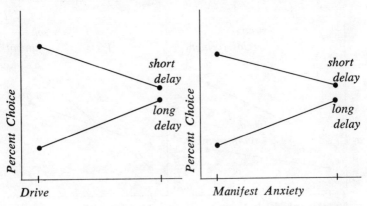

FIGURE 6.9: *Interactive effects of delay of reinforcement and drive level on strengths of differentially rewarded responses under conditions of low reaction potential*

FIGURE 6.10: *Interactive effects of delay of argument and manifest anxiety on strength of differentially reinforced attitudes under conditions of low reaction potential*

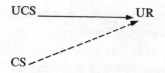

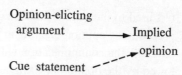

FIGURE 6.11: *Sequence of conditioned stimulus, unconditioned stimulus, and unconditioned response in classical conditioning*

FIGURE 6.12: *Sequence of cue statement, opinion-eliciting argument, and implied opinion in classical attitude conditioning*

experiment, with the results shown in Figure 6.10. The drive variable was Taylor manifest anxiety. As in selective learning, discrimination was better at low drive than at higher levels of drive.

CLASSICAL CONDITIONING

[A persuasive communication may explicitly state the opinion to be learned, or it may merely imply an opinion, leaving it to the subject to draw the unstated conclusion.] In the instrumental conditioning of attitudes, the opinion to be learned is explicitly stated in the communication. [In the classical conditioning of attitudes the opinion to be learned is merely implied by the communication, and the subject is left to draw the unstated conclusion for himself.] In this theory, the communication element which implies the opinion is called an opinion-eliciting argument. The technique for the construction of opinion-eliciting arguments is adapted from the work of McGuire. The opinion to be learned is the *conclusion* of a syllogism. The communication includes the *premises* of the syllogism (the opinion-eliciting argument), but not the conclusion. Figures 6.11 and 6.12 depict corresponding paradigms for a classical conditioning trial and a persuasion trial. Research based on this classical conditioning model requires persuasive communications which incorporate two elements: (1) the Opinion-Eliciting Argument; and (2) the Cue Statement, two neutral words which immediately precede the opinion-eliciting argument and will later constitute part of the test used to measure attitude acquisition. Since the cue statement precedes the opinion-eliciting argument, a subject listening to (or reading) the communication will first hear the cue statement, followed by the opinion-eliciting argument; and then draw the conclusion implied by the argument. This sequence of events may be regarded as analogous to the sequence: CS, UCS, UR. The cue statement is the CS, and the opinion-eliciting argument is the UCS which elicits the implied opinion—the UR. Through repetition of the sequence the implied opinion becomes conditioned to the cue statement and thus becomes a conditioned opinion as shown in Figure 6.12.

Following the logic of this paradigm further, the number of repetitions of this sequence is analogous to the number of conditioning trials, and the power of the opinion-eliciting argument to convincingly imply the opinion is analogous to the strength of the UCS. Figure 6.13 shows that CR probability is an increasing function of number of conditioning trials and UCS strength, and the diverging curves show how these two variables combine multiplicatively. Figure 6.14 shows the same relationships among the

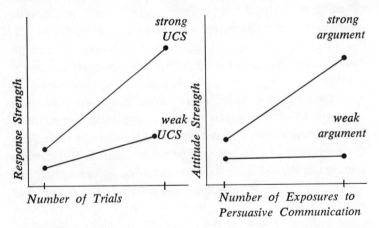

FIGURE 6.13: *Multiplicative effects of number of conditioning trials and UCS strength on strength of conditioned response*

FIGURE 6.14: *Multiplicative effects of number of persuasion exposures and strength of opinion-eliciting argument on speed of agreement*

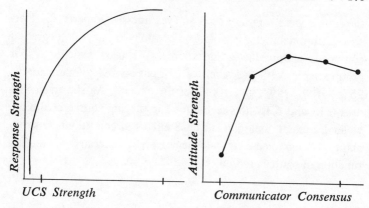

FIGURE 6.15: *Negatively accelerated increasing effect of UCS strength on strength of conditioned response*

FIGURE 6.16: *Negatively accelerated increasing effect of communicator consensus on speed of agreement with implied opinion*

corresponding persuasion variables, opinion-eliciting argument strength, and number of persuasion trials, one vs. three exposures to the persuasive communication. Probability of agreement was an increasing function of argument strength and persuasion trials, with these two variables combining multiplicatively.

In a second experiment on the classical conditioning of attitudes we employed a second analog of UCS strength. We have already noted that the power of the opinion-eliciting argument to convincingly imply an opinion is analogous to UCS strength. Figure 6.15 shows CR probability as a negatively accelerated increasing function of UCS-strength. Theoretically, then, probability of agreement should be a negatively accelerated increasing function of source credibility. But credibility is normally varied by comparing sources, such as the *New York Times* and the *Volkischer Beobachter,* which do not lend themselves to parametric study without dimensional analysis and scaling. We considered doing such a scaling, but first noticed that in credibility research the source has always been individual; a low credibility person or publication constitutes one experimental condition and a high credibility person or publication constitutes the other. If

174 : *A Reinforcement Learning Model*

the source were a *group,* such as eyewitnesses, experts, or reference-group members, it would be possible to vary the degree of consensus among the group source. We used experts as our group source, with five levels of consensus: 0% of the experts, 25%, 50%, 75%, and 100% of the experts. As shown in Figures 6.15 and 6.16, this ·technique for varying source credibility yielded a result analogous to UCS effects in conditioning: probability of agreement was a negatively accelerated increasing function of source credibility.

SUMMARY

Employing the general approach which Neal Miller has called extension of liberalized S-R theory, theoretical and experimental

TABLE 6.1: *Theoretical Analogies Between the Independent Variables in Instrumental Reward Learning and Instrumental Persuasion (Relation to Intervening Variables Also Indicated)*

Persuasion	Learning	Intervening Variable
1. Number of exposures to complete communication	Number of reinforced trials	*H*
2. Interval between exposures to complete communication	Intertrial interval	*I*
3. Number of exposures to argument	Number of reinforcements	*K*
4. Delay of argument	Delay of reinforcement	*K*
5. Length of opinion statement	Length of behavior chain	*K, I*
6. Strength of argument	Magnitude of reinforcement	*K*
7. Source credibility	Magnitude of reinforcement	*K*
8. Activeness of participation in argument	Vigor of goal response	*K*
9. Activeness of participation in statement of opinion	Response generalization	*H*

TABLE 6.2: *Theoretical Analogies Between the Independent Variables in Classical Conditioning and Classical Persuasion (Relation to Intervening Variables Also Indicated)*

Persuasion	Learning	Intervening Variable
1. Number of paired presentations of cue statement and argument (complete communication)	Number of reinforced trials	H
2. Interval between exposures to complete communication	Intertrial interval	I
3. Number of exposures to cue statement alone	Number of unreinforced trials	I
4. Number of exposures to argument alone	Number of exposures to UCS without CS	?
5. Differences in cue statement in persuasion and testing	CS change (stimulus generalization)	H
6. Activeness of participation in cue statement	CS intensity	H, I
7. Cue statement–argument interval	CS-UCS interval	H, I
8. Argument strength	UCS strength	D
9. Source credibility	UCS strength	D
10. Activeness of participation in statement of argument	UCS strength (?)	D
11. Length of argument	UCS duration	H

analogies were drawn between learning and persuasive communication. The theory includes more analogies than have yet been explored experimentally, and these are listed, for your reference, in Tables 6.1 and 6.2. Instrumental conditioning, selective learning, and classical conditioning were used as models. Theoretically, the functional relationships between the independent and dependent learning variables should also hold between the analogous persuasion variables. In general, the relations among the persuasion variables were found to be isomorphic with the relations among the corresponding learning variables. Thus, for example, delay of argument in persuasion was considered to be analogous to delay of reinforcement in instrumental conditioning and selective learning. As in selective learning, our subjects learned to choose the opinion response which had been "reinforced" with the shorter delay. In attitude "conditioning" a delay of argument gradient of the same shape as a delay of reinforcement gradient was discovered. Again, as in conditioning, delay combined multiplicatively with the number of persuasion "trials" to determine attitude strength. Results of other experiments also tend to support the theory.

7

An Experimental Analysis of Self-persuasion

DARYL J. BEM

Though Daryl J. Bem *is a relative newcomer to the attitude scene (he received his Ph.D. in 1964), he has aroused controversy enough for several oldsters: his "Skinnerian" reinterpretation of dissonance experiments has set off a running battle in the journals. Besides being original and controversial, he is also a witty writer. He has recently published an enjoyable as well as substantial book on attitudes and values. Bem is currently at Carnegie-Mellon University.*

Self-awareness, one's ability to respond differentially to his own behavior and its controlling variables, is a prod-

From *Journal of Experimental Social Psychology,* 1 (1965): 199–218, copyright 1965 by Academic Press, Inc. Reprinted by permission.

This research is drawn from part of a dissertation submitted to the Department of Psychology, University of Michigan, in partial fulfillment of the requirements for the degree of Doctor of Philosophy. The author is grateful to Harlan L. Lane and Theodore M. Newcomb, who served as co-chairmen of the Doctoral Dissertation Committee.

uct of social interaction (Mead, 1934; Ryle, 1949; Skinner, 1953, 1957). Among the responses that comprise self-aware-ness, verbal statements that are self-descriptive are perhaps the most common, and the general procedures by which the socializ-ing community teaches an individual to describe his own overt behavior would not seem to differ fundamentally from the meth-ods used to teach him to describe other events in his environ-ment. The community, however, faces a unique problem in train-ing the individual to make statements describing internal stimuli to which only he has direct access, for the conditioning of the ap-propriate verbal responses must necessarily be based on the pub-lic stimuli and responses that often accompany or resemble these private events. Skinner (1953, 1957) has provided a detailed analysis of the limited resources available to the community for training its members thus to "know themselves," and he has de-scribed the inescapable inadequacies of the resulting knowledge.

One implication of Skinner's analysis is that many of the self-descriptive statements that appear to be exclusively under the discriminative control of private stimulation may, in fact, remain under the control of the same public events which members of the community themselves must use in "inferring" the individu-al's inner states. In our well-fed society, for example, it is not un-common to find a man consulting his wrist watch to answer the question, "Are you hungry?" There is also direct experimental evidence that an individual relies on external cues for describing his emotional states (Schachter and Singer, 1962). Attitude statements may be similarly controlled. For example, when the answer to the question, "Do you like brown bread?" is, "I guess I do, I'm always eating it," it seems unnecessary to invoke a fount of privileged self-knowledge to account for the reply. In this example, it is clear that the discriminative stimuli controlling the attitude statement reside in the individual's overt behavior; indeed, the man's reply is functionally equivalent to the reply his wife might give for him: "I guess he does, he is always eating it."

It is the major thesis of this report, then, that an individual's belief and attitude statements and the beliefs and attitudes that an outside observer would attribute to him are often functionally equivalent in that both sets of statements are "inferences" from the same evidence: the public events that the socializing community originally employed in training the individual to make such self-descriptive statements. The three experiments reported below provide support for this hypothesis by demonstrating that an individual's belief and attitude statements may be predicted and controlled by manipulating his overt behavior and the stimulus conditions under which it occurs in ways that would lead an *outside* observer to infer that the individual held the "belief" or "attitude" we wish to obtain. The individual, in short, is regarded as an observer of his own behavior and its controlling variables; accordingly, his belief and attitude statements are viewed as "inferences" from his observations.

TACTS, MANDS, AND COMMUNICATOR CREDIBILITY

A descriptive statement, a verbal response that is under the discriminative control of some portion of the environment, is classified as a "tact" (Skinner, 1957). A speaker is trained to describe or "tact" his environment for the benefit of his listeners, who provide generalized social reinforcement in return. An individual's belief and attitude statements are often tacts of stimuli arising from himself (e.g., "I am hungry"), his behavior (e.g., "I am generous"), or the effects of stimuli on him (e.g., "It gives me goosepimples"). Attitude statements in particular have the properties of tacts of the reinforcing effects of a stimulus situation on the individual (e.g., "I detest rainy weather," "I'd walk a mile for a Camel").

Verbal responses that are under the control of specific reinforcing contingencies are called "mands." A speaker who emits a mand is asking for, requesting, or "manding" a particular reinforcer (cf. de*mand*s, com*mand*s). Only a characteristic consequence will serve to reinforce the response, and often this reinforcer is specified explicitly by the response (e.g., "Please pass the milk"). Mands need not be verbal in the usual sense; for example, pointing to the milk pitcher may be functionally equivalent to the vocal request. Mands are often disguised as tacts as in "I believe you have the sports page" or as in the case of the television announcer who praises a product he is selling; his verbal behavior is a mand for the salary he receives and may not at all be under the actual discriminative control of the features of the product he appears to be tacting. A lie is often a mand for escape from aversive consequences; it, too, is a mand disguised as a tact. Any particular verbal response, then, may have both mand and tact characteristics in differing degrees. Thus, until the controlling circumstances are specified, it is not possible to determine the functional classification of a remark like "Darling, you look beautiful tonight"; the probabilities are high that it is a subtle blend of mand and tact.

It is clear, then, that in attempting to infer a speaker's "true" beliefs and attitudes, the listener must often discriminate the mand-tact characteristics of the communication. This is, in fact, an important dimension of "communicator credibility." A communicator is credible to the extent that his communication is discriminated as a set of tacts, and his credibility is vitiated to the extent that he appears to be manding in the form of disguised tacts. Thus, a communication attributed to J. Robert Oppenheimer is more persuasive than the same communication attributed to *Pravda* (Hovland and Weiss, 1951); the white coat and stethoscope on the television announcer are intended to indicate to the viewer that the announcer is one whose verbal behavior is under discriminative control of the product, not one who is manding money. Not only is a credible communicator more likely to persuade his listeners, but to the extent that his verbal responses appear to be "pure" tacts, they will be judged, by definition, to be his own "true" beliefs and attitudes. We turn now to evidence that the beliefs and attitudes of the communicator himself may be viewed as self-judgments based partially upon his credibility as a communicator; and, to the extent that this is so, they will coincide with judgments of his beliefs and attitudes that outside observers would make.

In an experiment by Festinger and Carlsmith (1959), two experimental groups of 20 undergraduates were employed as subjects. In the $1 condition, the subject was first required to perform long repetitive laboratory tasks. He was then hired by the experimenter as an "assistant" and paid $1 to tell a waiting fellow student that the tasks were enjoyable and interesting. In the $20 condition, the subjects were hired for $20 to do the same thing. A panel of judges, in a blind rating procedure, rated the $20 persuasive communications as slightly but insignificantly more persuasive than $1 communications. Attitude measurement showed that subjects paid $1 evaluated the tasks and the experiment *more* favorably than did $20 subjects. We may interpret these findings within the present framework by considering the viewpoint of an outside observer who hears the individual making favorable statements about the tasks, and who further knows that the individual was paid $1 or $20 to engage in this behavior. When asked to judge the "true" attitude of the communicator, an outside observer would almost certainly judge a $20 communication to be a mand, behavior not at all under the control of the actual features of the laboratory task the individual appears to be tacting. Although a $1 communication also has mand properties, an outside observer would be more likely to judge it than the $20 communication to be a set of tacts, and hence, by definition, to be the "true" attitudes of the individual. If one places our hypothetical outside observer and the communicator in the same skin, the findings obtained by Festinger and Carlsmith are the result.

Blind evaluations of the persuasive communications were an elegant control feature of the Festinger-Carlsmith design, and, as mentioned, showed $1 communications to be no more persuasive than $20 communications *when the mand-tact conditions under which the verbal behavior was emitted were not available to the observer*. But this is precisely the information which makes one communicator more credible than another.

Cohen (Brehm and Cohen, 1962, p. 73) performed an experiment similar to the Festinger-Carlsmith study in order to rule out the interpretation that the $20 payment in the latter study was so large that it engendered suspicion and resistance, leading subjects to think, "It must be bad if they're paying me so much for it." (See also Rosenberg, 1965.) Since this alternative interpretation is not unlike the mand-tact conceptualization offered here, it is relevant to examine Cohen's subsequent experiment in some detail.

Cohen's subjects were offered $.50, $1, $5, or $10 to write an essay against their initial opinions on a current issue. The post-essay belief statements essentially duplicated the Festinger-Carlson results: the higher the inducement, the less the belief statement coincided with the view advocated in the essay. (The $5 and $10 conditions did not differ significantly from the control group, who were simply asked their opinions on the issue.) The crux of Cohen's argument resides in the fact that significant differences in post-essay belief statements emerged between the $.50 and the $1 conditions, and between them and the control condition. Since these payments were small and close to one another, Cohen's argument implies, the mand-tact discrimination could not account for the results.

This is, of course, an empirical question. The following study was designed to answer it by demonstrating that the belief statements made by Cohen's subjects when they were asked for their "true" opinions may be viewed as judgments based on the mand-tact characteristics of their own behavior; that is, on their own credibility as communicators.

Experiment I:

An Interpersonal Replication of the Essay Study

If the suggested interpretation of Cohen's results is correct, then an external observer should be able to replicate the true belief statement of one of Cohen's subjects with an interpersonal judgment if this observer is told the behavior of the subject and the apparent controlling circumstances of that behavior.

The subjects in the present study thus served as external observers; each subject judged one—and only one—volunteer in one of Cohen's experimental conditions.

METHOD

Sixty undergraduates were randomly assigned to "$.50," "$1," and "control" conditions. The first two groups were given the following instructions on a single sheet of paper; it consists of a description of the experimental situation employed by Cohen:

> In the spring of 1959 there was a student "riot" at Yale University in which the New Haven Police intervened, with resulting accusations of police brutality toward the students. The issue was a very bitter and emotional one, and a survey of student opinion showed most of the student body to be extremely negative toward the police and their actions and sympathetic toward the students. As part of a research project, a student member of a research team from the Institute of Human Relations at Yale selected a student at random and asked him to write a strong, forceful essay entitled "Why the New Haven Police Actions Were Justified," an essay which was to be unequivocally in favor of the police side of the riots. The decision to write such an essay or not was entirely up to the student, and he was told that he would be paid the sum of $.50 ($1.00) if he would be willing to do so. The student who was asked agreed to do so, and wrote such an essay. The scale shown below was used in the original poll of student opinion on the issue. From this description, estimate as well as you can the actual opinion of the student who was willing to write the essay. Indicate your estimate by drawing a line through the appropriate point on the scale.

> "Considering the circumstances, how justified do you think the New Haven police actions were in the recent riot?"

| . . . . | . . . . | . . . . | . . . . | . . . . | . . . . | . . . . |

Not	Very little	Little	Somewhat	Quite	Very	Completely
justified	justified	justified	justified	justified	justified	justified
at all						

The control Ss in the present study received the same instructions except that the entire second paragraph was deleted and the third paragraph was altered to read: "From this description,

estimate as well as you can the actual opinion of a student selected at random on the Yale campus. . . ."

In Cohen's experiment the subjects first wrote the essay and
were then asked to indicate their own opinions on the scale. The
scale employed in the present study is identical to Cohen's. The
"control" condition in the present study also provides a check on
the adequacy with which the situation on the Yale campus has
been described.

RESULTS AND DISCUSSION

Figure 7.1 shows the interpersonal judgments of Ss in the present experiment compared to the belief statements collected by
Cohen. Two-tailed probability levels based on t tests are also
shown. It is seen that Cohen's results are closely replicated.

These results show that the mand-tact interpretation of the
general inverse relation between amount of payment and subsequent belief statements is still viable: the lower the payment, the

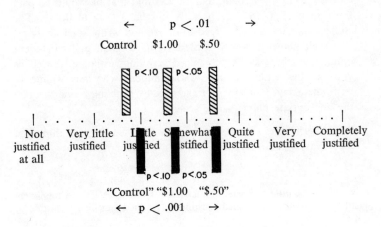

FIGURE 7.1: *A comparison of "actual" beliefs and interpersonal
judgments of belief*

less the mand properties of the observed behavior predominant in the eyes of both intra- and inter-personal observers. To the extent that the behavior has non-mand properties, it will be discriminated by an observer (including the individual himself) as indicating the "true" beliefs of that individual.

It should be noted that Ss in the experiment just presented did not actually read any of the essays written by Cohen's Ss. The successful interpersonal replication of his results, then, suggests that it may not have been necessary for his Ss to write the essays; that is, the behavior of *volunteering* may be the source of discriminative control over the beliefs. The "communication" may be contained in the commitment to write the essay, and it is the *commitment* that has the crucial mand or non-mand properties, depending upon the payment offered. Brehm and Cohen (1962, pp. 115–16) cite a number of studies which, indeed, do demonstrate that commitment alone is sufficient; the essays themselves do not have to be written. In order to provide direct support for our interpretation that the individual's subsequent belief statement in such experiments may be viewed as self-judgments based on his behavior of *volunteering* and its mand characteristics, it seemed desirable to attempt an interpersonal replication of a study in which persuasive communication *per se* did not play a part. The study chosen is of additional interest because the dependent variable is a judgment of hunger, a tact that is not only self-descriptive, but is typically considered to be under the exclusive control of private internal stimuli.

Experiment II:

An Interpersonal Replication of the Hunger Study

Volunteer male Ss in an experiment by Brehm (Brehm and Cohen, 1962, pp. 133–36) were required to go without food for a number of hours before an individual experimental session disguised as an investigation on hunger and intellectual performance. At the beginning of the session, the S indicated on a questionnaire scale how hungry he felt. After engaging in a number of tasks, the *S* was asked to volunteer for further testing, which would entail continued food deprivation. Half of the *S*s were offered $5 for volunteering; others were offered nothing. A second self-evaluation of hunger, administered after the *S* had volunteered, showed that those offered the money rated themselves significantly more hungry than those who had volunteered for nothing.

As before, we interpret these results by assuming the standpoint of an outside observer who sees the *S* volunteering, and is then asked to judge the volunteer's hunger. If the observer were to see an *S* volunteering for the sum of $5, he would discriminate the mand properties of that behavior, which is to say that he would be able to conclude very little about the *S*'s hunger; the internal discriminative stimuli arising from "hunger," the observer would assume, would not be a controlling variable of the decision to volunteer. If the observer had been told the volunteer's initial hunger rating, he would probably conclude that the *S* had simply increased his hunger somewhat over the intervening time. The behavior of the unpaid volunteer, however, has no obvious mand properties; *specific monetary* reinforcement is not a controlling variable. Hence, by volunteering, the *S* tells the outside observer (and himself) that he is not very hungry; his volunteering, relative of course to *S*s paid $5, is not a mand.

If this interpretation of the Brehm results is correct, then external observers should be able to replicate with interpersonal judgments the self-ratings of hunger obtained by Brehm. The design of the present experiment is the same as the interpersonal replication of the essay study; each *S* in the present experiment judges only one "other."

METHOD

Fifty male college students were randomly assigned to a "$5" or a "no-pay" condition. Those in the "$5" condition were given the following instructions on a single sheet of paper.

Volunteer male subjects in a psychology experiment on the effect of hunger on motor and intellectual functioning were required to go without food from the time they got up in the morning until the afternoon testing session. The volunteers received experimental credit points in their introductory psychology course for this experiment.

When the subject arrived, he was shown the sandwiches, cookies, and milk on the testing table and told he would be able to eat as much of these as he wanted after the testing session. The subject then indicated how hungry he was on the rating scale shown below; the arrow shows the *average* degree of hunger for all the subjects who participated in this research at the beginning of this session.

"How hungry are you?"

$$\downarrow$$

| .... | .... | .... | .... | .... | .... | .... |

Not at   Very   Slightly Moderately Quite   Very   Extremely
all   slightly

After giving this rating, the subject engaged in a number of motor and intellectual tasks. One of the subjects was then asked if he would be willing to return for further testing in the evening; this, it was explained, would require him to continue going without food until about eight or nine that evening. He was told, "Unfortunately, we cannot give you any more experimental credit points for the evening testing session. However, we can pay anyone willing to come back since we do need your help. The amount is $5.00."

This individual agreed to continue his participation. From this description, try to estimate how hungry this particular person must have been at the end of the first session just described. Indicate your estimate by drawing a line through the appropriate point on the scale above.

Subjects in a "no-pay" condition received identical instructions except that the reported offer of $5 was replaced by the following: "You get your point for having taken part this afternoon so don't think you have to come again this evening. But we would appreciate your help. If, however, you don't feel like doing it, that's okay because we can get someone else to do it."

The scale and reported instructions to the volunteers are identical to those employed by Brehm. The arrow given on the present instruction sheet represents the initial hunger rating of Brehm's $5 subjects.

RESULTS AND DISCUSSION

Figure 7.2 shows the interpersonal judgments of *S*s in the present experiment compared to the self-rating data collected by Brehm. (Brehm's result for the no-pay condition has been expressed as a displacement from the arrow rather than from the actual initial hunger rating of his no-pay *S*s.) The separation between the results of the treatments in Brehm's study was statistically significant at the .01 level; the separation in the interpersonal data is significant at the .025 level (two-tailed *t* test). It is clear that Brehm's results for intrapersonal judgments are closely replicated by the results for interpersonal judgments in the present study.

Self-judgments of hunger (Brehm)

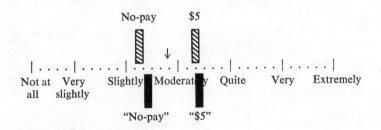

Interpersonal judgments of hunger

FIGURE 7.2: *A comparison of self-judgments and interpersonal judgments of hunger*

We conclude that the self-ratings of hunger obtained by Brehm were partially under the control of the mand characteristics of the behavior of volunteering, and that the judgments made by Brehm's subjects vis-à-vis their own behavior does not differ significantly from judgments based on their behavior made by an external observer.

ALTERNATIVE MANIPULATIONS OF THE SELF-CREDIBILITY PARAMETER

The crux of the present interpretation is that the control over beliefs exercised by an individual's own behavior will vary as the contingencies of specific reinforcement for engaging in the behavior are made more or less prominent as a controlling variable. As the contingencies of reinforcement are made more subtle, less discriminable, the mand properties of the S's own behavior will be lessened and the behavior will, thereby, have maximum control over his subsequent beliefs. In the studies discussed in detail so far, this self-credibility discrimination has been manipulated by varying the magnitude of reinforcement offered for engaging in the overt behavior: the larger the reinforcement, the more likely it was that the S would discriminate his own behavior as a mand. We turn now to studies which employed a number of different stimulus operations, all with the effect of manipulating the mand properties of the induced behavior.

In an experiment by Aronson and Carlsmith (1963), school children approximately four years of age gave preference rank-orderings on a set of five toys. The experimenter then told the subject that he could play with any of the toys but one while the experimenter ran an errand. The forbidden toy was the one which ranked second in the child's preference ordering. Children assigned to a mild-threat condition were further told that the experimenter would be annoyed if the child played with the forbidden toy; children assigned to a strong-threat condition, were told that if they disobeyed, the experimenter would be very angry,

190 : *An Experimental Analysis of Self-persuasion*

take all of the toys away, never come back, and think that the child was "just a baby." The experimenter then left the room and observed the child through a one-way mirror for ten minutes. None of the subjects played with the forbidden toy. After this interval, preference orderings on the five toys were again obtained from the subjects. The final preference ranking of the forbidden toy was the dependent variable under investigation. It was found that subjects in the mild-threat condition assigned significantly lower final preference rankings to the toy than did children in the strong-threat condition. Rankings obtained 45 days later still showed some evidence of the differential effects of the treatments.

In interpreting these results, it is again instructive to assume the standpoint of an outside observer who sees the child playing with all the toys but one; in addition, we assume that the observer has been told that the child was given a mild (strong) threat of aversive consequences if he played with the toy. The outside observer is now asked to estimate the child's ranking of the forbidden toy. We may infer that the behavior of avoiding the toy on the part of subjects in the mild-threat condition has less the property of a mand (for withholding aversive consequences) than the behavior of subjects in the strong-threat condition. Thus, a hypothetical observer of a subject in the mild-threat condition would be more likely to assume that the actual reinforcing properties *of the toy* were partially controlling the observed behavior than would an observer judging the behavior of a subject in the strong-threat condition. The former observer would then assign a lower preference rating to the toy than the latter observer. These are the obtained findings, which are, then, consistent with the interpretation that the final ranking of the toy given by the child himself is primarily a self-judgment based on his own behavior and its controlling variables, rather than a tact of the reinforcing properties of the toy being ranked.

The studies which have been discussed so far are among several "forced compliance" experiments conducted within the framework of Festinger's theory of cognitive dissonance (1957). Each of these studies yields data consistent with the present analysis: when the operations employed are submitted to a careful analysis in terms of the discriminative stimuli presented to the subject, then those conditions in which specific reinforcing contingencies are enhanced or made more prominent (the mand conditions) are always found to yield weaker control over the subsequent belief statements than those conditions in which the subject is given "no good reason" for engaging in the behavior. For example, other experiments have manipulated the degree of choice permitted the subject, degree of commitment evoked, amount of justification given, and the reinforcing properties of the experimenter—all with the same results (Brehm and Cohen, 1962, pp. 303–6): when the contingencies of reinforcement are made less significant or more subtle, the non-mand properties of the behavior predominate and subsequent belief statements may be predicted by assuming them to be the inferences of an observer of the behavior.

Other studies from the literature are also amenable to the self-credibility interpretation. King and Janis (1956) compared improvised versus non-improvised role playing in producing belief change and found that subjects who read a communication and then played the role of a sincere advocate of the communication's point of view changed their beliefs more than those who read the fully prepared script aloud. It seems likely that the subjects who simply read the script clearly discriminated that their behavior was under the control of the text (cf. Skinner, 1957), whereas in the case of the subject who actually played out the role, every measure possible was taken to insure that he was surrounded by stimuli that would characteristically control the behaviors of an individual who "believed" the point of view. It should also be noted that subjects who were permitted to "improvise" would be expected to select precisely those arguments that had initial tact properties for themselves. It seems consonant with our analysis, then, to find that these subjects were more "persuasive" to themselves than the script readers.

In an experiment by Scott (1957), pairs of students were asked to debate different issues in front of a class; each student argued the position contrary to his initial beliefs. The experimenter manipulated the conditions so that a predetermined member of each pair "won" the debate. Later measurement of belief showed that the "winners" changed in the direction of the position that they had defended in the debate, but "losers" did not; in fact, "losers" shifted slightly toward the "winning" side. In a replication of the experiment in which a panel of judges rather than a class vote "decided" the winner of the debates, some of the debaters defended positions they actually held (Scott, 1959). Among these subjects, "winners" shifted still further in the direction of their arguments, and "losers" again shifted slightly in the direction of the "winning" side, a shift that was against the arguments they themselves presented *and* their initial beliefs.

Since the winners had been reinforced by winning and the losers had not, Scott interprets these results as showing that the reinforcement of overt verbal responses leads to a change in the beliefs. Such an interpretation, however, runs into difficulty in accounting for the results of the dissonance experiments previously described, which show an inverse relation between reinforcement and belief change. The present analysis suggests that the (falsified) class vote or judges' decision gave an additional tact property, or measure of credibility, to the beliefs stated in the "winning" argument; hence, the "winner" himself discriminated these beliefs as tacts, which is to say as his "true" beliefs. The fact that "losers" also shifted slightly toward the winning side is consistent with this interpretation. Further support for this interpretation comes from a study by Kelley and Woodruff (1956). College students who heard a recording of "prestigeful" members of their college group applaud a speech that opposed their initial beliefs changed their beliefs more than did a control group that was told that the applauding audience was a group of townspeople. These subjects thus based their credibility discriminations of the communicator on the judgment of other listeners, just as the debaters in the debate studies, it is suggested, based the credibility of their own communications on the decisions of the judges. The self-perception interpretation is thus consistent with the data from both the debate experiments and the dissonance theory experiments.

Experiment III:

Self-credibility and the Control of Attitude Statements

The stimulus operations that we have interpreted as controlling self-credibility discriminations in all the experiments discussed and replicated so far have always had other functional properties. Thus, money payoffs and the winning of debates also have reinforcing properties; manipulations of justification, choice, commitment, etc. involve a veritable tangle of complex and ambiguous stimulus operations. The present experiment was designed to provide more direct support for the present formulation by "raising stimuli from birth" in the laboratory that would have no functional properties other than those we have imputed to the stimulus operations in the other experiments discussed.

The dependent variable in this study is an attitude statement concerning the "funniness" of magazine cartoons. The cartoons employed are those that the S has previously marked as "neutral"; that is, neither funny nor unfunny. During the experimental session, which is disguised as a tape recording session for the preparation of experimental stimulus materials, the S is required to state that each cartoon is either "very funny" or "very unfunny." Each overt statement is made in the presence of a visual stimulus (a colored light) that has been previously paired with the S's verbal behavior: one of the colored lights, which we shall call the truth light, had always been illuminated previously when the S was giving true answers to a set of questions concerning personal information. The other light was always illuminated when the S was giving false answers to the questions; we shall call this light the lie light. After the S has made an overt statement about the cartoon, he rates his "true" attitude on a rating scale.

The prediction is that the S's "true" attitude will be controlled by his overt statements to a greater degree when the statement is emitted in the presence of the truth light than when it is emitted in the presence of the lie light. A postexperimental questionnaire tests for the S's "awareness" of any of the obtained effects. It will be noted that each S is his own control, and that each S provides a complete replication of the experiment.

METHOD

Eight college students were hired for two forty-minute sessions on consecutive days to "help prepare materials for use in experimental research on voice-judgment." In the first session, the S ranked each of 200 cartoons for "funniness" on the 100-millimeter scale shown below by drawing a short vertical line across the scale line at any appropriate point.

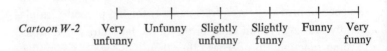

Cartoon W-2 Very unfunny Unfunny Slightly unfunny Slightly funny Funny Very funny

The cartoons, arranged two to a page in a loose-leaf notebook, were taken from *The New Yorker, The Saturday Evening Post, Look,* and *McCall's* magazines. This session, then, provided a baseline measure for the dependent variable, ratings of funniness of cartoons.

In the experimental session the following day, the S was seated at a desk in a small acoustically tiled recording room for the alleged purpose of making a tape recording of his voice for the voice-judgment experiments. The S's first task was to fill out a form with forty-nine questions concerning personal information. The instructions and sample items from this form are reproduced below:

This information form will provide some of the materials you will be recording on tape for the voice-judgment experiment. It should be filled out completely and accurately. THIS INFORMATION WILL REMAIN CONFIDENTIAL AND ANONYMOUS. YOUR NAME WILL NOT APPEAR ON THE TAPE OR ELSEWHERE IN THE EXPERIMENT.

    (1) First Name _____

    (10) Are you generally favorable or unfavorable to fraternities and sororities? _____

(22) Do you feel that full socialism would be preferable to the free enterprise system in America? _____

(29) Do you believe in a Supreme Being? _____

After obtaining the completed information form, *E* left the recording room, and all further communication with the *S* was conducted with an intercom. The following training procedure was then employed to establish two lights as discriminative stimuli which would indicate that verbal behavior in the presence of the one was tacting ("truth-telling") and in the presence of the other, lying, a form of behavior which is characteristically a mand. The following instructions were given to the *S*:*

As I mentioned, you are going to be making a tape of your own voice to be used in some research we will be doing on an individual's ability to judge another person's voice. In particular, we are going to be examining an individual's ability to judge whether the speaker on the tape is telling the truth or not. To do this, some of the things you will say on the tape will be true statements; others will be untrue. The procedure will be as follows: I will ask you questions, one at a time, from the list of information you just filled out. After I ask you a question, I will start the tape recorder, and you should answer the question into the microphone in front of you. Whenever I turn on the tape recorder, one of two colored light bulbs in the ceiling fixture will also go on automatically. If the amber light goes on [amber light turned on], you are to answer the question truthfully; if, however, the green light turns on [green light turned on; amber light turned off], you should make up an untrue answer and speak it into the microphone as convincingly and as naturally as possible. My questions will not be recorded on the tape, so your answers must be complete statements, not just single-word answers. For example, I will ask: "What is your first name?" When the ceiling light goes on, you should answer, "My first name is such-and-such." If the light is amber, then you would, of course, give your real first name. If the light is green, you would make up some other name. As you can see, we wanted this to be spontaneous, which is why you will not know until the tape actually starts whether you are going to give a true or an untrue answer;

---

* Instructions were designed to sound matter-of-fact so that it would not be apparent to *S* that they were being read verbatim. Hence, in written form they seem wordy and ungrammatical.

you have to be on your toes. The lighting circuitry is set to select the two colored lights automatically and in random sequence. I will be checking your responses on your information form; when you respond in the appropriate way, I will stop the tape, the colored light will go out, and we will proceed to the next question. If you happen to make a mistake, or do not answer with a complete sentence, we will repeat that item. Are there any questions? [Pause.] Okay, remember the amber light means you are to give a true answer; the green light, an untrue one.

The training procedure then proceeded as described. Half of the questions required untrue responses, and half required true responses. The two lights were reversed for some *S*s: green light for true responses, amber light for false responses. At the end of the training session, *E* continued as follows:

We have now completed all the questions on the information form. In the second part of our voice-judgment experiments, the subjects will be asked to look at some of the cartoons you judged earlier. The cartoons we have decided to use have been placed in the notebook in front of you. The subjects will be asked to give their opinions of each cartoon on a rating scale like the one on the notebook cover by drawing a line through the scale line at the appropriate point. You will note that this scale is less detailed than the ones you used earlier. [See scale below.] Before judging each cartoon, the subject will listen to a comment made by you on the tape stating that you found the cartoon very funny or very unfunny. We are interested in seeing whether your comment can influence the subject's opinion of the cartoon in the direction of your own opinion. Our procedure now, then, will be as follows: You will glance at each cartoon and decide whether it is funny or unfunny, that is, whether in your opinion it falls to the right or to the left of the neutral point on the scale. When you decide, tell me your decision and I will start the tape recorder. If you think the cartoon is a funny one, you should then record the comment, "I think cartoon such-and-such is a *very funny* cartoon." If the cartoon lies on the left side of the scale in your opinion, you should record the comment, "I think cartoon such-and-such is a *very unfunny* cartoon." In every case you should identify the cartoon by its code letter and say that it is either very funny or very unfunny, whichever is closer to your own opinion. Aside from that, however, you should use whatever words seem most natural and convincing to you, such as "I find cartoon such-and-such to be etc." or "I find cartoon such-and-such is . . . etc." Are there any questions? [Pause.] Just so you will know when I turn the tape recorder on and off, I will leave the ceiling recording lights hooked up to the tape recorder; so, the two colored lights will continue to flash on and off with the recorder in random sequence. Okay, glance at the first cartoon and let me know which half of the scale it falls in, and I will start the recorder for your comment.

The following scale was used in this session:

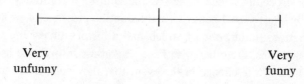

| Very | Very |
| unfunny | funny |

At this point, *S* glanced at the first cartoon, and indicated his binary decision. *E* then turned on the lie light; *S* made his comment, the colored light went out, and the white desk light went on simultaneously. *E* continued as follows:

It is also necessary that we have a record of your *exact* opinion of the cartoon at the time the comment was recorded. For this reason, you should now turn the page and mark your exact opinion of the cartoon on the scale provided by placing a mark through the scale line at the appropriate point. [*E* waited for this to be done.] Okay, turn to the second cartoon and tell me which half of the scale it falls in.

For each *S,* the twenty cartoons employed in this session had been ranked within ten millimeters of the neutral point (that is, between *Slightly funny* and *Slightly unfunny)* on the scale presented in the pre-experimental session. The cartoons were further matched and alternated in the sequence of presentation to control for the smaller variations around the neutral point. (This precaution was probably unnecessary because of the high variability of such rankings over time.)

The following sequence of lights was used for the 20 cartoons:

1. Lie	5. Truth	9. Lie	13. Truth	17. Lie
2. Truth	6. Lie	10. Truth	14. Lie	18. Truth
3. Truth	7. Lie	11. Truth	15. Lie	19. Truth
4. Lie	8. Truth	12. Lie	16. Truth	20. Lie

After the *S* followed the procedure for the first cartoon, *E* did not communicate further with him except to announce the code number of the next cartoon after the *S* had completed his ranking of the previous one.

The procedure, then, assessed the control of attitudes exercised by overt verbal behavior emitted in the presence of two discriminative stimuli, one of which had a history of pairing with true responses, the other with false responses. In order to assess awareness of the effects, in the event that they occurred, each *S* was instructed to respond in writing to the following four questions at the end of the session.

> Each of the attached sheets contains a question which will be helpful to us in revising our procedures for the voice-judgment experiment. Please do not look ahead to the next question until you finish the preceding one.
>
> As far as you can tell, did your ratings of the 20 cartoons you looked at today change from your previous ratings of them? If so, in what way?
>
> As far as you can tell, were your cartoon ratings today affected in any way by the other procedures involved? If so, in what way?
>
> Did you pay attention to the color of the recording lights during the cartoon portion of the session? As far as you can tell, did the recording lights affect your cartoon judgments in any way? If so, in what ways?

Each *S* was then paid $2.50 and told the true purpose of the experiment.

RESULTS AND DISCUSSION

The prediction is that the 10 cartoons commented upon by the *S* in the presence of the truth light would be ranked further from the neutral point in the direction of the self-persuasion ("very funny" or "very unfunny") than the 10 cartoons commented upon by the S in the presence of the lie light. This one-tailed hypothesis is tested on each S with the Mann-Whitney U test.

Because separate analyses of attitudes toward the cartoons called "very funny" and "very unfunny" yielded comparable results, these data have been combined; the scores given in Table 1 represent mean absolute deviation in millimeters from the neutral point (0) in the direction of the self-persuasion on the 100-millimeter scale. Accordingly, the scores can range from 0 to 50, where a score of 50 represents a rating of either "very funny" or "very unfunny," depending upon the S's overt statement. The Ss' responses to the final awareness question are also displayed.

It is seen in Table 7.1 that seven of the eight Ss were persuaded to a greater extent by comments made in the presence of the truth light than by comments made in the presence of the lie light. The null hypothesis (no difference between attitude ratings affected by the truth versus lie treatments) is rejected by a sign test applied to the relative position of these ratings on the scale of each S ($p = .035$; one-tailed). In addition, the results from five of the Ss considered individually attain a significance level smaller than 5% by a one-tailed Mann-Whitney U test.

The reverse trend displayed by S 7 is due primarily to the final cartoon—a lie-light cartoon—which was marked at 48 (very funny). On the awareness questionnaire she responded: "I didn't think any of them were too funny so toward the end maybe I tried to think that they were funny so that I wouldn't seem so unhappy."

In pretesting the experimental procedures, a foreign student (Chinese undergraduate) served as an S. A slightly different procedure was employed with him in that only twelve cartoons, which he had previously marked as neutral, were employed, and E dictated the comment which was to be made for each cartoon rather than first obtaining the S's preference. For this reason, the attitude rating can be displaced from the neutral point in the negative direction, that is, in the direction away from the overt

TABLE 7.1: *A Comparison of the Effectiveness of Self-Persuasion in the Presence of the Truth Light and in the Presence of the Lie Light*

Subject	Mean deviation (in millimeters) from the neutral point in the direction of the self-persuasion		One-tailed Mann-Whitney U test	Response to the awareness question: "Were your ratings affected by the color of the lights?"
	Truth light ($N = 10$ cartoons)	Lie light ($N = 10$ cartoons)		
1. (Male, 21 yr.)	23	14	$U = 16$ $p < .01$	"The lights, as far as I know, did not affect me."
2. (Male, 22 yr.)	4	3	$U = 20$ $p < .05$	"I do not believe so."
3. (Male, 20 yr.)	24	14	$U = 24$ $p < .05$	"I made my judgment before the recording light came on—I don't think the light affected my judgment in any way."
4. (Male, 27 yr.)	35	27	$U = 29$ $p < .06$	"No."

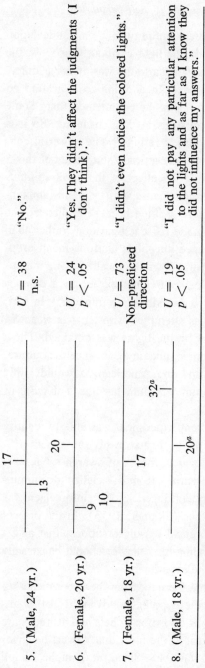

5. (Male, 24 yr.)	13	17	$U = 38$ n.s.	"No."
6. (Female, 20 yr.)	9, 10	20	$U = 24$ $p < .05$	"Yes. They didn't affect the judgments (I don't think)."
7. (Female, 18 yr.)	17		$U = 73$ Non-predicted direction	"I didn't even notice the colored lights."
8. (Male, 18 yr.)	20^a	32^a	$U = 19$ $p < .05$	"I did not pay any particular attention to the lights and as far as I know they did not influence my answers."

[a] Subject made two incorrect overt statements at the beginning of the series. The analysis is based on the remaining nine truth-light and nine lie-light cartoons.

comment "Very funny" or "Very unfunny." The mean deviation from the neutral point for the lie-light cartoons was -9; the mean deviation for the truth-light cartoons was $+28$, a difference significant at the .004 level. In addition to indicating no awareness of the effect of the lights, he commented that "Some of the cartoons are not too obvious in their meanings. So it is quite hard to give them the correct ratings." The powerful control exercised by the lights over the attitude statements of this S is thus interpreted as reflecting the effect of the weak stimulus control exercised by the cartoons themselves ("stimulus ambiguity"). The control is even more striking because E dictated the comment which was to be made for each cartoon, rather than first obtaining the S's preference; this adds a strong mand property to the subsequent behavior. (It will be recalled that a manipulation of "amount of choice" was cited earlier as a demonstrated manipulation of the self-credibility parameter.) In fact, when this same procedure was attempted with ten American Ss, no effect of stimulus control by the lights was obtained. These interpretations are not, of course, unequivocal, since the cultural differences between this S and the American Ss would imply variation of many more parameters than just the ambiguity of the cartoons.

None of the Ss in the present experiment was able to identify the effect of his comments or the lights on his subsequent attitude statements. Again, it is evident that "self-awareness" is a set of behaviors which must be learned from a socializing community that sets up the necessary contingencies of reinforcement for establishing the discriminations (Skinner, 1953). In the present experiment, there is no theoretical reason to suppose that an S's tact of the conditions controlling his behavior should be causally relevant to the outcome of the experiment.

In sum, it is concluded that the data from the experiments reported provide support for the hypotheses advanced at the outset: self-descriptive statements known as beliefs and attitudes are often under the partial control of the individual's overt behavior and its apparent controlling variables. Since these public stimuli and responses are those which the socializing community itself must use initially in training the individual to "know himself," the individual's belief and attitude statements are functionally equivalent to those that an outside observer would attribute to him. They are "inferences" from the same evidence. The two interpersonal replications of experiments by Brehm and Cohen (1962) illustrated the similarity between an individual's "true" beliefs and attitudes and the inferences drawn by an outside observer of his behavior. The final experiment demonstrated the direct control over an individual's attitude statements exerted by his own overt behavior and the stimulus conditions in which it occurs. Finally, it is suggested that the present functional analysis also provides an alternative formulation of several other experiments in the literature, especially the "forced compliance" studies conducted within the framework of Festinger's theory of cognitive dissonance (1957).

REFERENCES

ARONSON, E., and J. M. CARLSMITH. 1963. "Effect of the Severity of Threat on the Devaluation of Forbidden Behavior," *Journal of Abnormal and Social Psychology,* 66, 584–88.
BREHM, J. W., and A. R. COHEN. 1962. *Explorations in Cognitive Dissonance.* New York: Wiley.
FESTINGER, L. 1957. *A Theory of Cognitive Dissonance.* Evanston, Ill.: Row, Peterson.
FESTINGER, L., and J. M. CARLSMITH. 1959. "Cognitive Consequences of Forced Compliance," *Journal of Abnormal and Social Psychology,* 58, 203–10.
HOVLAND, C. I., and W. WEISS. 1951. "The Influence of Source Credibility on Communication Effectiveness," *Public Opinion Quarterly,* 15, 635–50.
KELLEY, H. H., and CHRISTINE L. WOODRUFF. 1956. "Members' Reactions to Apparent Group Approval of a Counternorm Communication," *Journal of Abnormal and Social Psychology,* 52, 67–74.
KING, B. T., and I. L. JANIS. 1956. Comparison of the Effectiveness of Improvised vs. Non-improvised Role-playing in Producing Opinion Change," *Human Relations,* 9, 177–86.
MEAD, G. H. 1934. *Mind, Self and Society.* Chicago: University of Chicago Press.

ROSENBERG, M. J. 1965. "When Dissonance Fails: On Eliminating Evaluation Apprehension from Attitude Measurement," *Journal of Personality and Social Psychology*, 1, 28–42.

RYLE, G. 1949. *The Concept of Mind*. London: Hutchinson.

SCHACHTER, S., and J. SINGER. 1962. "Cognitive, Social, and Physiological Determinants of Emotional State," *Psychological Review*, 69, 379–99.

SCOTT, W. A. 1957. "Attitude Change Through Reward of Verbal Behavior," *Journal of Abnormal and Social Psychology*, 55, 72–75.

————. 1959. "Attitude Change by Response Reinforcement: Replication and Extension," *Sociometry*, 22, 328–35.

SKINNER, B. F. 1953. *Science and Human Behavior*. New York: Macmillan.

————. 1957. *Verbal Behavior*. New York: Appleton-Century-Crofts.

8 Processes of Opinion Change

HERBERT C. KELMAN

Herbert C. Kelman, *whose instrumental theory of attitude change is one of the first and best of its kind, is now involved in wider arenas. A strong critic of experiments in which subjects are deceived unnecessarily, he has written extensively on the ethics and the applications of social psychology. To him must go the credit for the awakening of many researchers to their responsibilities both to their subjects and to society as a whole. A native of Austria and—like many prominent social psychologists—for some time resident at the University of Michigan, he is now Richard Clarke Cabot Professor of Social Ethics at Harvard University.*

A persistent concern in the analysis of public opinion data is the "meaning" that one can ascribe to the observed

From *Public Opinion Quarterly,* 25 (1961): 57–78. Reprinted by permission.
  This paper is based on a research program on social influence and behavior change, supported by grant M-2516 from the National Institute of Mental Health.

distributions and trends—and to the positions taken by particular individuals and segments of the population. Clearly, to understand what opinion data mean we have to know considerably more than the direction of an individual's responses or the distribution of responses in the population. We need information that will allow us to make some inferences about the characteristics of the observed opinions—their intensity, their salience, the level of commitment that they imply. We need information about the motivational bases of these opinions—about the functions that they fulfill for the individual and the motivational systems in which they are embedded.[1] We need information about the cognitive links of the opinions—the amount and the nature of information that supports them, the specific expectations and evaluations that surround them.

The need for more detailed information becomes even more apparent when we attempt to use opinion data for the prediction of subsequent behavior. What is the likelihood that the opinions observed in a particular survey will be translated into some form of concrete action? What is the nature of the actions that people who hold a particular opinion are likely to take, and how are they likely to react to various events? How likely are these opinions to persist over time and to generalize to related issues? What are the conditions under which one might expect these opinions to be abandoned and changed? Such predictions can be made only to the extent to which we are informed about the crucial dimensions of the opinions in question, about the motivations that underlie them, and about the cognitive contexts in which they are held.

INFERRING THE MEANING OF OPINIONS

In a certain sense, the need for more detailed information about opinions can (and must) be met by improvements and refinements in the methodology of opinion assessment. A great deal of progress in this direction has already been made in recent years.

Thus, many widely accepted features of interviewing technique are specifically designed to elicit information on which valid inferences about the meaning of opinions can be based: the creation of a relaxed, nonjudgmental atmosphere; the emphasis on open-ended questions; the progressive funneling from general to specific questions; the use of probes, of indirect questions, and of interlocking questions; and so on. These procedures facilitate inferences (1) by maximizing the likelihood that the respondent will give rich and full information and thus reveal the motivational and cognitive structure underlying the expressed opinions, and (2) by minimizing the likelihood that the respondent will consciously or unconsciously distort his "private" opinions when expressing them to the interviewer.

Similarly, when attitudes are assessed by means of questionnaires, it is possible to approximate these methodological goals. In part, this is accomplished by the instructions, which can motivate the subject to respond fully and honestly and assure him of confidentialness or anonymity. In part it is accomplished by the use of indirect and projective questions, and by the inclusion of a series of interrelated items in the questionnaire. And, in part, it is possible to make inferences about the meaning of opinions by the use of various scaling devices in the analysis of the data.

There is no question about the importance of these methodological advances, but in and of themselves they do not solve the problem of inference. They increase the investigator's ability to obtain rich and relatively undistorted information on which he can then base valid inferences. But, no matter how refined the techniques, they do not provide direct information about the meaning of the opinions and do not permit automatic predictions to subsequent behavior: the investigator still has to make inferences from the data.

To make such inferences, the student of public opinion needs a theoretical framework which accounts for the adoption and expression of particular opinions on the part of individuals and groups. Such a framework can serve as a guide in the collection of data: it can provide a systematic basis for deciding what information is relevant and what questions should be asked in order to permit the drawing of inferences. Similarly, it can serve as a guide for interpreting the data and deriving implications from them.

The need for such a framework is particularly apparent when one attempts to make predictions about subsequent behavior on the basis of opinion data. For example, in a relaxed interview situation a particular respondent may express himself favorably toward socialized medicine. What are the chances that he will take the same position in a variety of other situations? To answer this, we would need a theoretical scheme for the analysis of interaction situations, in terms of which we could make some inferences about the structure and meaning of this particular interview situation as compared to various other situations in which the issue of socialized medicine might arise. How would we expect this same respondent to react to a concerted campaign by the American Medical Association which links federal insurance programs with creeping socialism? To answer this, we would need a theory of opinion formation and change, in terms of which we could make some inferences about the characteristics of opinions formed under different conditions.

Progress in the analysis of public opinion, then, requires theoretical development along with methodological improvements. For this development, it should be possible to draw on some of the current theoretical thinking and associated research in social psychology. There are two foci of social-psychological theorizing and research that would appear to be particularly germane to the analysis of public opinion. One is the study of processes of social interaction as such. Such diverse approaches to the analysis of social interaction as those of Getzels,[2] Goffman,[3] and Jones and Thibaut,[4] for example, can be useful for conceptualizing the determinants of *opinion expression*. Thus, by using one or another of these schemes, the investigator can make some formulations about the expectations that the respondent brought to the interview situation and the goals that he was trying to achieve in this interaction. On the basis of such a formulation, he can make inferences about the meaning of the opinions expressed in this situation and about their implications for subsequent behavior—for example, about the likelihood that similar opinions will be expressed in a variety of other situations.

The second relevant focus of social-psychological theorizing and research is the study of processes of social influence and the induction of behavior change. Theoretical analyses in this area can be useful for conceptualizing the determinants of *opinion formation* and *opinion change*. They can help the investigator in making formulations about the sources of the opinions expressed by the respondent—the social conditions under which they were adopted, the motivations that underlie them, and the social and personal systems in which they are embedded. On the basis of such a formulation, again, he can make inferences about the meaning and implications of the opinions ascertained.

The model that I shall present here emerged out of the second research focus—the study of social influence and behavior change. It is, essentially, an attempt to conceptualize the processes of opinion formation and opinion change. It starts with the assumption that opinions adopted under different conditions of social influence, and based on different motivations, will differ in terms of their qualitative characteristics and their subsequent histories. Thus, if we know something about the determinants and motivational bases of particular opinions, we should be able to make predictions about the conditions under which they are likely to be expressed, the conditions under which they are likely to change, and other behavioral consequences to which they are likely to lead, Ideally, such a model can be useful in the analysis of public opinion by suggesting relevant variables in terms of which opinion data can be examined and predictions can be formulated.

THE STUDY OF SOCIAL INFLUENCE

Social influence has been a central area of concern for experimental social psychology almost since its beginnings. Three general research traditions in this area can be distinguished: (1) the

study of social influences on judgments, stemming from the earlier work on prestige suggestion;[5] (2) the study of social influences arising from small-group interaction;[6] and (3) the study
of social influences arising from persuasive communications.[7] In
recent years, there has been a considerable convergence between
these three traditions, going hand in hand with an increased interest in developing general principles of social influence and socially induced behavior change.

One result of these developments has been that many investigators found it necessary to make qualitative distinctions between different types of influence. In some cases, these distinctions arose primarily out of the observation that social influence
may have qualitatively different effects, that it may produce different kinds of change. For example, under some conditions it
may result in mere public conformity—in superficial changes on
a verbal or overt level without accompanying changes in belief;
in other situations it may result in private acceptance—in a
change that is more general, more durable, more integrated with
the person's own values.[8] Other investigators found it necessary
to make distinctions because they observed that influence may
occur for different reasons, that it may arise out of different motivations and orientations. For example, under some conditions
influence may be primarily informational—the subject may conform to the influencing person or group because he views him as
a source of valid information; in other situations influence may
be primarily normative—the subject may conform in order to
meet the positive expectations of the influencing person or
group.[9]

My own work can be viewed in the general context that I have
outlined here. I started out with the distinction between public
conformity and private acceptance, and tried to establish some of
the distinct determinants of each. I became dissatisfied with this
dichotomy as I began to look at important examples of social influence that could not be encompassed by it. I was especially impressed with the accounts of ideological conversion of the "true
believer" variety, and with the recent accounts of "brainwash-

ing," particularly the Chinese Communist methods of "thought reform."[10] It is apparent that these experiences do not simply involve public conformity, but that indeed they produce a change in underlying beliefs. But it is equally apparent that they do not produce what we would usually consider private acceptance—changes that are in some sense integrated with the person's own value system and that have become independent of the external source. Rather, they seem to produce new beliefs that are isolated from the rest of the person's values and that are highly dependent on external support.

These considerations eventually led me to distinguish three processes of social influence, each characterized by a distinct set of antecedent and a distinct set of consequent conditions. I have called these processes *compliance, identification,* and *internalization.*[10]

THREE PROCESSES OF SOCIAL INFLUENCE

Compliance can be said to occur when an individual accepts influence from another person or from a group because he hopes to achieve a favorable reaction from the other. He may be interested in attaining certain specific rewards or in avoiding certain specific punishments that the influencing agent controls. For example, an individual may make a special effort to express only "correct" opinions in order to gain admission into a particular group or social set, or in order to avoid being fired from his government job. Or the individual may be concerned with gaining approval or avoiding disapproval from the influencing agent in a more general way. For example, some individuals may compulsively try to say the expected thing in all situations and please everyone with whom they come in contact, out of a disproportionate need for favorable responses from others of a direct and immediate kind. In any event, when the individual complies, he does what the agent wants him to do—or what he thinks the agent wants him to do—because he sees this as a way of achieving a desired response from him. He does not adopt the induced behavior—for example, a particular opinion response—because he believes in its content, but because it is instrumental in the production of a satisfying social effect. What the individual learns, essentially, is to say or do the expected thing in special situations, regardless of what his private beliefs may be. Opinions adopted through compliance should be expressed only when the person's behavior is observable by the influencing agent.

Identification can be said to occur when an individual adopts behavior derived from another person or a group because this behavior is associated with a satisfying self-defining relationship to this person or group. By a self-defining relationship I mean a role relationship that forms a part of the person's self-image. Accepting influence through identification, then, is a way of establishing or maintaining the desired relationship to the other, and the self-definition that is anchored in this relationship.

The relationship that an individual tries to establish or maintain through identification may take different forms. It may take the form of classical identification, that is, of a relationship in which the individual takes over all or part of the role of the influencing agent. To the extent to which such a relationship exists, the individual defines his own role in terms of the role of the other. He attempts to be like or actually to *be* the other person. By saying what the other says, doing what he does, believing what he believes, the individual maintains this relationship and the satisfying self-definition that it provides him. An influencing agent who is likely to be an attractive object for such a relationship is one who occupies a role desired by the individual—who possesses those characteristics that the individual himself lacks —such as control in a situation in which the individual is helpless, direction in a situation in which he is disoriented, or belongingness in a situation in which he is isolated.

The behavior of the brainwashed prisoner in Communist China provides one example of this type of identification. By adopting the attitudes and beliefs of the prison authorities—including *their* evaluation of *him*—he attempts to regain his identity, which has been subjected to severe threats. But this kind of identification does not occur only in such severe crisis situations. It can also be observed, for example, in the context of socialization of children, where the taking over of parental attitudes and actions is a normal, and probably essential, part of personality development. The more or less conscious efforts involved when an individual learns to play a desired occupational role and imitates an appropriate role model would also exemplify this process. Here, of course, the individual is much more selective in the attitudes and actions he takes over from the other person. What is at stake is not his basic sense of identity or the stability of his self-concept, but rather his more limited "professional identity."

The self-defining relationship that an individual tries to establish or maintain through identification may also take the form of a reciprocal role relationship—that is, of a relationship in which the roles of the two parties are defined with reference to one another. An individual may be involved in a reciprocal relationship with another specific individual, as in a friendship relationship between two people. Or he may enact a social role which is defined with reference to another (reciprocal) role, as in the relationship between patient and doctor. A reciprocal-role relationship can be maintained only if the participants have mutually shared expectations of one another's behavior. Thus, if an individual finds a particular relationship satisfying, he will tend to behave in such a way as to meet the expectations of the other. In other words, he will tend to behave in line with the requirements of this particular relationship. This should be true regardless of whether the other is watching or not: quite apart from the reactions of the other, it is important to the individual's own self-concept to meet the expectations of his friendship role, for example, or those of his occupational role.

Thus, the acceptance of influence through identification should take place when the person sees the induced behavior as relevant to and required by a reciprocal-role relationship in which he is a participant. Acceptance of influence based on a reciprocal-role relationship is similar to that involved in classical identification in that it is a way of establishing or maintaining a satisfying self-defining relationship to another. The nature of the relationship differs, of course. In one case it is a relationship of identity; in the other, one of reciprocity. In the case of reciprocal-role relationships, the individual is not identifying with the other in the sense of taking over *his* identity, but in the sense of empathically reacting in terms of the other person's expectations, feelings, or needs.

Identification may also serve to maintain an individual's relationship to a group in which his self-definition is anchored. Such a relationship may have elements of classical identification as well as of reciprocal roles: to maintain his self-definition as a group member an individual, typically, has to model his behavior along particular lines and has to meet the expectations of his fellow members. An example of identification with a group would be the member of the Communist Party who derives strength and a sense of identity from his self-definition as part of the vanguard of the proletarian revolution and as an agent of historical destiny. A similar process, but at a low degree of intensity, is probably involved in many of the conventions that people acquire as part of their socialization into a particular group.

Identification is similar to compliance in that the individual does not adopt the induced behavior because its content per se is intrinsically satisfying. Identification differs from compliance, however, in that the the individual actually believes in the opinions and actions that he adopts. The behavior is accepted both publicly and privately, and its manifestation does not depend on observability by the influencing agent. It does depend, however, on the role that an individual takes at any given moment in time. Only when the appropriate role is activated—only when the individual is acting within the relationship upon which the identification is based—will the induced opinions be expressed. The individual is not primarily concerned with pleasing the other, with giving him what he wants (as in compliance), but he is concerned with meeting the other's expectations for his own role performance. Thus, opinions adopted through identification do remain tied to the external source and dependent on social support. They are not integrated with the individual's value system, but rather tend to be isolated from the rest of his values—to remain encapsulated.

Finally, *internalization* can be said to occur when an individual accepts influence because the induced behavior is congruent with his value system. It is the content of the induced behavior that is intrinsically rewarding here. The individual adopts it because he finds it useful for the solution of a problem, or because it is congenial to his own orientation, or because it is demanded by his own values—in short, because he perceives it as inherently conducive to the maximization of his values. The characteristics of the influencing agent do play an important role in internalization, but the crucial dimension here—as we shall see below—is the agent's credibility, that is, his relation to the content.

The most obvious examples of internalization are those that involve the evaluation and acceptance of induced behavior on rational grounds. A person may adopt the recommendations of an expert, for example, because he finds them relevant to his own problems and congruent with his own values. Typically, when internalization is involved, he will not accept these recommendations *in toto* but modify them to some degree so that they will fit his own unique situation. Or a visitor to a foreign country may be challenged by the different patterns of behavior to which he is exposed, and he may decide to adopt them (again, selectively and in modified form) because he finds them more in keeping with his own values than the patterns in his home country. I am not implying, of course, that internalization is always involved in the situations mentioned. One would speak of internalization only if acceptance of influence took the particular form that I described.

Internalization, however, does not necessarily involve the adoption of induced behavior on rational grounds. I would not want to equate internalization with rationality, even though the description of the process has decidedly rationalist overtones. For example, I would characterize as internalization the adoption of beliefs because of their congruence with a value system that is basically *irrational*. Thus, an authoritarian individual may adopt certain racist attitudes because they fit into his paranoid, irrational view of the world. Presumably, what is involved here is internalization, since it is the content of the induced behavior and its relation to the person's value system that is satisfying. Similarly, it should be noted that congruence with a person's value system does not necessarily imply logical consistency. Behavior would be congruent if, in some way or other, it fit into the person's value system, if it seemed to belong there and be demanded by it.

It follows from this conception that behavior adopted through internalization is in some way—rational or otherwise—integrated with the individual's existing values. It becomes part of a personal system, as distinguished from a system of social-role expectations. Such behavior gradually becomes independent of the external source. Its manifestation depends neither on observability by the influencing agent nor on the activation of the relevant role, but on the extent to which the underlying values have been made relevant by the issues under consideration. This does not mean that the individual will invariably express internalized opinions, regardless of the social situation. In any specific situation, he has to choose among competing values in the face of a variety of situational requirements. It does mean, however, that these opinions will at least enter into competition with other alternatives whenever they are relevant in content.

It should be stressed that the three processes are not mutually exclusive. While they have been defined in terms of pure cases, they do not generally occur in pure form in real-life situations. The examples that have been given are, at best, situations in which a particular process predominates and determines the central features of the interaction.

ANTECEDENTS AND CONSEQUENTS
OF THE THREE PROCESSES

For each of the three processes, a distinct set of antecedents and a distinct set of consequents have been proposed. These are summarized in Table 8.1. First, with respect to the antecedents of the three processes, it should be noted that no systematic quantitative differences between them are hypothesized. The probability of each process is presented as a function of the same three determinants: the importance of the induction for the individual's goal achievement, the power of the influencing agent, and the prepotency of the induced response. For each process, the magnitude of these determinants may vary over the entire range: each may be based on an induction with varying degrees of importance, on an influencing agent with varying degrees of power, and so on. The processes differ only in terms of the *qualitative* form that these determinants take. They differ, as can be seen in the table, in terms of the *basis* for the importance of the induction, the *source* of the influencing agent's power, and the *manner* of achieving prepotency of the induced response.

1. The processes can be distinguished in terms of the basis for the importance of the induction, that is, in terms of the nature of the motivational system that is activated in the influence situation. What is it about the influence situation that makes it important, that makes it relevant to the individual's goals? What are the primary concerns that the individual brings to the situation or that are aroused by it? The differences between the three processes in this respect are implicit in the descriptions of the processes given above: (*a*) To the extent that the individual is concerned—for whatever reason—with the *social effect* of his behavior, influence will tend to take the form of compliance. (*b*) To the extent that he is concerned with the *social anchorage* of his behavior, influence will tend to take the form of identification. (*c*) To the extent that he is concerned with the *value con-*

gruence of his behavior (rational or otherwise), influence will tend to take the form of internalization.

2. A difference between the three processes in terms of the source of the influencing agent's power is hypothesized. (*a*) To the extent that the agent's power is based on his *means control,* influence will tend to take the form of compliance. An agent pos-

TABLE 8.1: *Summary of the Distinctions Between the Three Processes of Opinion Change*

	Compliance	Identification	Internalization
Antecedents:			
1. Basis for the *importance of the induction*	Concern with social effect of behavior	Concern with social anchorage of behavior	Concern with value congruence of behavior
2. Source of *power of the influencing agent*	Means control	Attractiveness	Credibility
3. Manner of achieving *prepotency of the induced response*	Limitation of choice behavior	Delineation of role requirements	Reorganization of means-ends framework
Consequents:			
1. Conditions of performance of induced response	Surveillance by influencing agent	Salience of relationship to agent	Relevance of values to issue
2. Conditions of change and extinction of induced response	Changed perception of conditions for social rewards	Changed perception of conditions for satisfying self-defining relationships	Changed perception of conditions for value maximization
3. Type of behavior system in which induced response is embedded	External demands of a specific setting	Expectations defining a specific role	Person's value system

sesses means control if he is in a position to supply or withhold means needed by the individual for the achievement of his goals. The perception of means control may depend on the agent's *actual* control over specific rewards and punishments, or on his *potential* control, which would be related to his position in the social structure (his status, authority, or general prestige). (*b*) To the extent that the agent's power is based on his *attractiveness,* influence will tend to take the form of identification. An agent is attractive if he occupies a role which the individual himself desires[12] or if he occupies a role reciprocal to one the individual wants to establish or maintain. The term "attractiveness," as used here, does not refer to the possession of qualities that make a person likable, but rather to the possession of qualities on the part of the agent that make a continued relationship to him particularly desirable. In other words, an agent is attractive when the individual is able to derive satisfaction from a self-definition with reference to him. (*c*) To the extent that the agent's power is based on his *credibility,* influence will tend to take the form of internalization. An agent possesses credibility if his statements are considered truthful and valid, and hence worthy of serious consideration. Hovland, Janis, and Kelley[13] distinguish two bases for credibility: expertness and trustworthiness. In other words, an agent may be perceived as possessing credibility because he is likely to *know* the truth, or because he is likely to *tell* the truth. Trustworthiness, in turn, may be related to over-all respect, likemindedness, and lack of vested interest.

3. It is proposed that the three processes differ in terms of the way in which prepotency is achieved. (*a*) To the extent that the induced response becomes prepotent—that is, becomes a "distinguished path" relative to alternative response possibilities—because the individual's choice behavior is limited, influence will tend to take the form of compliance. This may happen if the individual is pressured into the induced response, or if alternative responses are blocked. The induced response thus becomes prepotent because it is, essentially, the only response permitted: the individual sees himself as having no choice and as being re-

stricted to this particular alternative. (*b*) To the extent that the induced response becomes prepotent because the requirements of a particular role are delineated, influence will tend to take the form of identification. This may happen if the situation is defined in terms of a particular role relationship and the demands of that role are more or less clearly specified; for instance, if this role is made especially salient and the expectations deriving from it dominate the field. Or it may happen if alternative roles are made ineffective because the situation is ambiguous and consensual validation is lacking. The induced response thus becomes prepotent because it is one of the few alternatives available to the individual: his choice behavior may be unrestricted, but his opportunity for selecting alternative responses is limited by the fact that he is operating exclusively from the point of view of a particular role system. (*c*) Finally, to the extent that the induced response becomes prepotent because there has been a reorganization in the individual's conception of means-ends relationships, influence will tend to take the form of internalization. This may happen if the implications of the induced response for certain important values—implications of which the individual had been unaware heretofore—are brought out, or if the advantages of the induced response as a path to the individual's goals, compared to the various alternatives that are available, are made apparent. The induced response thus becomes prepotent because it has taken on a new meaning: as the relationships between various means and ends become restructured, it emerges as the preferred course of action in terms of the person's own values.

Depending, then, on the nature of these three antecedents, the influence process will take the form of compliance, identification, or internalization. Each of these corresponds to a characteristic pattern of internal responses—thoughts and feelings—in which the individual engages as he accepts influence. The resulting changes will, in turn, be different for the three processes, as indicated in the second half of the table. Here, again, it is assumed that there are no systematic quantitative differences between the processes, but rather qualitative variations in the subsequent histories of behavior adopted through each process.

1. It is proposed that the processes differ in terms of the subsequent conditions under which the induced response will be performed or expressed. (*a*) When an individual adopts an induced response through compliance, he tends to perform it only under conditions of *surveillance* by the influencing agent. These conditions are met if the agent is physically present, or if he is likely to find out about the individual's actions. (*b*) When an individual adopts an induced response through identification, he tends to perform it only under conditions of *salience* of his relationship to the agent. That is, the occurrence of the behavior will depend on the extent to which the person's relationship to the agent has been engaged in the situation. Somehow this relationship has to be brought into focus and the individual has to be acting within the particular role that is involved in the identification. This does not necessarily mean, however, that he is consciously aware of the relationship; the role can be activated without such awareness. (*c*) When an individual adopts an induced response through internalization, he tends to perform it under conditions of *relevance of the values* that were initially involved in the influence situation. The behavior will tend to occur whenever these values are activated by the issues under consideration in a given situation, quite regardless of surveillance or salience of the influencing agent. This does not mean, of course, that the behavior will occur every time it becomes relevant. It may be outcompeted by other responses in certain situations. The probability of occurrence with a given degree of issue relevance will depend on the strength of the internalized behavior.

2. It is hypothesized that responses adopted through the three processes will differ in terms of the conditions under which they will subsequently be abandoned or changed. (*a*) A response adopted through compliance will be abandoned if it is no longer perceived as the best path toward the attainment of social rewards. (*b*) A response adopted through identification will be

abandoned if it is no longer perceived as the best path toward the maintenance or establishment of satisfying self-defining relationships. (c) A response adopted through internalization will be abandoned if it is no longer perceived as the best path toward the maximization of the individual's values.

3. Finally, it is hypothesized that responses adopted through the three processes will differ from each other along certain qualitative dimensions. These can best be summarized, perhaps, by referring to the type of behavior system in which the induced response is embedded. (a) Behavior adopted through compliance is part of a system of external demands that characterize a specific setting. In other words, it is part of the rules of conduct that an individual learns in order to get along in a particular situation or series of situations. The behavior tends to be related to the person's values only in an instrumental rather than an intrinsic way. As long as opinions, for example, remain at that level, the individual will tend to regard them as not really representative of his true beliefs. (b) Behavior adopted through identification is part of a system of expectations defining a particular role —whether this is the role of the other which he is taking over, or a role reciprocal to the other's. This behavior will be regarded by the person as representing himself, and may in fact form an important aspect of himself. It will tend to be isolated, however, from the rest of the person's values—to have little interplay with them. In extreme cases, the system in which the induced response is embedded may be encapsulated and function almost like a foreign body within the person. The induced responses here will be relatively inflexible and stereotyped. (c) Behavior adopted through internalization is part of an internal system. It is fitted into the person's basic framework of values and is congruent with it. This does not imply complete consistency: the degree of consistency can vary for different individuals and different areas of behavior. It does mean, however, that there is some interplay between the new beliefs and the rest of the person's values. The new behavior can serve to modify existing beliefs and can in turn be modified by them. As a result of this interac-

tion, behavior adopted through internalization will tend to be relatively idiosyncratic, flexible, complex, and differentiated.

RESEARCH BASED ON THE MODEL

The model itself and its possible implications may be seen more clearly if I present a brief summary of the research in which it was used. This research has moved in three general directions: experimental tests of the relationships proposed by the model, application of the model to the study of personality factors in social influence, and application of the model to the analysis of a natural influence situation.

Experimental Tests of the Proposed Distinctions Between the Three Processes

The relationships proposed by the model can be tested by experiments in which the antecedents postulated for a given process are related to the consequents postulated for that process. The first experiment on this problem[14] varied one of the antecedents—the source of the influencing agent's power—and observed the effects of this variation on one of the consequents—the conditions of performance of the induced response. Subjects (Negro college freshmen) were exposed to a tape-recorded interview dealing with an aspect of the Supreme Court decision on school segregation. Four versions of this communication were developed and played to different groups of subjects. The four communications contained the same message, but they differed in the way in which the communicator was introduced and presented himself at the beginning of the interview. These differences were designed to vary the source and degree of the communicator's power: in one communication the speaker was presented as possessing high means control, in the second as possessing high attractiveness, in the third as possessing high credibility, and in the fourth (for purposes of comparison) as being low in all three of these sources of power.

The subjects filled out attitude questionnaires designed to measure the extent of their agreement with the communication. To vary the conditions of performance, we asked each subject to complete three separate questionnaires, one under conditions of salience and surveillance, one under conditions of salience of the communicator but without surveillance, and a third under conditions of nonsurveillance and nonsalience. It was predicted that attitudes induced by the communicator high in means control would tend to be expressed only under conditions of surveillance by the communicator (the mediating process here being compliance), attitudes induced by the communicator high in attractiveness would tend to be expressed only when the subject's relationship to the communicator was salient (the mediating process here being identification), and attitudes induced by the communicator high in credibility would tend to be expressed when they were relevant in content, regardless of surveillance or salience (the mediating process here being internalization). These predictions were confirmed to a most encouraging degree.

One implication of this study for the analysis of public opinion is that we can make certain predictions about the future course of a given opinion if we know something about the interpersonal circumstances under which it was formed. An interview might reveal the predominant dimensions in terms of which the respondent perceives those individuals and groups to whom he traces the opinion in question. For example, does he see them primarily as potential sources of approval and disapproval? Or as potential reference points for his self-definition? Or as potential sources of information relevant to his own concern with reality testing and value maximization? From the answers to these questions we should be able to predict the future conditions under which this opinion is likely to come into play.

The study also suggests possible "diagnostic" devices that would make it possible to infer the process by which a particular opinion was adopted and hence the level at which it is held. If, for example, an opinion is expressed only in the presence of certain crucial individuals, one can assume that it is probably based on compliance and one can make certain further inferences on that basis. In other words, by observing the "conditions of performance of the induced response" (one of the consequents in our model), we can deduce the process on which this response is based.

It would, of course, be considerably easier and safer to make such inferences if several diagnostic criteria were available. It would be useful, therefore, to derive—from the list of consequents postulated by the model—further indicators in terms of which compliance-based, identification-based, and internalized opinions can be distinguished from one another, and to test the validity of these indicators. This is particularly true for identification and internalization. Since both of these processes, presumably, produce changes in "private belief," it is difficult to pin down the distinction between opinions based on them. There is a need, therefore, to develop a number of indicators that can capture the qualitative differences in the nature of opinions produced by these two processes, subtle though these differences may be. A second experiment addressed itself to this problem.[15]

The experimental situation, again, involved the use of tape-recorded communications. Three versions of the communication were used, each presented to a different group of college students. In each of the communications a novel program of science education was described and the rationale behind it was outlined. The basic message was identical in all cases, but the communications differed in terms of certain additional information that was included in order to produce different orientations. In one communication (*role-orientation* condition) the additional information was designed to spell out the implications of the induced opinions for the subject's relationship to certain important reference groups. Positive reference groups were associated with acceptance of the message, and —in a rather dramatic way—negative reference groups were associated with opposition to it. The intention here was to create two of the postulated antecedents for *identification:* a concern with the social anchorage of one's opinions, and a delineation of the requirements for maintaining the desired relationship to one's reference groups (see Table 1). In the second communication (*value-orientation* condition) the additional information was designed to spell out the implications of the induced opinions for an important value—personal responsibility for the consequences of one's actions. The communication argued that acceptance of the message would tend to maximize this value. The intention here was to create two of the postulated antecedents of *internalization:* a concern with the value congruence of one's opinions, and a reorganization of one's conception of means-ends relationships. The third communication was introduced for purposes of comparison and contained only the basic message.

On the basis of the theoretical model it was predicted that the nature of the attitude changes produced by the two experimental communications would differ. Role orientation would presumably produce the consequences hypothesized for identification, while value orientation would produce the consequences hypothesized for internalization. A number of measurement situations were devised to test these predictions: (1) In each group, half the subjects completed attitude questionnaires immediately after the communication, under conditions of salience, and half completed them a few weeks later, under conditions of nonsalience. As predicted, there was a significant difference between these two conditions of measurement for the role-orientation group but not for the value-orientation group. (2) The generalization of the induced attitudes to other issues involving the same values, and to other situations involving similar action alternatives, was measured. The prediction that the value-orientation group would show more generalization than the role-orientation group on the value dimension tended to be confirmed. The prediction that the reverse would be true for generalization along the action dimension was not upheld. (3) Flexibility of the induced attitudes was assessed by asking subjects to describe their doubts and qualifications. As predicted, the value-orientation group scored significantly higher on this index. (4) Complexity of the induced attitudes was assessed some weeks after the communication by asking subjects to list the things they would want to take into account in developing a new science education program. The total number of items listed was greater for the role-orientation group, but the number of items showing an awareness of relevant issues (as rated by a naïve judge) was clearly greater in the value-orientation group. (5) Half the subjects in each group were exposed to a countercommunication presenting a new consensus, the other half to a countercommunication presenting new arguments. It was predicted that the role-orientation group would be relatively more affected by the first type of countercommunication, and the value-orientation group by the second. The predicted pattern emerged, though it fell short of statistical significance.

The results of this study are not entirely unambiguous. They are sufficiently strong, however, to suggest that it should be possible to develop a number of criteria by which identification-based and internalized attitudes can be distinguished from one another. On the basis of such distinctions, one can then make certain inferences about the meaning of these attitudes and further predictions about their future course.

The Relation Between Personality Factors and Social Influence

This research starts with the assumption that the specific personality variables that are related to the acceptance of influence will depend on the particular process of influence involved. There is a further assumption that relationships depend on the type of influence situation to which the person is exposed. In other words, the concern is with exploring the specific personality variables that predispose individuals to engage in each of the three processes, given certain situational forces.

In the first study of this problem[16] we were interested in the relationship between one type of personality variable—cognitive needs and styles—and the process of internalization. We wanted to study this relationship in a situation in which people are exposed to new information that challenges their existing beliefs and assumptions. This is a situation in which at least some peo-

228 : *Processes of Opinion Change*

ple are likely to re-examine their beliefs and—if they find them to be incongruent with their values in the light of the new information—they are likely to change them. A change under these particular motivational conditions would presumably take the form of internalization.

It was proposed that people who are high in what might be called the *need for cognitive clarity* would react more strongly to a situation of this type. They would be made uncomfortable by the incongruity produced by such a situation and the challenge it presented to their cognitive structures. The *nature* of their reaction, however, may differ. Some people may react to the challenge by changing their beliefs, while others may react by resisting change. Which of these directions an individual would be likely to follow would depend on his characteristic *cognitive style*. A person who typically reacts to ambiguity by seeking clarification and trying to gain understanding (a "clarifier") would be likely to open himself to the challenging information and perhaps to reorganize his beliefs as a consequence. A person who typically reacts to ambiguity defensively, by simplifying his environment and keeping out disturbing elements (a "simplifier"), would be likely to avoid the challenging information.

Measures of cognitive need and cognitive style were obtained on a group of college students who were then exposed to a persuasive communication that presented some challenging information about American education. Change in attitudes with respect to the message of the communication was measured on two occasions for each subject: immediately after the communication, under conditions of salience, and six weeks later under conditions of nonsalience.

We predicted that, among people high in need for cognitive clarity, those whose characteristic style is clarification would be the most likely to manifest attitude change in the induced direction, while those whose characteristic style is simplification would be the most likely to manifest resistance to change and possibly even negative change. This difference should be especially marked under conditions of nonsalience, which are the conditions necessary for a reasonable test of internalization.

Among the people who are low in need for cognitive clarity, it was predicted that cognitive style would be unlikely to produce consistent differences since they are less motivated to deal with the ambiguity that the challenging information has created.

The results clearly supported these predictions. High-need clarifiers showed more change than high-need simplifiers (who, in fact, changed in the negative direction). This difference was small under conditions of salience, but became significant under conditions of nonsalience—suggesting that the difference between clarifiers and simplifiers is due to a difference in their tendency to internalize. Among low-need subjects, no consistent differences between the two style groups emerged.

This study suggests that one can gain a greater understanding of the structure of an individual's opinions on a particular issue by exploring relevant personality dimensions. In the present case we have seen that, for some of the subjects (those concerned with cognitive clarity), the opinions that emerge represent at least in part their particular solution to the dilemma created by incongruous information. In studies that are now under way we are exploring other personality dimensions that are theoretically related to tendencies to comply and identify. If our hypotheses are confirmed in these studies, they will point to other ways in which emerging opinions may fit into an individual's personality system. Opinions may, for example, represent partial solutions to the dilemmas created by unfavorable evaluations from others or by finding oneself deviating from the group. Since these relationships between opinions and personality variables are tied to the three processes of influence in the present model, certain predictions about the future course of the opinions for different individuals can be readily derived.

The Application of the Model to the Analysis Of a Natural Influence Situation

We are currently engaged in an extensive study of Scandinavian students who have spent a year of study or work in the United States.[17] We are interested in the effects of their stay here on their self-images in three areas: nationality, profession, and interpersonal relations. Our emphasis is on learning about the processes by which changes in the self-image come about or, conversely, the processes by which the person's existing image maintains itself in the face of new experiences. Our subjects were questioned at the beginning of their stay in the United States and at the end of their stay, and once again a year after their return home.

This study was not designed as a direct test of certain specific hypotheses about the three processes of influence. In this kind of rich field situation it seemed more sensible to allow the data to point the way and to be open to different kinds of conceptualizations demanded by the nature of the material. The model of influence did, however, enter into the formulation of the problem and the development of the schedules and is now entering into the analysis of the data.

In a preliminary analysis of some of our intensive case material, for example, we found it useful to differentiate four patterns of reaction to the American experience which may affect various aspects of the self-image: (1) An individual may change his self-image by a reorganization of its internal structure; here we would speak of a change by means of the process of *internalization*. (2) His self-image may be changed by a reshaping of the social relationships in which this image is anchored; here we would speak of a change by means of *identification*. (3) The individual may focus on the internal structure of the self-image but maintain it essentially in its original form; here we would speak of the process of *confirmation*. Finally, (4) he may maintain his self-image through a focus on its original social anchorage; here maintenance by the process of *resistance* would be involved. We have related these four patterns to a number of variables in a very tentative way, but the analysis will have to progress considerably farther before we can assess the usefulness of this scheme. It is my hope that this kind of analysis will give us a better understanding of the attitudes and images that a visitor takes away from his visit to a foreign country and will allow us to make some predictions about the subsequent history of these attitudes and images. Some of these predictions we will be able to check out on the basis of our post-return data.

CONCLUSION

There is enough evidence to suggest that the distinction between compliance, identification, and internalization is valid, even though it has certainly not been established in all its details. The specification of distinct antecedents and consequents for each of the processes has generated a number of hypotheses which have met the experimental test. It seems reasonable to conclude, therefore, that this model may be useful in the analysis of various influence situations and the resulting opinion changes. It should be particularly germane whenever one is concerned with the quality and durability of changes and with the motivational conditions that produced them.

I have also attempted to show the implications of this model for the analysis of public opinion. By tying together certain antecedents of influence with certain of its consequents, it enables us to infer the motivations underlying a particular opinion from a knowledge of its manifestations, and to predict the future course of an opinion from a knowledge of the conditions under which it was formed. Needless to say, the usefulness of the model in this respect is limited, not only because it is still in an early stage of development but also because of the inherent complexity of the inferences involved. Yet it does suggest an approach to the problem of meaning in the analysis of public opinion data.

NOTES

1. For discussions of the different motivational bases of opinion, see I. Sarnoff and D. Katz, "The Motivational Bases of Attitude Change," *Journal of Abnormal and Social Psychology,* 49 (1954): 115–24;

232 : *Processes of Opinion Change*

and M. B. Smith, J. S. Bruner, and R. W. White, *Opinions and Personality* (New York: Wiley, 1956).

2. J. W. Getzels, "The Question-Answer Process: A Conceptualization and Some Derived Hypotheses for Empirical Examination," *Public Opinion Quarterly,* 18 (1954): 80–91.

3. See, for example, E. Goffman, "On Face-work: An Analysis of Ritual Elements in Social Interaction," *Psychiatry,* 18 (1955): 213–31, and "Alienation from Interaction," *Human Relations,* 10 (1957): 47–60.

4. E. E. Jones and J. W. Thibaut, "Interaction Goals as Bases of Inference in Interpersonal Perception," in *Person Perception and Interpersonal Behavior,* ed. R. Tagiuri and L. Petrullo (Stanford, Calif.: Stanford University Press, 1958), pp. 151–78.

5. See, for example, S. E. Asch, *Social Psychology* (New York: Prentice-Hall, 1952).

6. See, for example, D. Cartwright and A. Zander, eds., *Group Dynamics* (Evanston, Ill.: Row, Peterson, 1953).

7. See, for example, C. I. Hovland, I. L. Janis, and H. H. Kelley, *Communication and Persuasion* (New Haven: Yale University Press, 1953).

8. See, for example, L. Festinger, "An Analysis of Compliant Behavior," in *Group Relations at the Crossroads,* ed. M. Sherif and M. O. Wilson (New York: Harper, 1953), pp. 232–56; H. C. Kelman, "Attitude Change as a Function of Response Restriction," *Human Relations,* 6 (1953): 185–214; J. R. P. French, Jr., and B. Raven, "The Bases of Social Power," in *Studies in Social Power,* ed. D. Cartwright (Ann Arbor, Mich.: Institute for Social Research, 1959), pp. 150–67; and Marie Jahoda, "Conformity and Independence," *Human Relations,* 12 (1959): 99–120.

9. See, for example, M. Deutsch and H. B. Gerard, "A Study of Normative and Informational Social Influence upon Individual Judgment," *Journal of Abnormal and Social Psychology,* 51 (1955): 629–36; J. W. Thibaut and L. Strickland, "Psychological Set and Social Conformity," *Journal of Personality,* 25 (1956): 115–29; and J. M. Jackson and H. D. Saltzstein, "The Effect of Person-Group Relationships on Conformity Processes," *Journal of Abnormal and Social Psychology,* 57 (1958): 17–24.

10. For instance, R. J. Lifton, " 'Thought Reform' of Western Civilians in Chinese Communist Prisons," *Psychiatry,* 19 (1956): 173–95.

11. A detailed description of these processes and the experimental work based on them will be contained in a forthcoming book, *Social Influence and Personal Belief: A Theoretical and Experimental Approach to the Study of Behavior Change,* to be published by John Wiley & Sons.

12. This is similar to John Whiting's conception of "status envy" as a basis for identification. See J. W. M. Whiting, "Sorcery, Sin, and the Superego," in *Nebraska Symposium on Motivation,* ed. M. R. Jones (Lincoln: University of Nebraska Press, 1959): pp. 174–95.

13. *Communication and Persuasion,* p. 21.

14. H. C. Kelman, "Compliance, Identification, and Internalization: Three Processes of Attitude Change," *Journal of Conflict Resolution*, 2 (1958): 51–60.
15. H. C. Kelman, "Effects of Role Orientation and Value Orientation on the Nature of Attitude Change" (paper read at the meetings of the Eastern Psychological Association, New York City, 1960).
16. H. C. Kelman and J. Cohler, "Reactions to Persuasive Communication as a Function of Cognitive Needs and Styles" (paper read at the meetings of the Eastern Psychological Association, Atlantic City, 1959).
17. Lotte Bailyn and H. C. Kelman, "The Effects of a Year's Experience in America on the Self-image of Scandinavians: Report of Research in Progress" (paper read at the meetings of the American Psychological Association, Cincinnati, 1959).

9

An Uncertainty Model
of Attitude Change

BERTRAM L. KOSLIN
RICHARD PARGAMENT
PETER SUEDFELD

*When the uncertainty model of opinion change was
being developed,* Bertram L. Koslin *was Assistant
Professor of Psychology at Princeton University and*
Richard Pargament *was his graduate student.* Koslin
*is now Vice President for Research of the Riverside
Research Institute in New York City, where Pargament is Assistant Manager, Social Systems Division.
Their current work is primarily in areas of urgent social problems, and has included research on the effects
of school desegregation. The third author,* Peter Suedfeld, *the editor of this volume, is Professor of Psychology at Rutgers University, The State University
of New Jersey. This chapter, written especially for
inclusion here, is the first systematic exposition of
the complete uncertainty theory.*

This research was supported by NIH Grant MH 13838–01.

234

In recent years, much research has been carried out to determine the relationship between attitude change and the amount of change advocated in communications. Several studies have reported that the amount of attitude change is directly related to the amount of change advocated in communications (Ewing, 1942; Fisher, Rubinstein, and Freeman, 1956; Goldberg, 1954; Hovland and Pritzker, 1957; Zimbardo, 1960). Other studies suggest that attitude change decreases as the amount of change advocated in a communication increases (Cohen, 1959; Hovland, Harvey, and Sherif, 1957). Finally, some studies have reported a curvilinear relationship between attitude change and amount of change advocated (Carlson, 1956; Insko, Murashima, and Saiyadain, 1966). The curvilinear relationship occurs in the following manner: When a small amount of opinion change is advocated in a communication, a recipient slightly changes his views. When a moderate amount of opinion change is advocated, the recipient changes his opinions to a greater extent. When a still larger amount of opinion change is advocated, however, the recipient changes his opinions to a lesser extent or perhaps not at all. Thus over a continuum of discrepancy (i.e., amount of change advocated), a curvilinear function of attitude change is formed.

Although a great many models have been suggested to account for the relationship between attitude change and the amount of change advocated, no clear picture has yet emerged to show how the recipient's own position, communication discrepancy, communicator credibility, and many other variables interact in affecting opinion change. The uncertainty model described here attempts to account for the interactive effects of several variables upon curvilinear attitude change.

UNCERTAINTY

Uncertainty is a state of mind that arises when one does not know how to order alternatives or how to choose among them. We assume that an individual can tolerate only a limited amount of uncertainty, and that when uncertainty rises above his tolerance level (U_o), he tries to reduce it. Thus the view underlying the model is that opinion change occurs to reduce uncertainty (above U_o) concerning the validity of various alternative positions on some social issue. The amount of opinion change that occurs is assumed to be directly related to the degree of uncertainty that an individual experiences. When an individual does not experience uncertainty, he is not motivated to change his opinion.

Uncertainty may occur with respect to one's own position, the appropriateness of the alternative opinions advocated by a discrepant communication, and a large number of other factors. The extent to which the recipient has formulated arguments and counterarguments and the prestige of the communicator are some of the moderator variables that may serve to increase or reduce uncertainty produced by a communication at a given discrepancy from the recipient's preferred position.

Discrepant Communications and Opinion Rehearsal

The effects of communication discrepancy and rehearsal upon uncertainty are shown in Figure 9.1. It is unnecessary to illustrate communication discrepancy on both sides of the recipient's most preferred position, since predictions and explanations for one side apply equally well to the other. In other words, the uncertainty curves are symmetric around the recipient's most preferred position.

U_o indicates a hypothetical recipient's initial level of uncertainty before entering the attitude change situation. Points above U_o on the y axis indicate an increase ($U+$) in uncertainty from the initial level; points below the line indicate a decrease ($U-$) in uncertainty. Discrepant communications have been plotted from the recipient's most preferred position along the x axis. The recipient's least preferred positions on the discrepancy continuum are indicated on either side of the most preferred position. The least preferred positions bound the range of opinions on the

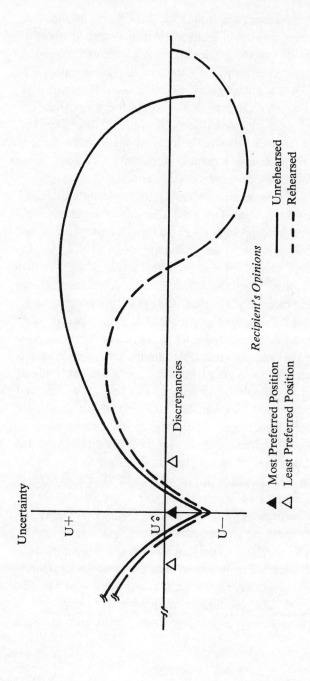

FIGURE 9.1: *The hypothetical relationship between communication discrepancy and uncertainty for rehearsed and nonrehearsed opinions.*

discrepancy continuum which the recipient believes he can comfortably endorse without being logically inconsistent. It is apparent in Figure 9.1 that the greater the range of endorsed positions, the greater the uncertainty and the greater the inconsistency. What, then, is the advantage of endorsing more than one position? The psychological gain that a recipient obtains from endorsing a range of opinions is some measure of flexibility, and thus the more he wants to avoid being rigid, the more likely he is to endorse more than one opinion. Flexibility, however, as we have seen, is paid for by a reduction in certainty.

The symbolic notations concerning the recipient's preferred positions may be illustrated with the following example: a recipient's most preferred position might be that all segregated school districts should voluntarily integrate their student bodies as rapidly as possible. One of his least preferred positions might be that federal funds may be withheld from districts to encourage them to integrate immediately. His other least preferred position might be that school districts may be permitted to delay integration up to five years while they prepare for it. The least preferred positions define the range of acceptable alternatives. Outside of this range of acceptable alternatives would be positions such as "School districts should be federalized to effect immediate and complete integration," or, on the other side of the acceptable range, "School districts may delay integration indefinitely."

Unrehearsed opinions are those that the recipient has accepted without being aware of the arguments that support them. Cultural truisms (for example, brush your teeth after every meal) are good examples of opinions that are accepted without rehearsal or awareness of the relevant arguments (McGuire, 1964).

For such an unrehearsed opinion as a cultural truism, the relationship of uncertainty to communication discrepancy is presumed to be curvilinear, reaching a maximum at a moderate discrepancy level. The curvilinear relationship of uncertainty to communication discrepancy follows from the manner in which the discrepant message is evaluated by the recipient. Messages that merely or partially restate the recipient's opinions would be somewhat supportive, and would therefore produce little additional uncertainty concerning the recipient's position on the issue. More discrepant but still plausible communications that neither overlap the recipient's opinions nor are judged to be appreciably different from them would engender the greatest amount of aditional uncertainty. Communications that are appreciably different would be considered implausible and might produce interpersonal conflict with the communicator, but they would produce less additional uncertainty concerning the validity of the recipient's own opinions. Thus if a communication merely asserted that people should never brush their teeth, little if any additional uncertainty would be induced because the message would be rejected outright.

When individuals are committed to uphold particular opinions and have been motivated to discredit contrary opinions, uncertainty and communication discrepancy are related in the way indicated by the rehearsed opinion curve in Figure 9.1. The additional uncertainty induced by discrepant communications is lower for rehearsed opinions than for unrehearsed opinions. When the recipient is prepared for discrepant communications, he has few doubts about their plausibility. Extreme messages that the individual is prepared to discount should actually reduce the uncertainty he had when he entered the attitude change situation. It is apparent that the better prepared an individual is to hear opinions he definitely opposes, the greater the possibility that extreme arguments will reduce uncertainty. Knowing what one is against helps to reduce uncertainty concerning one's preferred position. Eventually, very extreme communications would lose relevance altogether (Bevan and Darby, 1955; Koslin, Pargament, and Levine, 1967) and would have no effect upon uncertainty.

It is possible to derive opinion change predictions from the curves describing the relationships between uncertainty and communication discrepancy for rehearsed and unrehearsed opinions indicated in Figure 9.1. These predictions have been derived for the right side of the recipient's preferred position. However, the predictions apply equally well to the other side.

UNREHEARSED OPINIONS

When a recipient is exposed to a discrepant communication concerning an issue on which his opinions have not been rehearsed, additional uncertainty is produced. The recipient could reduce this uncertainty by broadening the range of opinions that he is willing to endorse so as to include the opinion advocated in the communication. Because previously held opinions might now be inconsistent with the newly endorsed opinion, the recipient might have to relinquish some of his previously held opinions. This form of uncertainty reduction could be depicted graphically by moving the least preferred position indicated in Figure 9.1 on the right hand side farther to the right so that it corresponded to the newly endorsed opinion. The other least preferred position would also have to be moved to the right to a position that the recipient felt was logically consistent with his newly endorsed opinion. If this change occurred, it would mean that positions that the recipient previously endorsed would now be discrepant, and therefore could potentially induce uncertainty. Since this self-induced uncertainty could be reduced only by reindorsing previously held views, and the communication-induced uncertainty could be reduced only by abandoning original commitments, a conflict situation would result.

One way to resolve the conflict is to relax the requirements for logical consistency concerning the opinions the recipient endorses. The conflict can be resolved by increasing the range of opinions that the recipient is willing to accept (that is, by expanding the size of the interval between his least preferred positions). We could indicate this resolution graphically by moving the least preferred position which is closer to the communication toward the opinion advocated, without changing the other least preferred position.

Another way of resolving the conflict is to tolerate the uncertainty that results from abandoning previously endorsed positions (if greater uncertainty can thus be avoided) by moving the most preferred position toward the opinion advocated in the communication.

The means of reducing uncertainty that is most likely to be chosen is a compromise of some sort between the available modes of uncertainty reduction. The extent to which one mode of uncertainty reduction is favored depends upon a number of variables. For example, if the individual has publicly committed himself to a position prior to receiving the discrepant message, he will be less likely to move his most preferred position toward the communication than if no one would be aware of his shift in position.

The mode of uncertainty reduction used by the recipient will also depend upon the distance between the opinions that he held previously and the opinion advocated in the communication. Although mildly discrepant communications induce little additional uncertainty, they readily allow the recipient to move his least preferred position toward the position advocated by the message. Thus, for mildly discrepant communications, the ratio of actual change to the amount of change advocated should be fairly large. Although moderately discrepant communications induce considerable additional uncertainty, they are more difficult to endorse. To endorse moderate communications, the recipient would have to move one least preferred position so as to abandon previously endorsed views. Thus, the recipient is apt to move his most preferred position slightly toward the source, while stretching his least preferred position as much as possible in the same direction. Thus the ratio of the amount of opinion change observed to the amount of change advocated should be less for moderate than for mild discrepancies. Because extreme discrepancies induce little uncertainty, the recipient is merely apt to heighten his uncertainty tolerance level without changing the position of his most preferred opinion. This slight increase in tolerance for uncertainty should result in even less change. Thus the ratio of amount of change obtained to the amount of change advocated should be a decreasing function of communication discrepancy.

REHEARSED OPINIONS

The preceding discussion concerning unrehearsed opinions applies equally well to rehearsed opinions over the appropriate interval of the discrepancy continuum. The only qualitatively new possibility is that a highly discrepant communication can reduce uncertainty from the initial amount that the recipient had before entering the attitude change situation, as previously indicated. To the extent to which rejecting an extreme opinion reduces uncertainty, the individual may opt to take a more logically consistent position by reducing the range of positions he endorses. Thus, with extreme communications, the model predicts a boomerang effect, that is, a shift away from the opinions advocated by the communicator. The likelihood of obtaining a boomerang effect is greater for rehearsed than for unrehearsed opinions.

Communicator Prestige

In addition to the discrepancy of the communication, the prestige of the communicator would also be expected to affect the amount of uncertainty that is induced by a communication. To the extent that the recipient's beliefs about the credibility of a positively valued communicator are more stable than his beliefs about his own opinions on an issue, uncertainty will be resolved by changing opinions in the direction advocated by the communicator. The magnitude of the difference in opinion change produced by communicators of high and low prestige should be proportional to the total amount of uncertainty. In other words, the more uncertain the recipient is of the validity of his own opinions, the more he will be influenced by the prestige of the communicator.

Belief Instability

Koslin, Stoops, and Loh (1967) introduced belief instability concerning the validity of the recipient's own opinions as a mediating variable between communication discrepancy and uncertainty. Belief instability results from communications that attack or refute the beliefs, evidence, or information upon which the recipient has based his opinions. Since it is assumed that the recipient employs his beliefs to support the validity of his opinions, an increase in belief instability should result in increased uncertainty.

One of the ways in which communication attacks may operate is by increasing the apparent reasonableness of discrepant opinions, thus weakening the recipient's belief system (McGuire, 1964). If persuasive attacks refute the beliefs supporting the recipient's own opinions or refute the beliefs that prevent an individual from endorsing contrary views, uncertainty should result. The recipient should become less certain than he was earlier about the validity of his own opinions (or about the invalidity of opposing opinions, depending upon the nature of the attack). If the recipient does not know as well as he did prior to the attack what he does and does not believe (belief instability), he will be less sure of the comparative validity of different opinions. He will now be less sure that mildly to moderately discrepant messages do not overlap his own opinions. He will also be less sure that moderate to large discrepancies represent invalid points of view.

Figure 9.2 illustrates the expected relationship between uncertainty and communication discrepancy for unrehearsed opinions based on low, medium, and highly stable beliefs. The less stable the individual's beliefs, the greater the uncertainty that discrepant communications may be expected to produce. As indicated earlier, the range of discrepancies producing uncertainty is also expected to be greater for recipients having less stable beliefs.

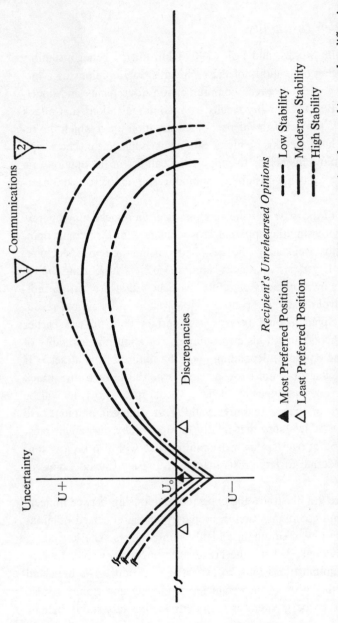

FIGURE 9.2: *The hypothetical relationship between uncertainty and discrepancy for those subjects who differ in initial levels of belief stability on an unrehearsed issue. The numbers at the top of the figure indicate communication attacks at various distances from the recipient's most preferred position.*

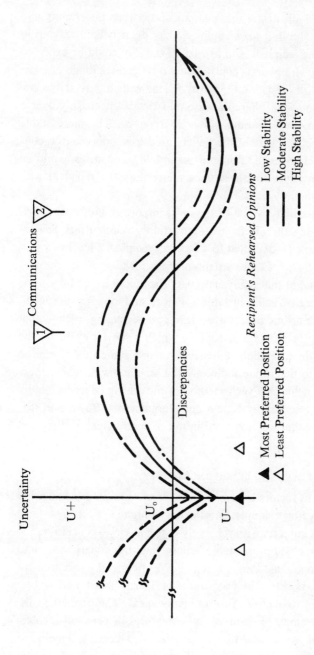

FIGURE 9.3: *The hypothetical relationship between uncertainty and discrepancy for those subjects who differ in initial levels of belief stability on a rehearsed issue. The numbers at the top of the figure indicate communication attacks at various distances from the recipient's most preferred position.*

Figure 9.3 illustrates the relationship between uncertainty and discrepancy for *rehearsed* opinions based on beliefs varying in stability. The recipient with low belief stability could be expected to find his own opinions contradicted by a greater range of communication discrepancy than a recipient with highly stable beliefs, and he should therefore also experience uncertainty over a broader range of communication discrepancy. The more stable recipient, being aware of the beliefs used to support and to contradict beliefs over the range of possible discrepancies, could be expected to experience less uncertainty than the recipient with low belief stability.

Belief instability is one of the most important moderator variables affecting the discrepancy-uncertainty relationship. Several variables may be expected to affect the recipient's level of belief instability. Some of these are discussed below.

It is apparent that many aspects of the model depend upon the measurement of belief instability before and/or after the introduction of various persuasive messages. A scaling method that engages the beliefs (standards) by which a subject evaluates the extent to which opinion statements possess some quality can be employed to determine indirectly the stability with which these beliefs are held. One such method of measuring belief instability has been presented by Koslin and Pargament (1969), and it is this method that we have used in the research which is discussed here.

INITIAL LEVELS OF BELIEF INSTABILITY

Numerous factors influence the recipient's initial level of belief instability. For example, Koslin and Pargament (1969) have shown that subjects with relatively extreme views concerning the Vietnam war had more stable beliefs than individuals with more moderate opinions. Pargament (1967) attempted to account for these findings using the procedures of Sherif, Sherif, and Nebergall (1965) to measure subject involvement. The predictor variables—extremity of opinions, two measures of personal involvement, and a participation variable—produced a significant multiple correlation of .53. Thus the more extreme the opinions of the recipient, the greater his involvement with groups espousing these opinions, and the greater his participation in social activities designed to carry them into action, the more stable his beliefs.

There are, however, many sources of belief stability, as McGuire (1964) has shown in his review of the variables contributing to resistance to change. One of the obvious ways in which participation in social activities may contribute to belief stability is by providing the individual with information with which he can defend his opinions. Personality factors such as those discussed in White and Harvey (1965) may also partially account for initial levels of belief stability.

COMMUNICATION ATTACKS AND THE INDUCTION OF BELIEF INSTABILITY

Communication attacks concentrating exclusively on the beliefs supporting the recipient's own position or on beliefs invalidating contrary opinions are more easily refuted than communications that attack the beliefs associated with more moderate opinions.

Severe attacks might actually reduce the instability of rehearsed beliefs. A rehearsed recipient should refute moderate to extreme attacks so well that he would derive from the exercise increased confidence in the beliefs supporting his own preferred opinions and in those beliefs that he uses to counterargue the opinions of others. In effect, the recipient says to himself, "Since I have successfully refuted these extreme arguments, my opinions must be even more valid than I thought they were." This reduction of belief instability would of course reduce the amount of uncertainty that could be aroused by a given level of communication discrepancy. The recipient is less well prepared for attacks in the moderate range than for extreme attacks because moderate attacks can be only partially refuted by beliefs supporting the recipient's own opinions or by those invalidating completely contrary views.

Thus beliefs may be seen as a continuum ranging from those beliefs that support the recipient's own opinions to those that invalidate contrary opinions. Since communications that attack moderately discrepant beliefs are expected to produce the greatest amount of belief instability, the relationship of belief discrepancy to belief instability should be curvilinear.

In accord with these predictions, Koslin, Suedfeld, and Pargament (1970) found that belief instability was a curvilinear function of belief discrepancy for a cultural truism concerning the wearing of automobile seat belts. When communications presented evidence against the wearing of automobile seat belts at speeds up to twenty-five miles per hour (a mildly discrepant attack), more belief instability was induced than in a control group that received no attack. When severe arguments opposing the wearing of seat belts under any driving conditions were introduced, less instability was induced than in a moderate attack condition (which resulted in the greatest amount of belief instability). In addition, the amount of belief instability was significantly $(r = .43)$ related to opinion change. (After the study, the recipients were told that the information in the communication attacks was false and that seat belts should be used under all circumstances.)

THE UNCERTAINTY MODEL IN MORE COMPLEX OPINION CHANGE SITUATIONS

In addition to making possible the predictions derived so far, the model may be expanded to account for other phenomena that affect attitude change.

Sequential Communications

An attack that produces instability (e.g., communication attack 1 in Figures 9.2 and 9.3) would raise uncertainty. The recipient would thus experience more uncertainty over all levels of discrepancy. By analogy, this situation would be equivalent to the recipient's experiencing the uncertainty levels associated with the low rather than the moderate stability curve in Figures 9.2 and 9.3. Similarly, communication attack 2 in Figures 9.2 and 9.3 would lower U_o and the recipient would be on a curve with lower levels of uncertainty over the discrepancy continuum. Thus for any two attacks on either rehearsed or unrehearsed beliefs, one could find the resultant uncertainty produced by the sequence by initially determining whether the first communication eventually raises or lowers the recipient onto a new uncertainty curve and then determining from the new curve the amount of uncertainty that the second communication would be expected to produce. Following this procedure, the reader should be able to deduce predictions for sequential communications. What would be the effect of a repetition of the original attack? What would be the effect of the introduction of two (or more) different attacks varying in degree of discrepancy on the opinion continuum?

DELAYED ATTACKS

In accord with McGuire's (1964) inoculation theory, it is assumed that when persuasive attacks are made on nonrehearsed beliefs (such as truisms), time is required for an individual to develop counterarguments. Therefore, rapidly introduced attacks on nonrehearsed opinions should produce greater instability of belief and resultant uncertainty than the same attacks introduced with a considerable delay between them.

The delay variable should function somewhat differently for rehearsed opinions. First, it is necessary to distinguish between short-term and medium-term delay. With periods of delay that allow the individual to sample his repertoire of beliefs (medium-term delay), the effect of a given attack should diminish. With short-term delay, there is less sampling time and a greater likelihood that the uncertainties produced by the attacks will "summate."

Since it should take less time to sample one's own repertoire of beliefs than to construct defenses, the difference between the results of attacks on rehearsed and nonrehearsed opinions should be greatest at the end of the medium-term delay. When individuals have been allowed time to construct defenses (long-term delay) for nonrehearsed opinions, however, the difference between the results of attacks on rehearsed and nonrehearsed opinions should be reduced.

The reader might attempt to relate the joint effect of multiple attacks and rehearsal time to the experiences of recipients exposed to debates as opposed to those addressed directly by communicators who are attempting to agitate people. We ourselves certainly hope to employ the uncertainty model to explain the processes whereby rather massive attitude change occurs during social movements such as revolutions.

The Spread of Uncertainty from One Dimension to Another

As we have seen, the model can predict differences between attacks on relatively stable versus unstable beliefs concerning various aspects of an issue. So far, the effects of attacking arguments and defensive counterarguments have been analyzed unidimensionally. However, it is possible that individuals may have varying amounts of belief instability with respect to different aspects or along different dimensions of a given issue. Also, for a rehearsed aspect, the amount of induced uncertainty would be depicted by the curve for rehearsed opinions in Figure 9.1, whereas for an unrehearsed aspect, the amount of induced uncertainty would be indicated by the unrehearsed opinion curve in Figure 9.1. An interesting research question concerns the extent to which discrepant communications along the more unstable (and/or less rehearsed) dimension affect opinion change on the stable (and/or rehearsed) dimension. It seems reasonable to hypothesize that communications on one dimension will affect the amount of uncertainty induced on another dimension to the extent that beliefs overlap between dimensions. Thus, the higher the correlation between aspects of an issue, the more the uncer-

tainty induced by communications on one dimension should
spread to other dimensions. From this hypothesis and previous
assumptions a variety of predictions can be deduced:

RELEVANCE-IRRELEVANCE PREDICTION

The dimensionalization of persuasive attacks allows for the
deduction of a relevance-irrelevance prediction concerning advocated change after persuasive attacks. A communication advocating opinion change after persuasive attacks should have a
greater effect the more it advocates change that is consistent
with the source of instability. Thus if belief instability is aroused
in regard to aspect A of an issue but not in regard to aspect B,
then a communication advocating opinion change along the A
dimension should have a greater effect than along the B dimension. The more strongly the two dimensions are correlated, however, the greater the probability that a communication advocating change along the B dimension will produce opinion change
when the attacks are on the A dimension.

SITUATIONAL VARIABLES

The uncertainty model also allows for the introduction of situational variables that may affect belief stability. One manipulation that should create situational uncertainty is the introduction
of persuasive attacks on an unrelated issue prior to the introduction of an attack on a target issue. If situational variables have
an effect, the more uncertainty that is induced by persuasive attacks on one issue, the more uncertainty should be induced by
any persuasive attack on a subsequent issue, even though the two
issues are not related. It also follows from previous assumptions
that a manipulation that links the previously unrelated issues
should induce more uncertainty than a manipulation that provides no such linkage. These hypotheses suggest that the uncertainty model may be used to study the complex processes of social agitation, in which the recipient is exposed to multiple communications that may or may not be interlinked.

REFERENCES

BEVAN, W., and C. L. DARBY. 1955. "Patterns of Experience and the Constancy of an Indifference Point for Perceived Weight," *American Journal of Psychology*, 68, 575–84.

CARLSON, E. R. 1956. "Attitude Change Through Modification of Attitude Structure," *Journal of Abnormal and Social Psychology*, 52, 256–61.

COHEN, A. 1959. "Communication Discrepancy and Attitude Change: A Dissonance Theory Approach," *Journal of Personality*, 27, 386–96.

EWING, T. N. 1942. "A Study of Certain Factors Involved in Changes of Opinion," *Journal of Social Psychology*, 16, 63–88.

FISHER, S., I. RUBINSTEIN, and R. W. FREEMAN. 1956. "Intertrial Effects of Immediate Self-committal in a Continuous Social Influence Situation," *Journal of Abnormal and Social Psychology*, 52, 200–7.

GOLDBERG, S. C. 1954. "Three Situational Determinants of Conformity to Social Norms," *Journal of Abnormal and Social Psychology*, 49, 325–29.

HOVLAND, C. I., O. J. HARVEY, and M. SHERIF. 1957. "Assimilation and Contrast Effects in Reactions to Communications and Attitude Change," *Journal of Abnormal and Social Psychology*, 55, 244–52.

———— and H. A. PRITZKER. 1957. "Extent of Opinion Change as a Function of Amount of Change Advocated," *Journal of Abnormal and Social Psychology*, 54, 257–61.

INSKO, C. A., F. MURASHIMA, and M. SAIYADAIN. 1966. "Communicator Discrepancy, Stimulus Ambiguity, and Influence," *Journal of Personality*, 34, 262–74.

KOSLIN, B. L., and R. PARGAMENT. 1969. "Effects of Attitude on Discrimination of Opinion Statements," *Journal of Experimental Social Psychology*, 5, 245–64.

————, ————, and S. LEVINE. 1967. "Effects of Learning on Judgment in the Presence of Discrepant Anchors," *Psychonomic Science*, 9, 565–66.

————, J. W. STOOPS, and W. D. LOH. 1967. "Source Characteristics and Communication Discrepancy as Determinants of Attitude Change and Conformity," *Journal of Experimental Social Psychology*, 3, 230–42.

————, P. SUEDFELD, and R. PARGAMENT. 1970. "Instability as a Mediating Variable in Opinion Change" (prepublication report).

MCGUIRE, W. J. 1964. "Inducing Resistance to Persuasion," in *Advances in Experimental Social Psychology*, ed. L. Berkowitz. New York: Academic Press.

PARGAMENT, R. 1967. "Opinion Extremity, Involvement, and Judgment Stability," (unpublished manuscript, Princeton University).

SHERIF, C., M. SHERIF, and R. E. NEBERGALL. 1965. *Attitude and Attitude Change.* Philadelphia: Saunders.

WHITE, B. J., and O. J. HARVEY. 1965. "Effects of Personality and Own Stand on Judgment and Production of Statements about a Central Issue," *Journal of Experimental Social Psychology,* 1, 334–47.

ZIMBARDO, P. G. 1960. "Involvement and Communication Discrepancy as Determinants of Opinion Conformity," *Journal of Abnormal and Social Psychology,* 60, 86–94.

Index

255